*ra* *Wa*

# Tracing the Way

*Spiritual Dimensions of the World Religions*

HANS KÜNG

Translated by John Bowden

continuum
LONDON • NEW YORK

**Continuum**

The Tower Building, 11 York Road, London SE1 7NX
370 Lexington Avenue, New York, NY 10017–6503

First published 2002

**British Library Cataloguing in Publication Data**
A catalogue record for this book is available
from the British Library.

ISBN: 0-8264-9423-4

Typeset by Centraserve Ltd, Saffron Walden, Essex
Printed and bound in Great Britain by
The Bath Press Ltd

# *Contents*

The dream of a lost paradise
Native inhabitants in a false light
'Primitive man' – uncivilized?
*Let's stop talking about 'primitive' cultures*
The earliest traces of religion
Even 'Stone Age people' have a cultural history
Women economically independent
Men are dominant in politics and ritual
People without religion?
'Primal religion' – nowhere to be found
The art of the Aborigines
What is in heaven?
And who formed the earth?
'Dreamtime'
The eternal law: tjukurpa
The fight between the snake woman Kuniya and the snake man Liru
Why women paint their bodies
What is totem and what is taboo?
The initiation dance: primal time and primal law
*Unwritten ethical norms*
A primal ethic
Colonization: Cook and the consequences
Triumph for the whites – tragedy for the blacks
Aborigines in the supermarket: the conflict between two cultures
Keeping the old religion alive
A question for native inhabitants throughout the world
Primal times: Australia and Africa
Human beings come from Africa
*We are all Africans under the skin*
The Late Stone Age revolution
Guardian spirits – only African?
Sacrificing goats even today
Spiritual healing – not automatic
*Against witchcraft*
Africa's great centuries

Social and political Buddhism: establishment of the Buddha kingdom
(Nichiren)
Social commitment lived out
*Buddhist ethic and global ethic*
Transition to a new global constellation
Archery: a demand on the individual

A Jewish wedding in New York
The riddle of Judaism
Jewish dress?
*A community of fate*
The homeland of the Jewish people
A people which did not always exist
Abraham: an immigrant
Abraham: the first leading figure of the prophetic religions
Strife over Abraham
Against commandeering Abraham
The hour of the birth of the people of Israel: the exodus
Moses: a second leading figure of the prophetic religions
The covenant on Sinai: the centre of Jewish religion
The solution to the riddle
The Sinai covenant presupposes a covenant with humankind
*The Decalogue – the basis for a shared fundamental ethic*
Israel: first of all a tribal society
Israel becomes a state
David: a third leading figure of the prophetic religions
The prophets in opposition to priests and king
The downfall of both kingdoms: the end of the monarchy
Israel becomes a theocracy
The destruction of Jerusalem and the temple
Why Judaism survived
The Jewish Middle Ages
The formation of Orthodox Judaism
Anti-Judaism in the Christian church
The Jews in medieval Germany: Worms
Jewish secret teaching: Kabbala
Jewish Enlightenment: Moses Mendelssohn
Exit from the ghetto
Modern Reform Judaism
The dispute over trends
Every individual has a name
A future for Jews in Germany
*The complicity of Christians*
The rebirth of the state of Israel
*The Palestine question*
Two olive branches
Judaism between secularism and fundamentalism
*The Decalogue as an ABC of human behaviour*
What will the future be?

# List of Illustrations

1. Krishna: for Hindus the ideal of true humanity
2. Daoist liturgy of the dead: the lantern in the middle symbolizes the soul which is to ascend on high
3. A 'possom man' draws his own quite personal possum history in the sand
4. Khajuraho: uninhibited depictions of orgiastic groups
5. Vivekananda: (with the dark turban) at the 1893 Chicago Parliament of the World's Religions
6. The Todaji Temple in Nara: the largest wooden building in the world
7. The Tai-ji diagram: the yin-yang symbol surrounded by the eight trigrams of the *Yijing*
8. The Temple of Heaven in Beijing
9. Roses mark the spots where the Jesuits of San Salvador University were brutally massacred by a death squad
10. A sand mandala: not work, but a meditative exercise
11. 'Emptiness'
12. Isaiah scroll from the Dead Sea
13. The Reform Synagogue in Berlin: a living synthesis between tradition and modernity
14. Kairouan: the oldest mosque in North Africa and the fourth holiest place in the Islamic world
15. The blessing of Easter bread in Moscow
16. Ritualized Sufi dance: an expression of being seized by God

# *Preface*

The world of the religions seems to be too vast even to survey, let alone comprehend. However, on our globe it is possible to distinguish three great river systems:
- the religions of Indian origin: Hinduism and Buddhism;
- the religions of Chinese origin: Confucianism and Daoism;
- the religions of Near Eastern origin: Judaism, Christianity and Islam.

The main figure in the first of these religions is the mystic, in the second the wise man, and in the third the prophet. So although all three systems overlap, a distinction is rightly made between Indian-mystic, Chinese-wisdom and Semitic-prophetic religions. In addition there are the tribal religions, which – although they had no means of producing writings – to some degree form the roots of all religions and continue to exist in different regions of the world.

This world of the religions seems to be immobile and static. However, in the course of the millennia all the great religions have undergone not only an organic development but revolutions, crises and transformations which can be established more or less clearly. In other words, they have undergone several epoch-making paradigm shifts. All these religions have a period of origin, an early form, a 'medieval' development and a transformation in the confrontation with modernity. And today they are all caught up in a transition to a new world era which one can call 'postmodern' or whatever. It is almost impossible to predict their future in the third millennium. We live in an exciting transitional period with as many fears as hopes.

The world of the religions seems to be confused and contradictory. However, despite all the differences in faith, teachings and rites, which cannot be overestimated, it is also possible to establish similarities, convergences and agreements. This is not just because people in all cultures are confronted with the same great questions: the primal questions about where the world and human beings come from and where they are going; about how to cope with suffering and guilt; about the criteria for life and action, the meaning of living and dying. It is also because people in the various cultures often receive similar answers from their religions. After all,

all the religions are at the same time both a message of salvation and a way of salvation. And in the end of the day, all the religions are the way in which believers view their lives, their attitude to them, and the way in which they live them.

But will it be at all possible to deal with this gigantic, complex world of the religions in relatively few pages? Will it be possible to relate, to describe, to explain all the developments that have taken place over so many millennia? I certainly did not want to write a history of the religions; there are plenty of those, often in many volumes, written by distinguished specialists, and I have consulted them time and again and quoted abundantly from them in previous works. This book is not the place for that. However, I do want to offer a survey of the religions, which is urgently needed today, and I have been preparing it for many decades. Indeed, my whole life has found its way into this book, and at the end I have attempted to indicate very briefly how.

Let me make clear from the start what this book is meant to be and what it is not meant to be.

– It is not mere reporting, which simply describes the situation of the religions in the different countries today. Rather, this book is an up-to-date account which starts from each religion in the present, constantly keeps the present in view in the journey through the centuries, and at the end returns to the present again.

– Nor is it a comprehensive history which sets out to offer the results of most recent research. It is, however, a systematic overall view of history which as succinctly as possible surveys the historical stages of each world religion and analyses their major paradigms and paradigm shifts. For the present can be understood only in the light of constellations from the past, which have often persisted side by side with each other.

In both text and pictures this book attempts to understand the religions as objectively as possible. This objectivity entails a holistic method. So as far as is possible and necessary, the social, political and historical contexts of each religion will be discussed: religions of which a greater knowledge can be presupposed (e.g. Christianity) can be described more briefly than those which are less well known to us (e.g. Indian and Chinese religion). However, the reporting of this book is not 'neutral', but committed in a quite specific direction. Indeed, 37 very personal statements are also scattered through the book (printed in boxes against a tinted background). I prepared them to make at various 'scenes' of the religions for a television series, but when I actually did make them, it was under the impact of special experiences, sometimes in difficult circumstances and in unpolished language.

This project has given me a tremendous opportunity to look for traces all over the world in the 4000-year-old history of the religions. These traces lead to peace and can help towards a life which is more in keeping with human dignity. They are traces of a common human ethic.

So this book is meant to offer reliable information, orientation in the confusing range of religions, and motivation towards a new attitude towards religion and the religions.

I certainly do not suppress the negative aspects of the religions, which I know all too well from personal experience. Their aggressive potential is well known and need not be trotted out here. Indeed, all this forms the starting-point for my efforts over peace between the religions. Perhaps readers, too, will be more interested in the positive function of religions. Why are billions of people all over the world religious? What is the origin and nature of these cultural phenomena which are to be found in all peoples and at all times? What developments have the great religions undergone and what in particular are their ethical constants, which day by day are an influence on countless people? What divides them, and above all what do they have in common? What is the contribution of the religions to an ethic which is now only slowly entering into human consciousness, a global ethic?

I hope that after reading this book readers may share with me the conviction that the goal of a world-wide understanding between the religions cannot and should not be a unitary world religion. There is no sign of anything like this anywhere on earth. Even in the new millennium the diversity of religions can lead to mutual enrichment.

The goal of a world-wide understanding between the religions should be a shared ethic for humankind, but this should not replace religion, as is sometimes falsely assumed. Ethics is and remains only one dimension within an individual religion and between the religions. So there should be no unitary religion, no cocktail of religions and no replacement of religion by an ethic. Rather, there should be an effort to achieve the peace which is so urgently required between the peoples from the various religions of this world. For there can be:

No peace among the nations without peace among the religions.
No peace among the religions without dialogue between the religions.
No dialogue between the religions without global ethical criteria.
No survival of our globe without a global ethic.

# I

# *Indigenous Religions*

## THE DREAM OF A LOST PARADISE

Sometimes we would like to drop out, escape the hustle and bustle and turn our backs on civilization. Why not seek other goals in life, attempt other forms of life?

We dream of a simple life in harmony with an untouched nature, in freedom, without ties, a natural life. This is the dream of a better world, the dream of a lost paradise.

But was there ever such a paradise? Did this ideal primal state of which the Bible tells ever exist? Was there this golden age of which other traditions of humankind speak, from which human beings have departed through their own fault? But where would such a paradise exist if this Golden Age took place? The natural sciences teach us that the world, the earth and human beings developed slowly over millions, indeed billions, of years.

## NATIVE INHABITANTS IN A FALSE LIGHT

Our search for traces of God first takes us to the centre of Australia, to the gigantic monolith Uluru, nowadays called Ayer's Rock, in the midst of a largely empty and uniform island continent the size of Europe. Australia lies in isolation between the Pacific and the Indian Oceans. But in the Ice Age this continent was still a unity with New Guinea in the north and Tasmania in the south, indeed also with Indonesia and the southern tip of Asia. It was only when the sea level rose around 100 metres after the Ice Age that Australia was separated from the land mass of Asia.

There have been traces of human life here for more than 100,000 years; the most recent discoveries of skeletons, stone implements and rock drawings indicate it. Indeed, it was here that *Homo sapiens*, that person with the external form of the present-day human being, developed first of all. This is asserted at least by some enthusiastic advocates of the multi-origin hypothesis, according to whom the development of human beings from the animal kingdom took place in various regions of this world quite independently of one another.

Its native inhabitants still live on the Australian continent: they are called 'Aborigines' (from the Latin *ab origine*, 'from the beginning'). They have left their mark in rock paintings and touched them up time and again: this is the oldest art tradition in the world. Today there are around 230,000 Aborigines in Australia, most of them in towns and a few also on reserves. There, a few attempt as best they can to live in the traditional style: in the way in which our ancestors also must have lived 10,000 years ago, when they still lived by hunting and gathering and their plunder included wild fruit, roots and small animals.

But how has it come about that these people, who have been living in Australia for so many millennia, have been calumniated, scorned and oppressed since their 'discovery' by the Europeans? Not least a report by the English pirate and explorer William Dampier is to blame for this. He was the first to come to the north-west coast of the Australian continent in 1688, after it had initially been discovered as early as 1606 by the Dutchman Willem Jansz and had at first been called 'New Holland'. In his diaries Dampier described the inhabitants there as the most wretched people in the world, without clothing and without houses. They might show strong solidarity within their small group, but they were ugly, and hardly to be distinguished from animals.

## 'PRIMITIVE MAN' – UNCIVILIZED?

The European 'explorers' reported that the Aborigines were people without culture and without religion, and that was also repeated by European scholars. But were they really without culture and religion?

It is true that many of the ways in which these people behave are basically different from ours. But does that make them worse? Are we to regard these people as uneducated and lazy simply because they prefer hunting, gathering, dancing and celebrating to rearing cattle and building houses? The Aborigines could retort:

– You 'civilized people' have developed agriculture and even industrialized it. We 'primitive people' have not cut down the forest and robbed the earth of plants, we have not striven for private property and have accumulated no possessions.

– You 'civilized people' have bred cattle and slaughtered millions of animals. We 'primitive people' have not domesticated animals or kept animals simply to kill and eat.

– You 'civilized people' have built houses, villages and finally giant cities. We 'primitive people' have renounced fixed homes and where possible garments to cover us, which would have isolated us from nature and its cycle.

No wonder that some people in the ecological, feminist and pacifist movements are attacked by the Aborigines' lifestyle, in which nature was spared, in which all were equal, had enough to eat and had to work relatively little. And we should not forget that the Romantics already attempted to idealize nature, which is often so cruel, and dreamed of being able to restore a primal state of paradise. But how could this still be possible in the present-day industrialized and urbanized world?

## LET'S STOP TALKING ABOUT PRIMITIVE CULTURES

Willem Jansz and the other explorers were certainly not romantics. A desire for gold and fame drove them to distant lands. We travellers of today are driven by another longing: the longing for a better, whole world. But a 'return to nature' is impossible. We cannot simply turn back history. However, perhaps it is worth seeing how these so-called 'primitive people' understand themselves. Perhaps they have preserved some of the things that we lost a long time ago.

We should not simply set 'primitive people' and 'civilized people' over against each other. For these Australian Aborigines also have a 'culture' though they developed no writing, no science and no technology. Their thought is quite logical, quite plausible, and in fact is stamped by a 'passion for order', for classifying things and relationships. It is already complicated to establish who may marry whom.

So let's stop talking about primitive peoples and cultures. Instead, let's talk of tribal cultures. For the views of these peoples, their worldview, their language and organization are not as primitive as we think. It is just that everything is more original.

Let's reflect that in our terminology 'primitive' means not only 'original' and 'primal' but also 'lowly', 'underdeveloped', 'rough' and the like. In the tribal cultures in particular – often in fact these are no longer limited to a tribe – great importance is attached to culture: after all, it is the central mark which distinguishes human beings from the animal world and savagery. Therefore we would also do better to avoid the term 'primitive religion' and use the term 'tribal religion' or even 'traditional religion', though the latter term is also used for the religions of higher cultures and cultures with writings.

## THE EARLIEST TRACES OF RELIGION

There is no reason for us Europeans to have any illusions: where do we come from? After all, by development, we too come from 'nature'. And what were we before writing, before written history, before science? First of all we were primitive 'Neanderthals' in the cold Europe of the Ice Age. With his receding forehead and partially different hereditary matter, Neantherthal man may not have been a direct ancestor of *Homo sapiens*, but he was at any rate a relative. He too already had an amazingly high culture: he buried his dead, cared for the old and sick, and had a presumably fully developed language. He died out around 30,000 years ago and gave place to *Homo sapiens*, present-day human beings.

Amazingly, in Australia too the 30,000-year-old male skeleton of a *Homo sapiens* has been found. He was smeared with ochre, a sign widespread all over the world for the idea of a life which continues after death. That means that this man had evidently been given a ritual burial. This is the first clear sign of the culture and religion of the Aborigines.

But what is 'culture'? Culture or civilization, understood comprehensively, always includes religion. Culture is the totality of knowledge and modes of experience which characterize a particular human society, whether these are technical, economic, scientific, social or religious.

## EVEN 'STONE AGE PEOPLE' HAVE A CULTURAL HISTORY

But we should be careful with our comparisons. Are the present Aborigines in Australia really Stone Age people? Have they really remained at the level of the first human beings? Are they a faithful image of the original form of society, as European scholars long thought? Not at all. These Aborigines, too, have changed. They can be classified in about 500 different groups. They speak more than 200 languages, often fundamentally different. They all have a long cultural history.

They are by no means pre-rational and pre-logical, as the first cultural anthropologists (those who investigated human beings and their culture) or ethnologists (those who investigated peoples) thought. Certainly they use a very simple technology, but this in no way implies a simple, indeed unchangeable and static culture. After all, by no means all of them live in a timeless state.

Rather, anthropologists of our day have established that from time to time the Aborigines have taken over rituals and songs, and also artistic styles and techniques, from other tribal groups. They have discovered new holy objects and have assimilated their myths to changed circumstances. And though they may use stone tools, they do not live in the Stone Age.

Thus their different cultures have also survived the two centuries of oppression by the Europeans, sometimes in their original form and sometimes in a changed form. To survive in the 'red heart' of Australia, in the greatest dry area of the southern hemisphere, means being familiar with nature down to the last detail, with its flora and fauna. The Aborigines had already brought with them from Asia to Australia a knowledge of fire, stone tools and implements.

Here under the earth's surface great masses of water from the rainy times of the Ice Age can still be found. However, the water comes to the surface only in quite specific, often hidden places, and often does so only occasionally. These watering places, which are vital to life, are the markers on the unwritten map of the Aborigines. Within the bounds of their hunting and gathering territory, they often travel as semi-nomads for hundreds of miles under the leadership of the men. Why? To find water at the right time at the right place, and also to find fruit or animals. So is this all in all a patriarchal male society? Certainly not.

## WOMEN ECONOMICALLY INDEPENDENT

The Aboriginal women are no less active than the men. Both sexes have a perfect knowledge of nature. But they observe a division of labour, even if this division is not rigorous. The women are gatherers. They know precisely which fruits ripen where and when; which plants, roots, berries, worms and insects are edible. And they teach their children to be at home in nature. The blue bush plants are said to help against headaches and skin diseases.

There is something hidden everywhere in nature. The honey ants, concealed in the earth, are a special delicacy. By tracks in the sand the women know where they can find insects up to ten centimetres long. These insects have been fed with sugary juice by their kind so that their crops swell up and finally they have 'honeypots' filled to the brim. The women dig them up, and now they and their children, not the ants themselves, consume the honey. The honey ant is especially important for particular tribal groups. It is the totem with which they have felt associated since primal times.

The sexes have equal rights when it comes to getting food. Is that perhaps an indication of the original domination of women? Is it support for the old thesis of the matriarchate which made particular reference to Australia when claiming that there was an original matriarchal society? No, more recent scholars have shown this up as a fiction. Or is it at least evidence for completely equal rights for women in the social process, as feminist anthropologists have sought to prove for the Australian Aborigines? This research has the undoubted merit of having thoroughly shaken the idea of a total male domination which was long prevalent among male anthropologists. It has brought out the autonomy of women, above all in the economic sphere. But,

## MEN ARE DOMINANT IN POLITICS AND RITUAL

It cannot be denied that the men are dominant in the political and also the ritual sphere. The regulations about marriage are the work of men. Only men can freely choose partners. And the old men – not the old women – are the guardians of the law. However, women are granted certain sexual freedoms in respect of other men. In particular they have their own secret ritual life and knowledge, their own ceremonies and holy objects. They can also perform healings. Above all, the older women know a good deal about the secret rites of the men.

But these specific women's domains do not yet amount to a matriarchy. The decisive rites and the particularly difficult healings are men's business. It is in the sounds drawn out of the thrumming wood of their instruments by the men that the Aborigines hear the voices of the ancestors, and these warn the women against treading on particularly holy places. In short, in the political and ritual sphere the women are bound by a network of rules defined and controlled by men.

The men are hunters. They know the habits of the kangaroos and possums – both marsupials. There were originally no more highly developed mammals in Australia. But, it may be asked, why do the men throw a stone into a water hole before they get water out of it? Out of reverence for nature: they ask the water spirits for permission. Is that only superstition? It is not just that: the water could be poisoned or the water hole dried out since the previous time. Nothing can be taken for granted. For the Aborigines, much can be explained only by mythology.

## PEOPLE WITHOUT RELIGION?

From primal times the mythology of the Aborigines has been visibly inscribed on the mountains and valleys of this land. Even now they have an almost religious relationship to the land. Religious? But is it really religion? The first anthropologists thought that the Aborigines were 'people without religion': *the* primitives, practising only magic, like the men who cover themselves with red ochre in order to assimilate themselves externally to the eternally young spirits.

It should be realized that the Aborigines of Australia were always something like a religious test case. Cultural anthropology (ethnography) evolved above all in the scholarly arguments over the Aboriginal tribes and here too fronts developed:

– Scholars of the late nineteenth century (like Sir James Fraser), whose scientific thought was moulded by ideas of evolution and progress, saw the whole of human history in a preconceived scheme of stages: first magic (thus in Australia) – only later religion – and in our time science. Fascinated by Darwin, they accepted without proof that the early human beings had all been people without God or gods. Only slowly had they developed from magical practices to religious customs and truths, to sacrifices and prayers. And enlightened only since the European 'discoveries', they would now, like the whites, finally progress to the pure truth of science. Thus the first cultural anthropologists collected a wealth of valuable information about the Aborigines, but interpreted it on the basis of their ideological scheme as belief in spirits and sheer magic.

– By contrast, other scholars, who believed in the Bible rather than Darwin, attempted to justify the opposite scheme of development: they argued that the original Australians had started from a primal monotheism. Only over time had this developed into polytheism and finally degenerated into mere magic. At any rate Australian tribes were still said to know a 'Great Father'.


## 'PRIMAL RELIGION' – NOWHERE TO BE FOUND

Both extreme theories have now been discarded. They are unfounded. Why? Because the cultures of the different tribal groups and with them the religions in reality developed in an utterly unsystematic way.

It would indeed be a prejudice to assume that religion developed quite generally out of magic; belief in spirits out of belief in souls; belief in the gods out of belief in spirits; and finally belief in God out of belief in the gods. Today there is agreement among scholars that phenomena and phases permeate one another. So rather than talking of phases and epochs ('one after another'), people speak of strata and structures ('one on top of the other') which can be found in quite different stages of development, phases or epochs.

And what about the 'primal religion' of human beings? Here too there is no agreement among scholars: empirically it cannot be found anywhere. For even the contemporary tribal peoples with their long, albeit unwritten, cultural history, are not just the 'primal peoples'. And no text, however holy, not even the Bible, provides historical information about the beginning of the world, human beings, religion, a 'primal people'. Instead of this the Bible in particular offers a message about God and man embodied in great poetry: about the greatness of the one Creator, about the divinely willed goodness of his creatures, and about the freedom, responsibility and guilt of human beings. So many people of course ask: don't the Australian Aborigines know such a God and Creator of the world and human beings? Can he perhaps even be found in their famous rock paintings?

## THE ART OF THE ABORIGINES

We have only to look at the depiction of a single leaf to be impressed by the art of the Aborigines. The same symbols, thousands of years old, are painted and touched up time and again. There are stylized plants, animals, human beings, but – as far as we can decipher the drawings – no gods, far less the one God.

On some rock pictures age-old routes are indicated leading right across the land, often from water hole to water hole, to which the Aborigines have given names. Two geometrical figures stand in the foreground:
– Depending on the narrative, circles, concentric circles, depict water holes, camp places, fire places, sometimes also a tree or a honey ant nest. At any rate they form the static element in the rock pictures.
– Lines stand for ways, spears, lightning, watercourses: they form the dynamic element. And what does the loincloth of a woman mean? Drawings like this serve to teach and to tell stories, but in general they have a ceremonial significance.

However, the deepest meaning of all is kept secret by the Aborigines. That also applies to the rich decorations which they put on sacred stones and pieces of wood which are called tjurungas. Granted, today these are now exploited commercially, usually in a different form, and are mostly put to a purely profane use. But in the end they have a religious significance.

What kind of religion did the Aborigines have and still have? At a very early stage they learned to kindle by themselves the fire which in the beginning human beings received through lightning from heaven. And this heaven – is it not empty?

## WHAT IS IN HEAVEN?

Professor T. G. H. Strehlow is probably the greatest expert on the tribes of central Australia. He spent his youth among the Aranda east of Uluru. He recorded hundreds of religious ceremonies and published a monumental work on the songs of Central Australia. He was the scholar who developed at length the currently normative view of the question of God, the world and human beings. According to him the tribes of Central Australia take two things for granted. Heaven and earth are eternal. And heaven and earth each have their own supernatural beings.

Do they have the one God? There are in fact tribes which believe in a Great Father (also called 'Eternal Youth'), who like all the inhabitants of heaven is immortal. But he is not like the God of the Bible. He has an emu's feet and moreover has a wife and child – according to some tribes even several wives and children. And what takes place below on earth leaves him and all the other original inhabitants of heaven untouched. Therefore neither the Great Father nor other heavenly beings are honoured on earth with prayers, songs and sacrifices.

## AND WHO FORMED THE EARTH?

Which powers and forces then formed the earth? Beyond question the great ancestor spirits of primal time. And they did not come from heaven but from the ground, in the form of human beings and animals. On gigantic travels they shaped the formless and monotonous earth into a landscape with hills, ways, watering places and mountains. They also created sun, moon and stars, and from preformed masses they created human beings, tribes and clans along with animals: ordinary animals like the ants and extraordinary animals like the amphibious thorny devil dragon. The great ancestor beings hunted, camped, fought, loved and performed particular rituals at particular places. They assigned the land to the tribal groups. But then, having grown weary, the ancestor spirits returned to the earth. Some sank into the water and others were elevated into heaven.

It is now for human beings to preserve the earth in the form and purity shaped by the ancestor beings: not to change it violently, but to spare it as far as possible. For the land is not just a material resource; it is land hallowed by the ancestor spirits. But all human beings are mortal, for they themselves or some dark forces have broken the link with heaven (the tree or ladder).

## 'DREAMTIME'

All this, they say, happened in 'dreamtime'. But is this 'dreaming' really the key concept for primal time? Western anthropologists were the ones who introduced 'dreaming' or 'dreamtime'. This is a term which does not exist at all in the primal Australian languages to denote the complicated situation to which it refers. The word *alcheringa* or *altjiranga* from Central Australian Aranda first used by Baldwin Spencer does not mean dreaming.

It means that original time when the ancestor spirits formed the physical world 'at the beginning of things' and simultaneously laid down the social, ethical, religious and ritual 'laws' to be followed as a way of life.

So it would be a misunderstanding of the word 'dreaming' to think that it suggests a single phenomenon, that it denotes a pre-logical or even fantastic sphere where the laws of logic allegedly do not apply. No, we do not have mythical realities here in the unreal sense of 'once upon a time'. It is not as if 'dreamtime' took place a long, long time ago; as if it were a fundamentally conservative principle which strictly determined everything today.

Subsequently 'dreaming' has been identified with everything possible: with the archetypes of the depth psychologist C. G. Jung, with Hindu karma, with 'green' theories about human beings and nature or with a new Christian 'creation spirituality'. But caution is needed: for the Aborigines 'dreaming' is not something dreamlike, past, unreal. It is the greatest reality, in which past, present and future form an indissoluble unity. For the eternal is invisibly present in the visible world. Human time and immutable eternity are more closely bound together among the Aborigines than in other cultures. This is the reason why there are no formal prayers and atonement offerings for deities outside the human world. Rather, the Aborigines find the eternal in the temporal: in a nature which is full of supernatural mysteries. The eternal, uncreated life force is at work in all things. This religion, which is bound up with nature, roots the individual in eternity. It gives the individual identity, the awareness of having a high personal value.

## THE ETERNAL LAW: TJUKURPA

The Anangu (from the Pitjantjarara tribe) living around the Uluru speak of 'tjukurpa', the 'law' given right at the beginning by the ancestor spirits. Tjukurpa embraces religion, ethics, rites, the whole way of life. 'Tjukurpa – this law – ' they say in their language, 'was given us by our grandfathers and grandmothers, our fathers and mothers, for us to observe in our heads and in our hearts.' This unwritten primal law has been handed on over time with the help of myths and songs, dances and ceremonies, body paintings and sand drawings, sacred objects and rock paintings.

The early anthropologists thought that the Aborigines spent their whole lives simply surviving. The opposite is true: for them, along with all the hunting and gathering, the whole of life from primal times was an uninterrupted sequence of ceremonies, dances and rituals. For the actions of the primal ancestors, the ancestor spirits – the subject of myth (which in Greek means narration), the tradition from the prehistory of a tribe or people – are handed on from generation to generation, but also adapted time and again to circumstances. For these people it is not very important whether all that is narrated is historical and plausible, whether or not it has a historical nucleus.

No, what is important for them is that what is narrated helps people to understand the world and themselves. And this does not happen through theoretical statements but through stories, images and rites which express the holy order of things that was given from the beginning and is never to be violated. For the Aborigines are convinced that what is good comes from primal times: all the material and spiritual goods which are to be preserved. After all, it is the ancestral beings who with their thought and action have laid down the norms for morals and customs. Cult and ceremonies are to repeat the events of primal times by song and drama.

## THE FIGHT BETWEEN THE SNAKE WOMAN KUNIYA AND THE SNAKE MAN LIRU

Does primal time mean a whole world, a paradise? No, on the contrary, here already there is good and evil, hatred and strife. The ancestor spirits are not gods nor are they moral examples. That is evident from the story which is still alive today of the battle between the giant snake Kuniya and Liru, a man who is a poisonous snake. As the Aborigines see it, this battle has left deep traces on the south side of Uluru. Since primal times they have told this story.

At that time the snake woman Kuniya came to Uluru to lay her eggs. But her nephew had so angered a host of poisonous Liru snakes that these threw Liru's spears at him; holes in the rock still bear witness to this. A spear fatally wounded him.

When Kuniya saw this she became sad, indeed angry, but a Liru warrior only mocked her. Thirsting for revenge, she roused herself to perform a powerful dance. To assuage her anger, first of all she spat poison in the sand and hurled it into the depths. But then she advanced on the Liru man and – now beside herself with rage – raised her hatchet and smote him, first gently and then fatally.

Even today the traces of the battle are pointed out on Uluru: fig trees and gum trees poisoned, snake tracks in the rock, Kuniya's two blows, and the shield of the dead Liru warrior, which has fallen on the ground. And finally there is the water hole to which Kuniya brought her dead nephew and where even today prayers for rain are offered to the ancestor snake. This is a holy place. Here is a true story of guilt and atonement, battle and death.

So all this is part of tjukurpa, the primal law, which to the present day is the foundation of the culture. Thus the conduct and actions of the primal powers have brought either life, happiness and salvation, or pain, destruction, death and disaster. At all events the battle between Kuniya and Liru is an event which even today is celebrated by the Australian Aborigines in stories, songs and ritual dances.

## WHY WOMEN PAINT THEIR BODIES

It is fascinating to see how the women from a Walpiri tribe north of Uluru, strictly segregated from the men, prepare for an initiation dance. They sing particular song cycles in their tribal language and paint mysterious symbols which are connected with primal times and primal law. They find these difficult to explain.

But why do these women paint their bodies – with ochre, clay and ashes? Not only for aesthetic and cosmetic reasons. The colour gives them a new skin and a different personality for the dance. These are all ceremonial actions: one does not paint without singing, and one does not dance without painting.

Here beyond question human sexuality plays a central role – as in all tribal religions. Sexual symbolism is an expression of the eternal male and female principles, indeed of that eternal uncreated life force which already manifested itself in the ancestor spirits and from there influences all living beings, so that new life is received and handed on time and again.

## WHAT IS TOTEM AND WHAT IS TABOO?

There is no doubt that animals play a quite special role in these paintings and dances. As we have already seen, for the Aborigines each individual comes from a quite definite primal being, an animal or a plant, the totem (to use a North American term), which as the animal from which the clan originates is also its guardian spirit. The kangaroo or the emu, a snake or a bird, are venerated as the primal ancestor of a whole tribe or clan. This is a collective totem which determines the totem relationship and regulates certain prohibitions relating to marriage (to combat incest). In accord with their totem, people call themselves kangaroos or snakes, and this at the same time raises the status of animals and plants.

So do the Aborigines make no distinction between human beings and animals? Ethnologists used to claim this, but it is nonsense. For the Aborigines, the connection between kangaroos and human beings is not biological but mythological. And it is no more to be taken literally than the transformation in our fairy tales of a king into a frog and vice versa.

But did the Aborigines perhaps have no knowledge of the biological origin of human beings? Ethnologists also used to claim this. But that too is nonsense. Alongside biological procreation and the mortal soul the Aborigines knew a second soul. The mother received this later at a particular place in the landscape. This other, immortal soul of the child comes from a primal being (say, in the first pains of pregnancy). It is the individual totem. It gives the child a home in the sphere of the eternal, remains its guardian spirit and communicates rights and duties. The 'place of conception' is of crucial significance for this 'conception totemism'.

For the Aborigines the totem is 'taboo' (a Polynesian word which means 'hallowed', 'untouchable'). As a result a totem animal may not be hunted, wounded or killed. But it can and should be depicted: on stones and wood, in dances and songs. And it should be celebrated to maintain one's own species. And because all the rituals are thought to have been ordained by the ancestor spirits, the ceremonial songs, body paintings and rituals are to remain unchanged. But which ritual is the most important?

## THE INITIATION DANCE: PRIMAL TIME AND PRIMAL LAW

The most important rite is initiation into adulthood, which takes place in stages. The child becomes the youth and the youth becomes the man. The girls are initiated by the mothers in a separate rite, above all into the mysteries of life: menstruation, deflowering, pregnancy and birth.

The boys are parted from their mothers through dance. Separated from the community they are to go through the land and gradually be initiated by experienced older men into the mysteries of the ancestor spirits, the land, the tribe, hunting and sexuality. Tests of courage are required in these puberty rites, especially in hunting, but also by adding scars, which are regarded as signs of beauty and strength. And above all, circumcision is performed.

The boy will return to his mother a different person from when he went away: as a grown man. Now he is initiated into tjukurpa, the primal law, into particular myths, rites, rules and precepts which come from primal times. As a young adult he has quite definite rights, but also responsibilities.

### UNWRITTEN ETHICAL NORMS

And in fact that is not very different from what we attempt to teach our children. Tjukurpa, the 'law', is meant to tell them what their place in life is, what is good and what is bad. In Australia, too, no people is without religion, far less without an ethic, i.e. without quite definite norms and standards. Of course, these are unwritten norms, handed down in stories, parables and comparisons. In the end every human society builds on them.

The 'primitive peoples' did not receive any table of commandments, say with the statement 'You shall not steal', but they do have a sense of reciprocity, justice and generosity (for example in the exchange of gifts).

- They do not have a commandment, 'You shall not kill', but they do have a deep reverence for all life (for example in resolving conflicts and punishing violence).
- They do not know a commandment, 'You shall not commit adultery', but they do know particular rules for the life of the sexes together (for example a prohibition of incest and a rejection of libertinism).
- They do not know a divine commandment, 'Honour your father and mother', but they do have a great respect for parents (and at the same time a love of children).

## A PRIMAL ETHIC

It is striking that certain basic human standards seem to be the same all over the world. Unwritten ethical norms form the rock on which human society is built. We can call this a primal ethic, which forms the core of a common ethic of humankind, a global ethic. So a global ethic does not have its foundation only in the basic norms of the different religions and regions today (synchronically). It also has its foundation in the basic norms of tribal cultures which already became established in prehistoric times (before the institution of written sources) (diachronically). But even if one may not of course regard every norm as an element of an ethic which has already been given, to bring out the continuity in all the transformations it can be said that the present-day universal ethic in space is ultimately based on a primal ethic in time.

So it is not surprising that the founding fathers of descriptions of peoples (ethnographies), those great travellers to whom since antiquity we have been indebted for reports on alien cultures, were all fascinated on the one hand by the differences between cultures and on the other by the common basic human features which transcend all differences. For a long time cultural diversity and variability stood in the foreground for modern ethnology. Now, though, in connection with the debate on globalization, ethnologists see themselves challenged to bring out more clearly what unites human beings despite all their cultural differences. New comparative studies are being made.

Here the significance of myths and rites for ethics can hardly be overestimated. They already guarantee a certain basic order for the little tribal groups of Australia which rests on basic social factors. Of course there are no differentiated state forms of organization as there are in the urbanized high cultures of Mesopotamia, Egypt, India and China with their command of writing. Rather, there is more co-operation than subordination, more differentiation without inequality, more tolerance for other customs and views. So the tribal cultures were and are quite well organized in their own way. Four factors of order are still determinative:
- gender: for the division of work;
- age: for the social hierarchy;
- kinship: for marriage practices;
- the totem: for cohesion beyond the family (and at the same time as a protection for flora and fauna).

But where do specific ethical standards, values and norms come from? In the view of the Aborigines they certainly did not fall from heaven. They were shaped in the beginning by the ancestor beings, who were quite earthly. Seen in terms of the history of their development it is clear that the concrete ethical norms, values and insights came to be formed gradually, in a hugely complex dynamic social process. Where needs in life made themselves felt, where urgent inter-personal matters and necessities emerged, from the beginning there was a need for guidelines and regulations for action: particular conventions, instructions, morals – in short, specific ethical standards and norms. These were tried out in the course of the centuries. They had so to speak to be polished. Only after periods of acclimatization and testing was there a general recognition of such existential norms, which were perhaps also formulated in statements. However, in a completely changed time such polished norms, values and standards could not only be changed but also robbed of content and even dropped. And such a time was to come for the Aborigines of Australia.

## COLONIZATION: COOK AND THE CONSEQUENCES

The Aborigines have always climbed Uluru only at the beginning of a religious ceremony. In the end it is a holy mountain, associated with many stories about tjukurpa. But then the whites came. And nothing was holy any more: age-old values were devalued. New values, above all material values, were put in their place, and the promise of endless progress.

First came that bold explorer Captain James Cook, who around 200 years ago with his staff of scientists more than anyone else changed the map of the world peacefully and made it possible for the British to seize power. On his first circumnavigation of the world in 1770 he discovered the fertile east coast of Australia. At any rate, in contrast to William Dampier he gave a relatively positive account.

But the two centuries of blood, sweat and tears which followed the white invasion are all too familiar. The Aborigines were threatened with nothing less than total destruction. Certainly no one can overlook the epoch-making significance of the colonization of this continent, now called not 'New Holland' but 'Australia': the legendary great 'unknown southern land' which Ptolemy already conjectured as a counterbalance to the northern continent: *Terra australis incognita*. The Europeans brought their cultivated plants, their domestic animals and their working animals and above all their technology. But even white Australians today will hardly deny that the result of this colonization was deeply ambiguous.

## TRIUMPH FOR THE WHITES – TRAGEDY FOR THE BLACKS

On the one hand, despite all the difficulties and setbacks, white Australia had a tremendous economic and political success story:
– First of all Australia was a penal colony: the first 717 English convicts arrived in 1788, and by 1868 around 161,000 in all had been settled there.
– Then it became a powerful centre of the wool trade: by 1829 there were already 400,000 white Australians.
– As a result of the discovery of gold in 1851 there was a second great wave of immigration; there were already 1,000,000 inhabitants by 1860 and at the end of the gold rush at the beginning of the twentieth century there were 4,000,000 Europeans in Australia.
– At the end of the twentieth century there were more than 18,000,000 inhabitants, with one of the highest standards of living in the world: 95 per cent of them are white and only about 2 per cent are Aborigines.

On the other hand, as a result of the white immigration there is the economic, political and cultural tragedy of the black Australians:
– By European law the land of the Aborigines, about as large as the United States, is regarded as virtually uninhabited no man's land (*terra nullius*); in short it has been declared British crown property, divided and 'colonized'.
– The religious bond of the Aborigines to their land has been trampled on: by a new 'right to private property' and new place names.
– For a long time the Aborigines have not been accepted as negotiating

partners; rather, as 'British subjects' they have been deprived of their rights and put under the colonial administrations.

– The European cattle-breeders, superior in numbers, organization and above all in technology, have increasingly displaced the Aborigines from their ancestral land into barren regions; indeed, sometimes they have actually killed them off.

– European diseases which have crept in, like venereal diseases, smallpox and measles, have even more decimated the black population, which has no resistance to them.

– Of the estimated at least 300,000 Aborigines at the beginning of the occupation and settlement, in 1901 only 67,000 remained, now including very many as cattle-drivers and labourers.

– On the reserves and mission stations, founded in the second half of the nineteenth century, the Aborigines had to change completely to European ways of life. Hunting and gathering were forbidden, as were the religious rites and polygamy. All in all, this was a separation from 'dreamtime'.

– Since the middle of the twentieth century yet more cult places in the interior have been desecrated and destroyed through the exploitation of the minerals there.

– It is estimated that even in our century, by 1970 100,000 children of mixed race had been forcibly separated from their parents.

## ABORIGINES IN THE SUPERMARKET: THE CONFLICT BETWEEN TWO CULTURES

But hasn't the situation of the Aborigines slowly improved in the last third of the twentieth century? It certainly has. However, by comparison with the white population the deficits are still great. In 1967 the Aborigines finally achieved equal rights to those of the whites under the law, and in 1992 they also secured some recognition of their earlier rights to the land. But now the Australian government is also finding itself increasingly confronted with massive demands for land, and that is the origin of vigorous conflicts which are far from being settled. However, in their protests against blatant abuses, the Aborigines are also increasingly finding support among the whites. There have been minor reconciliations between white and black in churches, communities and schools. But the greater reconciliation of two cultures still lies far in the distance.

The government still wants itself to apportion the development rights for mineral resources, which are regarded as national property. Will it be possible for the radical demands of the Aborigines for a complete restructuring of the land to be carried through? Be this as it may, the efforts made by the Australian federal government for the Aborigines have increased greatly since the 1970s. At the same time numerous institutions created for the political, social, legal and medical spheres are administered by the Aborigines.

However, the granting of major financial subsidies has also led to struggles over power and distribution among the Aborigines themselves, since now a black élite in the cities has made itself the spokesman for the traditional Aborigines in the country, from whom it has become largely alienated. Only a few blacks want to move out of the towns and villages into the desert. Why should they once more get by hunting and gathering what they can quite easily buy in the supermarket? And why not use modern technology, means of transport and building methods? One thing is certain: the majority of the Aborigines do not want independence and isolation, but they do not want total integration and assimilation either. Is there a reasonable middle way?


## KEEPING THE OLD RELIGION ALIVE

Johnny Possum Tjaplejerrie too wants to share in the achievements of the modern world and at the same time remain himself. For it remains important for him that in origin he belongs spiritually to the ancestor 'possum' ('opossum'), a little climbing marsupial.

This totem binds Johnny not only to his family but also to all the possum people. He shares the same ceremonial centre and the same rituals with them. There is a quite specific tradition, for which every member of the tribe has a special responsibility.

As a possum man he has his own quite personal possum history, which he can draw in the sand. It shows:
– how he, indicated by possum tracks, goes to another camp;
– how four women there are in search of tobacco leaves;
– how he attempts to put these into a trance with a love song;
– how he finally gets his wife here.

But whether it is a possum story or a possum dance – a fight between two tribes over a water hole in which each dancer represents a possum – each colour, each movement has one or more meanings, often different for initiates and non-initiates. For many Aborigines these old myths, rites, symbols and centres do not conflict with modern civilization. And they see them as more than folklore and nostalgia. So they want to keep them alive. They also want to preserve the old names and holy places and get to know the myths, songs and ceremonies associated with them. So this religion – despite all the prophecies – has not died out. Yet . . .

# A QUESTION FOR NATIVE INHABITANTS THROUGHOUT THE WORLD

The Aborigines are in the midst of a great transformation of their culture. For most of them the original cultural roots of a tribe and a person still play a significant role. But what individuals make of these roots must be left to them. And the decisions that individuals make may differ, depending on whether they have risen into white society or live in one of the slums on the edge of the great cities. Or they may try to lead their lives as far as possible by the age-old traditions, on one of the reserves. Be this as it may, set between tradition and modern culture, the Aborigines themselves should be allowed to determine their way of life in the light of their great cultural heritage.

However, the question arises for all of them, and especially for the younger generation, whether the old myths, rites, symbols and centres – four essential elements of the tribal religions – are in the long run adequate as spiritual roots: for their own cultural identity, a really different world-view, an alternative way of life.

And this is not just a question for Australians but for native inhabitants all over the world: for the Maoris in New Zealand, for the Canadian Inuit, the Indians of North and South America, the Nenet in the Russian tundra, Mongolian tribes in China and the Ainu of Japan. This question also arises in a slightly different way on another continent, where 'native inhabitants' and Europeans, or at any rate traditional religion and modern culture, clash with each other, namely in Africa. Geographically and culturally we must now make a giant leap.

# PRIMAL TIMES: AUSTRALIA AND AFRICA

It is almost incredible that today Australia and Africa are separated from each other by around 5000 miles. Two billion years ago both formed a great southern continent (Gondwanaland), together with India, New Zealand, South America and the Antarctic.

In the late cretaceous age, around 130 million years ago or even later, this gigantic land mass broke up and its elements drifted further and further apart. Since then Australia and Africa have been separate continents. Africa remained the second largest continent: the USA, India and China could easily fit into it. The distance from south to north, from Capetown to Tangier, is again almost 5000 miles. Geologically Africa is a very old continent in which the geological history of our earth can be studied better than anywhere else. But historically, too, Africa is also an age-old abode of human beings – highly significant for the beginnings of human culture, which for those researching into primal history already begins in the Old Stone Age (the Palaeolithic Age) with the 'tool-making being'.

That is why the second half of this chapter takes us to black Africa, first of all to the largest river of Africa south of the Sahara, the Zambesi. This Zambesi is an unparalleled natural spectacle. From the centre of Africa it flows eastwards, and between Zambia and Zimbabwe it thunders down from a plateau more than 300 feet before flowing through Mozambique to the Indian Ocean. The Victoria Falls are the greatest curtain of water on earth.

They were discovered by the 'missionary, adventurer and explorer David Livingstone', according to the inscription on the monument directly beside the falls. Livingstone was the first European to see the Zambesi Falls in 1855 and he named them after Victoria, who was the British queen at the time. He had already seen the cloud of spray from the waterfalls from almost 40 miles away. And there he saw a view which made this otherwise matter-of-fact man remark, 'even the angels in flight would have to wonder at this'. We must remember that it was here that Livingstone lost his wife, who had accompanied him on all his bold travels, from the yellow fever which still threatens travellers today. At that time the burdens that all the explorers of the rivers and lands of Africa took upon themselves were certainly enormous. However, here we are interested in another question: can perhaps the biological beginnings of humankind as a whole be demonstrated on this ancient continent?


## HUMAN BEINGS COME FROM AFRICA

Human beings reflect endlessly on their origins, and investigate them – in religion, philosophy and science. Some scholars think that *Homo sapiens*, human beings as they are today, developed in many places in the world. But on the basis of overwhelming discoveries, including the most recent ones, most scholars are convinced that *Homo sapiens* comes from warm, tropical and sub-tropical Africa, rich in wild life, in all probability from the Great Rift Valley which runs through Africa and Syria, north of the Zambesi. So Africa is our common origin.

In the dawn of prehistory, 2,000,000 years before any culture with writing, this area saw the appearance of *Homo habilis*, the human being who was capable of cutting stones as tools. L. S. B. Leakey has excavated the earliest tools known to us in the volcanic tufa at the bottom of the Olduwai Rift in Kenya and on the basis of the strata has been able to date them to between 2,150,000 and 2,120,000 years ago. Since then countless more recent discoveries have been made. Africa kept pace with the development of the other continents in the Old and Middle Stone Ages. That is evident from increasingly refined stone tools and also rock drawings. In the region of the Zambesi, finds of tools and burial places allow us to follow clearly the development of *Homo habilis* until he becomes our direct ancestor, *Homo sapiens*.

**WE ARE ALL AFRICANS UNDER THE SKIN**

It was probably around 100,000 years ago that *Homo sapiens* set off on his long journey over the globe and displaced the Neanderthals in Europe and elsewhere. Nearest to him on the evolutionary scale in Africa was the chimpanzee, who in its own course of development formed three very different sub-species. By contrast, *Homo sapiens* had a uniform development. And whether we meet an Aborigine over in Australia or a Bushman in Africa, an Asian, a European or an American, these are not all different species of human being, but all are one and the same human race. And though our external characteristics may be very different, presumably we all have a common African origin. Under the skin we are all Africans.

## THE LATE STONE AGE REVOLUTION

No one should doubt any longer the great capacity of black Africa for culture and development. The impression, long cherished, that African culture is static and stationary is misleading. So is the impression that the black African peoples are historically passive. Rather, the history of black Africa, too, reveals a progressive dynamic. We need to remember two things:

– Here by the Zambesi, as all over southern Africa, there are hunters and gatherers: the real native inhabitants of Africa whom the Dutch rather disrespectfully called 'Bushmen'. They themselves, however, call themselves the San.

– But in contrast to Australia, since the great revolution in the Late Stone Age, i.e. for thousands of years, in Africa there have also been farmers and cattle breeders who established village cultures in fixed abodes.

Thus the 'Late Stone Age revolution' meant a transition not only to polished stone tools, bows and pottery but to 'production' (cultivating

plants, taming and keeping animals) and to 'capital' (in the form of beasts of burden, seeds and raw materials). And with agriculture and breeding animals came the concern to acquire private property. So-called 'just' wars could be fought, and the rule of the few over the many took shape. The natural landscape became cultivated land, and villages became towns.

Finally, 5000 years ago, at the turn from the fourth to the third millennium BC, there were complex early historical high cultures and high religions which formed cities and states by the great rivers. This was bound up with the invention of writing. As yet there is still no satisfactory explanation of why they formed on the Euphrates, later on the Indus and the Yellow River, but in Africa in this early period only on the Nile, and not at the same time on the Zambesi or elsewhere in black Africa. Here it was to be millennia before individual courts and secret societies had a script, and then they kept it away from ordinary people in order to hang on to power.

Still, between the eleventh and the fifth centuries BC, in Africa too farmers and cattle-breeders penetrated southwards from the north and drove out the San, the original inhabitants, into remote areas, usually deserts. They formed the linguistic family of the Bantu ('human beings'), though this comprises very different groups of peoples from Cameroon through Central and East Africa to South Africa. If we enter a Bantu village we note how the age-old social order still functions very well here. But what we are most interested in is the religion.

## GUARDIAN SPIRITS – ONLY AFRICAN?

Barely half the inhabitants of Zimbabwe, this state in the interior of South Africa, call themselves Christians. But all of them – whether Christian or non-Christian (perhaps under Christian or Muslim influence) – believe in Mwari, the one God and Creator. Mixed up with this we frequently find traditional African religion, according to which the world and human beings are governed by invisible forces which need to be taken into account. The relationship to the ancestor spirits is central here. They are closer to human beings than the remote Creator God.

We should not overlook the fact that the Bantu-speaking peoples still celebrate ancient rites at the end of the twentieth century in the middle of modern civilization; others have disappeared under European influence. Even here in almost 100 per cent black Zimbabwe, which consists of two tribal cultures, 77 per cent Shona and 18 per cent Ndebele, traditional African religion is still very much alive. This is a world full of spirits, like the world of the Christian Middle Ages.

In Zimbabwe, as everywhere else among the tribal religions of black

Africa, there is a broad spectrum of spirits, good and evil, predictable and unpredictable. There are ancestor spirits (*vadzimu*) which now function as guardian spirits for the family and especially the children. There are wandering spirits (*mashavi*) which, because they have not been buried correctly abroad, do not want to be forgotten. There are tribal spirits (*mhondoro*), which are concerned for the prosperity of a tribe and its head. The tribal religions are not utterly stamped with a fear of demons, as is often claimed. Besides, some pious or impious Europeans still think that they can ward off evil spirits and 'bad luck' and influence good spirits by particular rites, amulets and very much more.

The ancestors make themselves known through a medium, who is taken possession of by a spirit, the spirit medium (*svikiro*). Endowed by the spirit with particular gifts, only this medium can soothe the evil spirits, propitiate them or drive them away. How? Through prayer, song, dance, and sacrifices, perhaps by the sacrifice of a goat, as above all at the joyful harvest festival.

## SACRIFICING GOATS EVEN TODAY

The whole ceremony begins eight days earlier with sexual continence and then reaches a first climax on the evening before with singing, dancing and the drinking of beer, which is brewed by older women who can no longer become 'unclean' through menstruation.

Clearly this is not an anxious feast but a joyful one. However, it is no longer the medium but the ancestor spirit who now speaks from the medium with a deep voice. He calls for gratitude: 'People,' he says, 'you came to me and wanted rain. Now you have had rain and good harvests. So value what we have done for you and live in the traditional way.' The people answer the rainmaker with the cry, 'Goat, now we sacrifice you!'

We need to know that at first the spirits of the dead wander around angry and dangerous. But they can be brought home by appropriate rites and made guardian ancestors. The land belongs to the ancestors. The ancestors are responsible for the prosperity of the living. The ancestors give health, rain and good harvests.

But now it is time for the sacrifice. The helpers are ready and do the holy work. Blood flows. But only the medium may drink the blood. That gives him supernatural power to control the spirits. However, something else is important for the people: 'The goat is dead,' goes up the cry; 'there is meat to eat.' There is also beer, handed round in great jars as a sign of togetherness. And people dance and dance and rejoice: over the sacrifice and the soothing of the spirits. Meanwhile the goat is cut up – in a matter-of-fact way, without deeper significance and symbolism. The rainmaker gets the best bit – the liver. It is eaten raw. And finally, water is sprinkled; now the spirits can rest.


## SPIRITUAL HEALING – NOT AUTOMATIC

Human beings are religious by their whole origin. And the old cults made it possible, indeed still make it possible, to interpret the mysteries of life and death. The human longing for happiness, for salvation, for healing, is age-old. And what often seems to us to be meaningless and miraculous here has its own logic, its own function. It is not all superstition, magic or even the work of the devil, as Europeans thought. Moreover in the Bible, too, are not sicknesses often attributed to demons, to spirits? In the Bible, too, the healing of body and soul goes together: it is a psychosomatic event.

There are religious healings, i.e. faith healings, prayer healings and spirit healings, in all cultures. And in Africa in particular, people meet everywhere in hordes around the healers and interpreters, who often indicate their position to the spirits with a banner. The healer is thought to have spiritual powers to heal infirmities and to indicate who is to blame. A banner with a cross, holy water to drive away the spirits, scarlet colouring and a staff: some of the rituals of healing recall the exorcisms of the medieval church. Here too the healing power of God itself is called down by blowing the trumpets of Jericho. For only if God hallows the place and the water, only if God gives the healer the power, may the healer drive out the evil spirits and help those who suffer from sickness or misfortune. In the eyes of the wider family, those who avoid going to the healer are to blame for further misfortunes.

In Zimbabwe alone there are 50,000 such spiritual healers, medicine men, witch doctors. They are on the increase in reaction to modernization, and they have innumerable patients. Here are just two examples:
– A woman believes that she is a witch: she has done harm to others. The healer, usually in a trance, commands the spirits. She is touched with the healer's staff and sprinkled with holy water. In this way she senses the healing power and the spirits confess themselves beaten. Healed, the woman creeps by herself into the field.
– A second woman is sick, in her heart and stomach. But the spirits which have taken hold of her are stubborn and she resists vigorously. The woman is treated harshly, very harshly. But even salt water in her mouth and nose cannot heal her torments. The treatment must be postponed to another time. We can see that healing is not automatic. And the healing staff is not a magician's wand.

## AGAINST WITCHCRAFT

I don't know what you think, but such spiritual healing can seem very brutal, indeed inhuman, to us Europeans. But the Africans see it differently. They laugh and say that evil spirits can only be driven out with force.

Of course, things are not so harmless if a quite specific person is blamed for a sickness or even is said to have caused a bolt of lightning. Then our medieval witch trials can be repeated: a completely innocent person is condemned to severe punishment, sent away or even executed.

So in some African states credentials are required for such spiritual healing. At the same time the law prohibits anyone from being accused of witchcraft, though nevertheless this happens very often.

## AFRICA'S GREAT CENTURIES

There is still a widespread prejudice that the black Africans were 'savages' before mission and colonization. They were rough 'nature people' without any culture. That is just wrong. Quite apart from the old cultures of Egypt, Nubia and Ethiopia, the peoples of black Africa also developed. They achieved a level of culture which left the Aborigines of Australia far behind, a level which in fact in some respects can be compared with the European Middle Ages.

From the end of the twelfth to the end of the sixteenth century black Africa experienced an economic, political and cultural boom. These were its 'great centuries'. There was, for example, the construction of the city of Great Zimbabwe with its giant granite buildings. There is no greater and more impressive cultural monument south of the Sahara than this old capital. In our century it was to give its name to the whole land: *dzimba dza mabwe* – 'houses of stone', or *dzimba woye*, 'venerable houses'. Since 1986 the extensive site with its conical tower and citadel has been classified by UNESCO as part of the world's cultural heritage.

## THEY WERE BLACK AFRICANS

The great question is: who built it? There has been speculation about that for four centuries:

– The Portuguese, who in the sixteenth century were the first Europeans to penetrate into the interior, in search of gold, thought that in Zimbabwe they had found the Queen of Sheba's land of Ophir, from where King Solomon in Jerusalem had got his gold.

– The German explorer Carl Mauch, who in 1871 was the first European to investigate the ruins of Great Zimbabwe and reported on its amazing technical world, also attributed the ruins to the Queen of Sheba: a wooden doorpost reminded him of the house of cedar in the temple of Solomon, though in a confidential note only published posthumously he later came to doubt this.

– The founder of British Rhodesia, Cecil Rhodes, concluded from a comparison of the British empire with the Phoenician empire that Great Zimbabwe was of Phoenician origin. The dilettante researchers commissioned by his British South African Company likewise assumed Phoenician origin and an Arab master builder.

– The Rhodesian Ancient Ruins Society founded soon afterwards had Great Zimbabwe and 50 other ruined cities plundered in the search for treasure and assumed that 'Semitic colonists' had built Zimbabwe.

Be this as it may, it was thought that the builders certainly could not have been black Africans. This was the European prejudice down the centuries. It was not until 1950 that the first professional archaeologist, David Randall-McIver, shattered this presupposition which had hitherto been held. The British archaeologist asserted that the builders had been black Africans. Natives of the Shona tribe of the Karanga had built this city.

Subsequent researchers confirmed this. But the British colonial population would have nothing of it. As late as 1973 the highly regarded archaeologist Peter Garlake, who between 1964 and 1970 was state curator of monuments, was expelled from the country because of a book which provided broad documentation for an African origin. But today no one doubts any longer that black Africans, made rich above all by trading in gold, built Great Zimbabwe in the fourteenth century. It was a representative city of between 12,000 and 20,000 people, which reached its high point in the fifteenth century.

Many white people do not realize even today that despite the tremendous natural obstacle of the Sahara, right across the continent, through which only difficult and dangerous caravan routes led, in the European high Middle Ages the African peoples were also experiencing an upward trend in their culture. After a phase of itinerant movements and exchange with the outside world through the Arabs, the black African countries seem to have achieved a certain equilibrium.

At the time of the first bold Portuguese expeditions in the fifteenth century – at that time Portugal was the most advanced European sea power – there were already black kingdoms with differentiated social structures, a balance of power worked out between different interest groups, and a notable art and culture. These were more or less centralized systems of rule, but they were rarely one-man governments. For all the differences, they have been compared with the early medieval states of Europe: in western Sudan the kingdoms of Mali and Gao; in central Sudan the Haussa states and Kanem-Bornu; on the Gulf of Guinea the Yoruba and Benin kingdoms; in Central Africa the kingdom of the Congo; on the East African coast several city states; and later in Zimbabwe the Monomotapa kingdom, which was to include the population of Great Zimbabwe.

## ORACLE: 'WHAT DOES THE FUTURE HOLD?'

'What does the future hold? Will we have enough to eat?' That is the cry to the oracle in the oracle cave. That is what people asked then, and it is what they ask today. Could the oracle have foreseen that the inhabitants would one day leave their Great Zimbabwe without a fight: because of drought, because of the exploitation of nature, because of a crisis in the gold trade?

Yes, what would the future hold for this land, which would later one day bear a bird, the sign of Great Zimbabwe, on its coat of arms? 'What does the future hold? Will we have enough to eat?' The land would be conquered, and it would be called Southern Rhodesia.

## STAGNATION OF THE BLACK AFRICAN PEOPLES

At the end of the fifteenth century the Portuguese explorer Vasco da Gama discovered the sea route to India via East Africa (Mombasa/Malindi). This promised a new era for Africa. For in the sixteenth century developments within Africa were abruptly interrupted by the invasion of the Europeans. Now and only now was there stagnation and deformation of the black African peoples. This came about:

– first through the European mercantile companies which were allowed to trade slaves, especially on the west coast of Africa between the mouth of the Senegal and northern Angola (up to around 1800) and later also on the east coast (Zanzibar);

– then through the colonial imperialism of the European powers themselves, who in the nineteenth and twentieth centuries cut up the whole of Africa, including East Africa, for themselves like a cake.

In the nineteenth century, at any rate, the sale of Africans as slaves above all to the New World could be prevented, but their exploitation went on. If this slave trade robbed Africa of Africans, now conversely the

Africans were robbed of Africa. After a period when there was colonial trading, with naval and military bases on the coast, in the nineteenth and twentieth centuries extensive colonies were established, which amounted to self-contained African colonial kingdoms. That becomes clear in Zimbabwe in particular, where the British Empire established its rule. Precisely what happened?

## IMPERIALISTIC COLONIZATION

From a European perspective the second half of the nineteenth century was the age of heroic discoverers and explorers, who were in constant danger. They explored the mysterious sources of the Zambesi, the Niger and the Nile, central and eastern Africa. The great names here are Mungo Park, the Lander brothers, the learned German Heinrich Barth and the Scot David Livingstone, who went missing for a long time and was then finally discovered by the American journalist Stanley in Burundi. Their pioneer achievements, which involved unspeakable deprivations, make exciting reading.

However, from an African perspective it all looks different: the information brought by these explorers and researchers was used by the army, adventurers, merchants and businessmen. For them, no means was too wretched to bring Africa under the rule of some European 'empire': from deception and enforced 'protective treaties', through whisky and weapons, to the crudest force and unrestrained massacres. Am I exaggerating? You will understand better if I briefly relate the especially instructive history of 'Southern Rhodesia', now Zimbabwe.

## 'SOUTHERN RHODESIA': A PRIME EXAMPLE
## OF COLONIALISM

Fighting between tribes had brought about the downfall of the Mutapa kingdom long before British colonization began (the last Mutapa king died in 1902). As early as the fifteenth century the power centre of Great Zimbabwe had shifted to Kame, near Bulawayo. However, the campaign of conquest by the warlike Nguni tribes proved fateful for Zimbabwe. Having broken away from the Zulu king in South Africa, after twenty years of wandering over 1500 miles northwards, by 1840 they came to possess the whole south-west of Zimbabwe, which hitherto had been inhabited by the Shona. Under the name of Ndebele ('wanderers', 'destroyers' or possibly 'men with long shields'), they still have their centre in Bulawayo. The king of Matabeleland had numerous contacts with the whites, above all with his friend Robert Moffat from the London Missionary Society. Moffat was a great missionary and agronomist. However, although the king allowed a mission station in the neighbourhood, he and his whole people practised the traditional ancestor cult.

Meanwhile the fever for diamonds and gold among the whites of South Africa also began to reach northwards. Cecil Rhodes, son of an Anglican clergyman, and always ready to quote the Bible for his own ends, was the richest owner of diamond mines in South Africa (the De Beers Mining Company was founded in 1890 and ended up with 90 per cent of the world's diamond production). As a Member of Parliament, Finance Minister and finally Prime Minister of the British Cape Colony he became an energetic champion of British imperialism. His dream was to unite the whole of South Africa from the Cape to Cairo politically under the British flag (with the help of a railway line). In 1889 he founded the British South Africa Company, which in the following years 'acquired' the territory of Rhodesia, named after Rhodes.

'Acquired'? Yes, but with lies and deceit. In Bulawayo Cecil Rhodes made use of the insignificant son of the missionary Robert Moffat, named John, to conclude an exclusive 'treaty of friendship' (the 'Moffat treaty') in 1888 with King Lobengula, who trusted only missionaries among the whites. Lobengula was deceived into thinking that he remained master of his land by a mistranslation of the decisive passage. According to the original text, however, he had agreed not to conclude any treaties in future without the permission of the British government. The consequence was that in the same year a treaty could be wrung out of the king for exploiting mineral resources. As a translator for Rhodes' delegation, a missionary who was highly paid for his services insinuated that here the king was simply plugging a 'great hole' to prevent gold-diggers. In fact the treaty accorded the English unlimited prospecting and trading rights.

In other words, the king of Ndebele was hoodwinked into unwillingly signing away his kingdom to the British empire. Even two special delegates whom he sent to Queen Victoria in London could not reverse this. On the contrary, her royal charter went far beyond what Lobengula had conceded and recognized no frontiers to the north. So soon Zambia (with Malawi) to the north could be counted part of what was of course called Rhodes Land, or more precisely Northern and Southern Rhodesia.

Now the British were the rulers: everywhere there was an administration supported by the army. Their only obligation was to develop an infrastructure and free trade. Moreover as early as 1890 their first pioneer colonists arrived from South Africa. Two hundred and twelve white settlers and the same number of black mercenaries, along with five hundred British soldiers, erected their 'forts' in Zimbabwe. Finally they also built Fort Salisbury (named after the British Prime Minister), the new capital, present-day Harare. They also attacked Matabeleland on a trivial pretext. Unlike the Shona, the Ndebele offered bitter resistance. There was a war. Fifteen thousand Ndebele fell in Bulawayo under a hail of modern fire. The city went up in flames. The king fled to the mountains and died, probably by his own hand. The British government buildings were erected on the site of his residence.

For his opponent Cecil Rhodes, the last seven years were likewise a great disappointment. Because of a failed coup against the Boers in the Transvaal in 1895 (the Jameson Raid) he had to resign from all his political offices. The tensions between the British colonists and the Boers led in 1899 to the Boer War. The affair of the hitherto misogynist Rhodes with the intriguer Princess Radziwill, who was later imprisoned, escalated into a sensational trial. But Rhodes died in 1902, before the end of the war and the trial.

In an unprecedented triumphal procession he was now brought right through Africa from Cape Town to Zimbabwe. He was buried in Bulawayo, in the Matopo hills, at a place which he had chosen for himself and which he called 'View of the World' because of the glorious views. His well-considered will proved a surprise: he left almost all his gigantic fortune for scholarships so that students from the colonies, the USA and Germany could study at his former university, Oxford. 'Rhodes scholars' from all over the world, white and many coloured, are grateful to him for that.


## THE MOTIVES OF COLONIALISM AND IMPERIALISM

However, we should beware of nationalistic prejudices. In Europe at that time the thinking not only of the British but of all the great powers was imperialistic. For example, shortly after Rhodes' death the Germans in Namibia/German South West Africa carried out a terrifying campaign of extermination: of the 60,000 to 80,000 Hereros only 16,000 were left. The German losses were 2,000. Everyone wanted to join in the feverish competition for 'protectorates' and 'colonies'. One either 'acquired' them or 'bought' them through treaties, or one used force, seized them and occupied them.

And how were such violent actions justified? The plausible motives propagated everywhere to justify this colonialist subjection were: opening up the mysterious continent, suppressing the slave trade, preventing tribal wars which had been encouraged by widespread slave-hunts, civilizing the uncivilized and Christianizing unbelievers. Now it cannot be disputed that humanitarianism and the urge to do research may have been factors for some unbelievers. For only since this time have we Europeans had a deeper knowledge of the geography, geology, climate, economy and ethnography of Africa, and this benefits economic development. But what was the cost to Africa itself?

And what lay behind all the European curiosity? Greed for gold – in the widest sense of the phrase. One truly does not need to be a Marxist to find here the verification of a Marxist insight: the *Realpolitik* of naked economic interest predominated in the industrial states of Europe, in England, Holland, Belgium, France and finally Bismarck's Germany. In the middle of the industrial revolution the Europeans no longer primarily needed people on the plantations of North and South America. What they needed now was raw material for their own factories, and plantation workers and mine workers in Africa itself to extract it. And what about the churches? We cannot pass over their diverse entanglement in this process of colonization. They share the responsibility for this development.

## THE CHURCHES SHARE THE RESPONSIBILITY

'We are the finest race in the world, and the more of it that we inhabit, the better it is for all humankind.' This remark was made by Cecil Rhodes, the founder of colonial Rhodesia. And many people in Europe at that time thought as he did. The heathen had to be converted, the savages civilized. And that was the task of the churches.

But does that mean that I should blame my own uncle, who built a great mission station in this country in the 1930s and 1940s? Quite by chance we arrived there, in the bush near Fort Victoria. A signpost said 'Gokomere'. That was a name from my childhood and I thought, 'This must be that mission station.' And indeed it was: hundreds of children came to meet us as we approached, all well clothed. Clearly they were being given a good education here.

So it cannot be disputed that a large number of these missionaries and sisters made a quite personal effort, which involved many sacrifices, and worked not only for the conversion of the heathen but really for the Africans. And no African will dispute that the churches did much for education and health.

But conversely, of course, it also cannot be disputed that the churches and the missions smoothed the way for the European powers to bring all Africa under their imperial rule, indeed that they legitimated this imperial rule and gave it ideological and theological support. Only very much later did the churches realize that things could not go on like this. And they slowly detached themselves from colonialism and then took the side of the blacks in their great battle of liberation: for an African Africa, an Africa that belongs to the Africans.

It is understandable that the missionaries attacked the negative features of African religion. Here one thinks not only of animal sacrifice, intoxicating drinks and excessive ecstatic rites. One need only recall the misery of millions of women, with its roots in age-old tribal customs, which continues to oppress them even in present-day black African metropolises. Unfortunately it is still apologetically justified by many African women themselves: beginning with what is expected of them in polygamy and an abundance of children, and extending to the cruel practice of the circumcision of the clitoris even before marriage, to weaken sexual desire and at the same time as a guarantee of faithfulness.

But whether the missionaries wanted it or not, whether they themselves were stamped by the Catholic Middle Ages and the Counter-Reformation like the Jesuits or by the Protestant Reformation and the revival movement like the London Missionary Society, on the whole over past centuries they certainly subordinated all missionary initiatives in the economic, political and above all spiritual and cultural spheres to the goals of the colonial powers. Indeed, they supported the colonial policies of these powers by their preaching and theology, by their policy on land and land grants, by their own great plantations and businesses, their missionary trading companies and even mission ships – all of which of course presupposed European superiority.

## CHRIST AFRICANIZED

Only in the middle of the struggle for liberation by the blacks in the 1970s did Zimbabwe's now often attacked churches distance themselves from the colonial system and 'Africanize' their leaders. A new departure had taken place earlier in the sphere of art. For a long time, all over Africa people had been quite naturally proclaiming and painting a white Jesus, a white Mary and white saints. But in Zimbabwe as early as the 1930s, Edward Paterson, an Anglican clergyman and artist, had gained a following: he founded the Cyrene mission school for African boys and there introduced art into the curriculum. The pupils were to develop their own creativity without any stylistic preconditions.

It is not surprising that they depicted Jesus and the saints, and also Adam and Eve, as black. Nor did they use perspective, as had become customary in Europe since the Italian Renaissance. Instead, the surfaces were completely filled, usually in primary colours, with a special focus on many details. With good reason, the novel paintings of these pupils were shown in various exhibitions in Europe.

But if we observe the worship now in the same church, we may ask whether it does not seem more European than African. Indeed it does: for the official major churches of Africa the rooting, the 'inculturation', of Christianity remains a still almost insoluble problem. The creative potential of the African spirit is hardly used at all.

## AFRICAN CREATIVITY

One need think only of the famous artists' settlement of Tengenenge: in the 1960s a beginning was made in encouraging indigenous artists – not only from Zimbabwe but also from Zambia, Malawi and Mozambique. The artists' community of Tengenenge was founded in 1964 at a difficult time, when the tobacco farmer Tom Blomefield, thwarted by Western economic sanctions and the economic crisis, was looking for an alternative for his endangered tobacco farm. With his workers he began making sculptures from dark volcanic serpentine stone. To work artistically with stone like this was a novelty for most of the former itinerant labourers, some of whom went back to work on the farms at harvest time. But literally thousands followed their example; their work is unmistakable, and it is for sale in souvenir shops, on market stalls and indeed by the roadside.

Some of the African artists also gained an international reputation. One of the most important is Henry Munjaradzi, who did not emigrate to Europe or America like others, but remained in Zimbabwe. He produced a particularly impressive sculpture of 'The New-Born Child'. But first of all the European cubists and expressionists were needed to help Europeans to understand the significance of African painting and sculpture with its quite distinctive forms and its unusual power of expression. 'The Good Shepherd and The Lost Sheep' is another example. Ten years ago I was already so impressed by the sculptures of the artists of Zimbabwe that I brought one home: a man with big round eyes and an arm with big hands holding his head: a man with a headache – against headaches.

## THE AFRICAN INDEPENDENT CHURCHES

In 1880 the Europeans had possession of barely a tenth of Africa, but only twenty years later the whole of Africa (with the exception of Ethiopia, Liberia and, until 1912, Morocco) was in their hands. Of course, the imperialistic division of Africa was made in the face of bitter opposition from the blacks. This opposition was not least religious in motivation. Already from the beginning of the nineteenth century a new, African kind of Christianity began to establish itself in the face of the big official churches. It is here – and not in Latin America – that the first beginnings of Christian liberation theology are to be found.

Prophetic protest and a messianic belief in Christ were activated. They were fused with old African traditions and proved to be a great spiritual power through the dynamic religious capacity of Africans for experience. Pressing for change, they entered the political, social and cultural framework of colonialized African society. Indeed, whether with church leaders of the type of the chieftain, prophet or on occasions even the messiah; whether on the farms, in the cities or on the reserves; whether with men or women as local leaders; whether more political or more non-political, these religious movements formed the starting-point both for anti-colonial resistance and for independent Christian churches.

In other words, many black Christians, often exploited farmers, decided to protest on religious grounds about the European mission churches, so associated with the apparatus of colonial power, because of their failure to understand the African character, psyche, language, cultures, customs and sense of responsibility. Under the leadership of chiefs, black clergy, teachers or workers, they began to make themselves independent. The foreign missionaries seemed to be preaching a false God to these Africans, a God of oppression and exploitation. So they founded free African Independent Churches. Now the Africans could finally be themselves in worship: they could sing and move as they were accustomed; they could have their own apostles, prophets, healers and preachers.

From Nigeria to South Africa, at the weekend one can watch larger and smaller groups of believers dressed in white gathering for worship. At the 'Vapostoles' congregation at a crossroads in Harare, the capital of Zimbabwe, even outsiders can recognize that the blacks, and already the children, clearly feel more at home here than in the stiff, regulated services of the European mission churches. The whites may scorn these African churches as 'sects' and fight against them. But as can be seen all over black Africa, they have a tremendous following. Some evangelical congregations and many charismatic congregations are often passive. But in the social unrest in Zimbabwe in 1998, independent churches, too, signed the explosive pastoral letter of the church leaders on the state of the nation.

Long before theologians reflected on it, an unwritten black theology was being lived out in Africa and practised in distinctive African songs and dances, liturgies and sermons. Central statements of holy scripture were combined with traditional African concerns. So African nationalism could appear not only in Marxist but also in religious garb. That is why Africa has largely remained a religious continent.

## LAND OF STONES

Today Africa is regarded socially and economically as problem continent number one. Will there be an African renaissance? Will there also be a renaissance in Zimbabwe? Zimbabwe means 'house of stones', and the land of Zimbabwe 'land of stones': great stone doors, stone citadels, stone cathedrals, often absurdly balanced blocks of stones. Zimbabwe is also the land of Stone Age traditions: here the tradition of the ancestors holds sway, the old who will soon also be ancestors.

This is a people which like many in Africa is orientated more on the past, bound to traditional ordinances. In some East African languages originally there was no real word for the future as such. In this patriarchal order with an authoritarian one-man government the young, the women, the innovators, those orientated on the future, have not always had an easy time. To go against fossilized traditions and commit oneself to land reform calls for courage and resolution. But many Africans are dissatisfied and energetically long for a more democratic, less corrupt, fairer, more moral political system. Here we should remember that the autocratic systems of the post-colonial period are not the consequence of the 'great African century' but are a result of the ongoing existence of colonial bureaucratic and military institutions.

### A CONTINENT WITH A FUTURE

With its 750 million inhabitants, for all its immense problems black Africa is a continent with a future. It is waiting for development and investment. When I was in Zimbabwe ten years ago, Harare was still a sleepy provincial town. Today it is the metropolis of a land with considerable economic possibilities. However, no one expects the old tribal culture to disappear quickly and the traditional African religion completely to lose its significance. Rather, African thought and African religion will continue to have something to say to us in the future.

## HOPE: THE AFRICAN CONTRIBUTION TO A GLOBAL ETHIC

What, finally, do I hope for as black Africa's special contribution to a common ethic of humankind, a global ethic? My answer is that I hope that Africans will contribute for humankind in the new millennium:

– their marked sense of community and solidarity;
– their high esteem for traditional values and standards;
– their holistic view of the world and human beings in which both young and old have a place and in which progress and tradition are combined.

# II

# *Hinduism*

## A JOYFUL RELIGION

Hinduism seems to be a joyful religion. With great exuberance people cover themselves with red water and sweet-smelling powder. This powder, mixed with saffron dust, is said to stimulate pleasure. At all events red is a symbol of blood, the bearer of life and love.

It is indeed a joyful religion, which celebrates its feast of Holi under the spring moon. This is the last feast in the Hindu calendar at the end of the winter harvest. People offer good wishes for the beginning of spring and exchange presents. It is a festival of the renewal of life: even the stringent social restrictions are lifted for a short time. People dare to say things to one another that they would not say otherwise.

Some features probably derive from fertility cults like those which have long also existed in many other cultures. There is an age-old popular religion which has remained alive above all in the villages. God is not encountered in silence, meditation and inwardness, all of which we often associate with Hinduism. Rather, God is encountered in orgiastic festivity, with dancing and noise, usually in honour of the countless village gods.

However, just as we must not judge Christianity by the equally exuberant prelude to Lent, which in many countries similarly lasts for several days, so too we should not judge Hinduism simply by the carnival of the Holi festival.

## KRISHNA'S DANCE

In Vrindaban in north India the festival of Holi is celebrated in a quite special way: in honour of Krishna, an incarnation of the God Vishnu. For the Indians Krishna represents the ideal of true humanity. So Krishna is often compared with 'Chrishta', the Christ of Christians. But the differences are manifest – one only has to think of the youthfulness and exuberance of Krishna. In Vrindaban, according to the legend, he grew up among cowherds, because two infants had been exchanged and in this way he escaped King Kamsa's massacre of the children. With his beauty and his flute-playing he captivated the Gopis, the shepherd girls, and especially his beloved Radha. He showered a golden rain of flowers over them. But in dancing he multiplies himself, so that he can give himself to all his beloveds.

Here we meet the legendary origin of the mimic dances (*rasas*) which are still practised today. But we can leave to the Indian interpreters how this pastoral scene is to be understood: as a tender erotic love story or as the eternal cosmic interplay of love between God and his beloved, the individual soul, a notion which is to be found in the mysticism of many religions. At all events, many Hindus see this ring dance around a central figure as a depiction of the personal relations between the human being (in female form) and the deity (in male form): the feelings of worldly love and devotion (which are Radha's) raised to the level of love and dedication to God (in the form of Krishna). Be this as it may, Krishna is the most popular of all Hindu gods. But:

## WHO IS A HINDU?

The people who go to the temple of Vrindaban are Indians. Of around a billion Indians world-wide, about 980,000,000 live in India, and of them about 80 per cent are Hindus. Originally 'Hindus' and 'Indians' were the same. For the Greeks, who had arrived in the Indus valley with the campaign of Alexander the Great in 326 BC, simply called those who had settled by this river 'Indians'; they were also called 'Indians' by the Persians and Latins and later by those who spoke the modern European languages.

Today, however, a distinction is made between 'Indians' and 'Hindus'. Since the nineteenth century 'Hinduism' has come to denote only the Indian religion, although it is difficult to distinguish this from Indian culture, lifestyle and ideas. In fact Hinduism is a collective term for a great variety of diverse but not completely different religious traditions and currents in India – excluding particular religions.

So who is a Hindu? It is easier to say who is not a Hindu. At least that is the expedient adopted by the Indian legislators in their perplexity. A Hindu is an Indian who is not a Muslim (11% = around 110,000,000 of the population of India), a Christian (2.4% = around 20,000,000) or a Jew (the precise number is unknown). Strictly speaking we should also add that a Hindu is not someone who is a Sikh (2%), a Jain (0.5%), or a Buddhist (0.7%). After all these qualifications, Hindus still make up around four-fifths of all Indians!

Doesn't that immediately make clear what dangerous consequences it can have if fundamentalist Hindu groups (World Hindu Council, VHP) and even political parties (BJP) call for a state which is not only Indian but also Hindu? 'Hindi, Hindu, Hindustan go together: Hindustan for the Hindus.' That is an awkward slogan. It would force around a fifth of the present population of the state of India – from the Muslims through the Sikhs to the Christians – to the periphery of the nation and even exclude them from culture and politics. Hindu massacres of Muslims and more recently violent assaults on Christian churches and institutions and attacks on priests and nuns make one fear for the future of the Indian state, which has hitherto been so tolerant.

### THE ETERNAL ORDER

The term 'Hinduism' has been invented by us Europeans to denote the religion of India. In reality it does not denote a single Indian religion but a whole wealth, a confederation, of religions. The Indians themselves usually call their religion 'eternal order'. In the old, classical language of India, Sanskrit, this is *sanatana dharma* – a term which was very often used by Mahatma Gandhi. This central term, dharma, governs everything: it means order, law, obligation. However, that does not mean a legal order, but an all-embracing cosmic order which governs all life and which has to be observed by all human beings, regardless of the caste or class to which they belong.

This reminds us of something like the fundamental ethic which we can already find among the Aborigines in Australia: a fundamental order that is given *a priori*, from the beginning. But that already makes it clear that Hinduism is not primarily concerned with doctrines, with dogmas, with orthodoxy: Hinduism has no magisterium. Rather, it is about right action, the correct rite, custom: everything that makes up religion in life. And its concern is not with particular rights which one may expect others to observe, but with the great destiny of human beings, the responsibilities that a human being has towards family, society, God and the gods.

## STRENGTHS AND WEAKNESSES

The strengths of a religion of eternal dharma are manifest. It is extremely stable. Specific rites and customs can last for centuries. And wherever such a religion is sufficiently flexible, it can also integrate opposites instead of simply repelling them.

But its weaknesses are also unmistakable: the rites and doctrines of such a religion, its prescripts and practices, can become fossilized. All too often people today praise the old Indian ideals and in so doing overlook the acute social abuses. Specifically this means:

– The social élites given preference by the 'eternal order' are fond of insisting on the rights and privileges that have always been bestowed on them. In doing so they neglect their responsibilities and do everything they can to preserve their monopoly of power and knowledge.

– In the face of any change of structure and improvement of circumstances fundamentalists can insist at any time: 'It was always like this in India', 'it was never any different', 'if it were different it would be wrong'.

– But critical thinkers and reformers who want to change the status quo of the social order which has become historic (for example the role of women, of the uppermost castes, or those outside the caste system), have difficulties.

– And yet, the history of Indian religion also knows pressures towards reform and paradigm shifts, i.e. transitions into a new overall constellation which are often hardly perceptible because elements of earlier eras are taken over into the new in a different form. They are often difficult to demarcate because the dates of many writings cannot always be defined clearly.


## MOTHER GANGA

Everything in the cosmos has its dharma, its destiny, its order: the gods, human beings, animals, plants and even inanimate nature. Even the rivers and streams have their destiny. They are to flow, cleanse, bear, but also sweep away, indeed destroy.

From the mountains of the Himalayas, covered in snow, comes that great river which after more than 1500 miles finally flows out into the Gulf of Bengal. For Hindus there is no more important, no more sacred river than this, the Ganges. For them the Ganges is female, as opposed to the 'male sea'. They call it 'Mother Ganga', and they know a goddess Ganga. Ganges water is used in many religious ceremonies (*pujas*). The dying are often given a sip of Ganges water.

Ganges – 'the river of life'. For many Hindus it is an image of Hinduism itself in the way in which it flows lazily, apparently slowly but inexorably, sometimes sweeping away everything in a storm. It is always the same and yet it constantly changes. It is often clear and pure, often turbulent and murky. It fertilizes much but sometimes it overflows and drowns creatures in its waters. Still:

## WHY BATHE IN THE GANGES?

At a city of 200,000 inhabitants, around 125 miles north-east of the capital Delhi, the young Ganga emerges from the mountains into the lowland plain: Haridwar is one of the holiest cities in India. A famous pilgrimage centre since ancient times, it is the starting point for the whole mountain region, with pilgrim paths which go up as high as 14,000 feet.

'Haridwar' means 'gate of Hari': Hari is another name for the god Vishnu. He is said to have left his footprint here: 'Hari-ke-charan', 'Vishnu's footprint', and this is the main attraction of the city. The rivers in India have always been regarded as holy, but the approaches to the water which people use to drink and bathe are thought to be particularly holy if they have been visited by a holy being like Vishnu. So miracles can take place there.

Early in 2001, five million pilgrims came to Haridwar for the great festival of Kumbh Mela, which takes place about every four years. But why do such people go down into the river? Not primarily for reasons of hygiene but as a ritual obligation, to cleanse themselves from sins: 'Our spirit and our body,' the young Indian says, in that order: 'our spirit and our body are purified. And this gives us peace of the spirit, peace of the soul.'

From earliest times in fact Indians have used bathing (*snana*) as an act of cleansing (*sodhana*). Performed correctly, bathing creates bodily cleanness and at the same time spiritual holiness. It is better to bathe in the flowing water of a stream or river than in standing water or even in the sea, where all uncleanness collects. And what river could be more suitable for that, what river could be more effective than the holiest of rivers, Mother Ganga? Whatever water one may use, people say in India, one should regard it as Ganges water, even if it is not. On the holy bathing steps, the ghats (*ghatas*), by which believers gain access to the water, the bather is linked with earth and heaven.

Preferably in the morning, the bather makes his offering to the sun, the great giver of energy. He washes all over and thoroughly cleanses all his clothes. Then follows the rite of 'immersion' (*majjana*): for comprehensive cleansing the believer immerses himself completely in the water. Finally he offers his gift of water to the sun with both hands.

## AFTER THE INDUS CULTURE, THE ARYANS

A great culture developed by the Ganges as early as the period between 1000 and 500 BC. But the greatest of all Indian cultures is the Harappa culture in the Indus valley, the forerunners of which reach back into the fourth, indeed even into the seventh, millennium.

We know very little about the life of the Indus people who gave their name to the Indians. Still, it is certain that the Indus valley in present-day Pakistan is the third great cradle of human high culture, comparable to Mesopotamia and Egypt, where the high culture is similarly bound up with writing. This Indus culture had its heyday as early as the third or second millennium BC. But its script has not yet been deciphered. Only recently do scholars think that they have puzzled out some words. And we can only guess at what lies hidden in these writings.

However, there have been many discoveries of weapons, utensils of all kinds and above all several thousand steatite seals; most of these discoveries have been made in the cities of Mohenjo-Daro and Harappa, which gave its name to the culture. But what is the meaning on a seal, say, of the fabled unicorn, whose homeland in antiquity was always thought to be India? Or what is the function of a seated man on a seal: a 'lord of the beasts', a kind of proto-Shiva or a meditating 'yogi'? At all events many scholars think that certain Indian techniques of breathing and meditation, and elements of the fertility cult, go right back to the Indus culture. So possibly this is a preliminary stage of the Hindu religion.

We only know that the highly developed Indus cities, along with their agriculture, irrigation systems and crafts, were destroyed around 1750 BC. Was this because of sudden changes in the climate? Or because of a gradual inner collapse brought about by regionalization? Or through violence and war? The one thing that is certain is that between 1700 and 1200 a quite different people came into this region, nomadic tribes. They called themselves 'Arya', the noble. Where did they come from? Presumably their home was in South Central Asia, like all the many peoples who once belonged to the same language family and the same cultural sphere and who are therefore called Indo-Europeans (they used also to be called Indo-Germans): not only the Germans but also the Celts, Slavs and Balts, the Romans and Greeks and, along with the Iranians, the Indians.

At a very early stage the Indo-Europeans split up. In this way those who called themselves Aryans came into the Indus and then also the Ganges valley, probably over the plateau of Iran: they arrived in the upper valley between 1000 and 800 and also in the lower valley around 850. At that time, the population still consisted of hunters and gatherers, who had only progressed as far as bronze weapons. This was a dark-skinned native population, to which the fair-skinned Aryans, who could already work iron and ride horses, felt superior in every respect. However, the Aryans did not form great unitary kingdoms, like the Mesopotamians or the Egyptians, but many small kingdoms, which became larger units only many centuries later. From that time to the present day Indians have rated a fair skin more highly, and the native inhabitants have settled at the very bottom of the markedly hierarchical Indian society.

## A STRUCTURED SOCIETY

If we look at the many men and women in an Indian city, who differ so widely from one another, and if above all we look at the tremendous masses on this sub-continent, caused above all by overpopulation, we could assume that here was a largely formless mass which at best could be divided into the poor, who do not know where their next meal is coming from, and the rich, who live a life of abundance. But this division is far too simple: hardly any society is so structured through and through as Indian society. Every person here could immediately say what their place was in this society, and what their social status was. This depends in the first place on caste.

Europeans may immediately associate the caste system with back-wardness, injustice, exploitation or fatalism. However, they should remember that until well into the twentieth century we in Europe had four social strata which lived very different and separate lives; these strata used to be called 'estates'. First came the clergy (who even now attempt to preserve certain marks, clothes, privileges and responsibilities of their estate). Then there were the nobility, and after them, as the 'third estate', 'the people', the 'citizens', who were first able to establish their basic rights with the French Revolution. Last came the 'fourth estate', the working class, who obtained completely equal rights only in the twentieth century.

So from ancient times things have not been very different in India:
- at the top the 'clerical' elite of the Brahmins: the priests, poets, thinkers and scholars;
- then the aristocracy of the Kshatriyas, the warriors, the rulers;
- then the often rich Vaishyas: the merchants, farmers and craftsmen;
- at the bottom the mass of the Shudras: the servants, workers, proletariat – around 500 million;
- in addition there are the around 150 million who belong to no caste, the Dalits, the 'untouchables', whom Gandhi euphemistically called *harijan*, 'children of God'.

The Indians did not call these four strata of society 'estates' but 'varnas'. The term originally means 'colours' and is perhaps connected with their origin. At any rate it was the Portuguese colonizers who first called them 'castas', from the Latin *castus* (pure, chaste). This indicates a decisive fact. As formerly among the estates in Europe, so too in India people like to marry within their estate, in the same caste (endogamy), and if possible they prefer to eat with their equals (commensality). And just as in Europe at an early stage the estates formed countless smaller units (the different degrees of the clergy, the nobility, the guilds), so in India there was a development into sub-castes, which are called *jati* (birth). These are countless, and even now there is no clear classification of the castes. When they were first counted in 1881, around 25,000 caste names were registered for the central provinces alone.

## WHERE DO THE CASTES COME FROM?

What, we may ask, is the origin of the division of this whole society into castes? Historical research gives different answers to this:
– One answer is that it comes from professional specialization. But the caste order is certainly more than a social phenomenon, however much it may determine the choice of profession.
– Another answer is that it is an order of estates invented by the priests. But the caste order is not just a religious phenomenon, however much the Brahmins may have contributed to shaping and fixing it.

Rather, the whole historical development was fundamental. For there is no disputing the fact that the Aryans who immigrated into India wanted to dissociate themselves from the subjected native population, who had dark skins, and to preserve their 'purity'. At any rate, it was at that time that those social 'colours', 'varnas' or groups formed. At an early stage they saw themselves as religious institutions, had a hierarchical order and bore a communal name.

Already in the earliest Indian literature, the Rig Veda (in a relatively late part), religious reasons are given for the hierarchy of the castes. We can see this if we look at the hymn to 'Purusha', a cosmic primal being in human form from whom the whole world arose (Rig Veda 10.90). Whereas three-quarters of this remarkable being are spiritual and transcendent, a quarter is offered by the gods in sacrificial fire. In this way all that is comes into being: the collections of Vedic texts, the animals, the four classes of human being, and finally the stars, the elements, heaven and earth:

The One            The primal being (Purusha) has a thousand heads,
                   a thousand eyes, a thousand feet.
                   He pervaded the earth on all sides . . .
                   It is the man who is all this,
                   whatever has been and whatever is to be.
                   He is the ruler of immortality . . .

| | |
|---|---|
| Four Vedas | From that sacrifice in which everything was offered<br>the verse and chants were born,<br>and from it the formulas for sacrifice were born. |
| Animals | Horses were born from it, and those other<br>animals that have two rows of teeth;<br>cows were born from it,<br>and from it goats and sheep were born. |
| Classes of men | His mouth became the Brahmins;<br>his arms were made into the warriors,<br>his thighs the merchants, and from his feet<br>the servants were born . . . |
| Heaven and earth | From his navel the middle realm of space arose;<br>from his head the sky evolved.<br>From his two feet came the earth,<br>and the quarters of the sky from his ear. |

It should be noted, however, that in this text there is not yet the sharp demarcation between the castes which would exclude the marriage of members of different castes and a change of caste. This is first found in the influential 'Law Book of Manu' (*manusmrti*, presumably from the third century BC), which is attributed to Manu (man), the tribal ancestor of humankind. This law book became the foundation of Hindu society, its religion and modes of conduct. It is the first and most important work of the post-Vedic 'tradition' (*smrti*).

Only in the Middle Ages did that rigorous caste system become established which predetermines both marriage and the individual's choice of profession and social prestige. Right at the centre stands the notion of ritual cleanness. Its shadow side is a fear of pollution. Now even physical contact with lower castes, and not just eating together, far less sexual intercourse, made people unclean. Any uncleanness required appropriate cleansing, as far as that is possible. The Brahmins developed countless regulations for this: commandments, prohibitions, rites of cleansing, but also excommunication. It is particularly significant here that the lower castes were excluded even from studying the Indian holy scriptures, the Vedas.

## THE SPIRIT OF THE VEDAS STILL BLOWS TODAY

At the beginning of the twenty-first century it is no longer generally accepted that only members of the three upper castes may be initiated into the knowledge of the Vedas, hear and study their holy words. Traditionally, the initiation took place in a special ceremony – in some ways comparable to Christian baptism. A 'second birth' was celebrated when a cotton cord (probably the ritual remnant of a former garment) plaited from strands was hung over the left shoulder of the person to be initiated. Only those who were 'born a second time' in this way were authorized to hear the revealed holy words and to perform the appropriate rituals.

All over India today there are persons and groups who are attempting to bring greater unity to a land split into different population groups, castes, religions and parties. Thus in Haridwar there is the great spiritual centre of Shantikunj, which is associated with an academy to train 2000 students as teachers. It inspires a moral and spiritual revival movement to which 'all persons right across all limits of caste, faith, gender or religion are invited'. Here, with serious study of the modern humanities and sciences, there is opposition to the widespread ignorance, fanaticism, hatred, strife and divisions, and work is done towards understanding, harmony, unity in difference, peace and humanity. The main point of reference here – along the lines of the Arya Samaj ('Fellowship of the Aryans'), a nationalistic movement for social reform founded by Dayanand Sarasvati (1824–33) – is to Hinduism in its original form: to the authority of the Vedas, that sacred 'knowledge' which even today is still regarded by most believing Hindus as the source of all Indian culture.

What does a small group of students do in an early morning Vedic ritual? They turn to the rising sun, to the 'begetter' (Savitri, also the consort of Brahma and mother of the four Vedas), to the sun god, who brings light and life and drives away darkness and its dangers.

The individual verses are introduced by the primal syllable 'OM', the symbol of Hindu spiritual knowledge and power. Finally the most famous of all the invocations or mantras is recited. The members of the higher caste have this whispered into their ears at their initiation and are to pray it daily. This is the Gayatri (or Savitri) Mantra, one of the holiest verses of the Rig Veda (Book III, 62.10). This mantra is regarded as the quint-essence of Vedic revelation. There are several dozen translations of it:

OM, this glory of the god Savitri, towering over all,
the splendour of the divine,
let us meditate on it.
May it inspire us with knowledge.

The non-Hindu needs to know that this morning invocation does not just call down the blessing of the sun (*savitri*) on the earth. Rather, it is a mystical formula of comprehensive power and force which is therefore called the 'Vedamatri' = 'Mother of the Vedas'. Why? Because its three times eight syllables are said to contain the substance of all four Vedas and to possess purifying power. According to the traditional view an Aryan who, say, had eaten 'unclean food' had to pray the Gayatri 108 times or 1008 times to restore his purity, depending on the severity of the offence.

But in the young people's rite the positive element stands at the centre: the sun, which can give life but also destroy, is to give them the energy to become better people and also to be able to do good to others. However, in Hinduism people are not content with rites, but are also concerned to study the classical holy scriptures.

## THE HOLY SCRIPTURES OF THE HINDUS

At Gurukul University in Haridwar quite a number of people zealously study the Vedas, the sacred 'knowledge'. This earliest testimony to Aryan culture came into being over a long period, perhaps from 1500 BC, in its earliest strata probably in the context of individual priestly families. There among other things generally widespread notions and practices were 'approved' and gathered together. In the process they were more or less harmonized, partially systematized and supplemented by the collectors' own views. They had been handed down orally from generation to generation. In content, literary form and time of composition the Vedas today can be divided into roughly four collections (*samhita*): the four Vedas, which form the basis of Vedic religion:

- the Rig Veda ('knowledge of the verses'): hymns to the gods, largely composed in the Indus valley between 1700 and 1200 BC;
- the Sama Veda ('knowledge of the songs'): a handbook for training the person who led the singing at sacrifices;
- the Yajur Veda ('knowledge of the sacrificial formulae'): a collection of sacrificial texts;
- the Atharva Veda ('knowledge of the "fire priest"'): a late collection of non-priestly magic and occult texts and rituals.

In addition there is a series of interpretative texts with famous names:

- the Brahmanas ('interpretations of the Brahmins'): comprehensive collections of priestly literature to explain and introduce the sacrificial rituals, related to the individual Vedas;
- the Aranyakas (texts of 'the forest'): supplements to the Brahmanas, mystical and speculative descriptions and allegorical interpretations of the great rituals, which because of the alleged danger that they posed to the uninitiated were taught in the forests far away from the villages;
- the Upanishads: important speculative philosophical texts, initially parts of the Brahmanas and Aranyakas, but then detached, compiled as independent texts and in the course of time (down to the Middle Ages) supplemented with further texts.

These are extensive texts, in total around six times as long as the Bible. For the believing Hindu they have divine authority. They are regarded as *shruti*, as the 'heard', 'revealed' part of the Hindu religious tradition. They are contrasted with the *smrti*, 'recollection', the non-revealed texts, which are regarded as human attempts to understand the truths of revelation. But as part of their authentic development, faithful to the tradition, these have a comparable status and similarly enjoy great respect. With the 'Lawbook of Manu', which has already been mentioned, they include the Vedangas and Shastras, the epics and the Puranas.

All these writings were composed in Sanskrit, which means 'regulated, perfect, complete'. It is the sacred language of the Hindus. Is it 'the language of the gods'? In fact it is the language of the Aryan tribes which immigrated into India from the north-west. However, over the course of the centuries it was perfected and refined and came to have a highly differentiated terminology. But today Sanskrit, like Latin with us, is a dead language. It is still studied and cultivated by Brahmins and educated people as the classical language of the scriptures and literature of India. North Indian Hindi, since 1965 the official language of India, is strongly influenced by it. Sanskrit remains of fundamental significance for the religious tradition, not least for the religious rituals.


## THE RITUAL OF FIRE AND THE ETERNAL CYCLE

Ordinary people do not bother very much about the holy scriptures. Grand as the whole Indian tradition is, even today almost half of all Indians cannot read or write, and around half of the children of school age do not go to school. For all these people, it is above all the countless religious rites that are significant: they accompany the Hindu's whole life and can be performed in nature, at home or in the temple.

Even today believing Hindus perform their fire ritual, whether at a simple fireplace or, as in Gurukul University, at an artistically decorated altar. Fire was given the utmost veneration as early as in the Vedas. That is understandable. In the beginning human beings knew about the power of fire almost only from fires which followed bolts of lightning; and it was a decisive step in our cultural development (in ancient Greece associated with the Prometheus myth) when human beings learned to kindle fire themselves by friction and to use it in a controlled way. No wonder that fire plays a central role in the religious tradition of India from the start: fire in heaven as the sun, in the air as lightning, on earth as the fire in the hearth, in rituals as sacrificial fire, and in the burning of corpses as the medium which bears the souls of the dead into the heavenly world.

Fire appears in personified form in the god Agni: in the Vedas he is the first and oldest priest, who combines the three worlds of heaven, air and earth. Alongside Indra, the king of the gods, the god of the firmament, storm and war, Agni is the most important god. Many hymns are devoted to him and the Brahmin offers a sacrifice to him to maintain the cosmic order. Agni receives it, burns it and makes it rise to the gods. Everything is precisely regulated: the choice of the place for the sacrifice, the gathering of the firewood, the building of the fireplace, the preparation of the sacrificial gifts, the kindling and tending of the fire, and the accompanying songs, ritual actions and prayers.

Morning and evening prayer (the *samdhya*) was prescribed for every Aryan. For young people the fire was to be a symbol of growth, of striving upwards and of dedication. It was at the same time to be a symbol of the eternal cycle of nature. After all, fire strives upwards from the earth and with the burnt matter bears water, the vehicle of all life, to heaven, where it becomes clouds, and then finally returns to the earth as rain and there revives matter to new life. So isn't everything an eternal cycle with neither beginning nor end? Already in the Brahmana texts, against the background of this notion a teaching is laid down which in the Upanishads, as the 'doctrine of the five fires', attempts to give a first coherent answer to the question of where human beings come from and where they are going. There it is already developed into that cyclical notion about the other world which later, in an ethicized form as the 'doctrine of karma', found adherents far beyond Hinduism. Many people regarded it as the central dogma of Indian thought, although evidently it developed only over time.

## REINCARNATION AND BELIEF IN KARMA

Belief in a cyclical reincarnation of the dead, in a 'migration of souls', is not an Indian invention. It has long been part of the traditional material of many cultures all over the world. And in India too there is by no means agreement as to how one is to imagine the fate of the dead, nor has there been in the past. At any rate in the early Vedic period people initially believed that with the burning of the bodies the dead went directly either to the eternal damnation of the underworld or to the bliss of paradise in the heavenly world. But soon doubts began to arise: was it not to be feared that there would be a 'second death' even in heaven, and that the dead would have to return to a new existence on earth, with death to rise once again from there to heaven?

At all times there was speculation and controversy about what influenced this cycle. At first it was thought that there was a guardian on the moon, the gate to the heavenly world, who put questions to the dead about their life; the answers were decisive for their further fate. Later, in the view of the Brahmins it was above all the sacrificial actions of the dead during their lifetime that would govern their fate. The term 'act' now provided the decisive key word under which the Indian tradition of the karma theory (Sanskrit *kr* = 'act') was to be continued. Here the decisive development was that the understanding of action began largely to be detached from mythical and ritual notions. This was a complex process which can still be followed in the Upanishads: finally the way of life, the morally correct action of the dead during their lifetimes, became the decisive criterion for the manner of their reincarnation.

Even today the notion of a cyclical course of time and history is still powerfully suggestive to Indians and some non-Indians: are not all courses of events repeated in nature itself? The orbits of the planets, the seasons, the phases of the moon come and go. Night and day alternate. In the Indian view all this is also a warning sign that the great will not always remain great and the small will not always remain small. But of course, according to present-day physics nature not only has cyclical movements but also – from atomic nuclei to the stars – has a history in a particular direction which cannot be reversed: from the Big Bang there is a history of billions of years which is moving towards an end.

However, Indian mythology, too, for example as it has been handed down in the Lawbook of Manu, also starts from an 'end' of this world. According to it we are in the last of four world ages (*yuga*), in the sixth millennium of Kaliyuga. But no apocalyptic fear can arise in India. Why? Because according to a system of numbering devised later, after our year 2000 there will still be around 426,000 human years to go until after 12,000 divine years (= 4,320,000 million human years) a divine age (*mahayuga*) will come to an end. And one thousand such divine ages are only one Brahma day, which after an annihilation of the world will be followed by the equally long Brahma night of the repose of the worlds. Only then is a world age (*kalpa*) completed. In this way the circle of uniform cycles of time, which succeed one another, comes to an end – immediately to begin all over again.

| World age | Duration | Twilight | Divine years | Human years |
|---|---|---|---|---|
| Kritayuga | 4,000 | 2 × 400 | 4,800 | 1,728,000 |
| Tretayuga | 3,000 | 2 × 300 | 3,600 | 1,296,000 |
| Dvaparayuga | 2,000 | 2 × 200 | 2,400 | 864,000 |
| Kaliyuga | 1,000 | 2 × 100 | 1,200 | 432,000 |
| 1 Mahayuga | | | 12,000 | 4,320,000 |
| 1 Kalpa | | | 24 million | 8.64 billion |

## THE CRISIS OF THE VEDIC VIEW OF THE WORLD: THE UPANISHADS

These are all subtle theories and speculations, far removed from the wild and luxuriant sacrificial mysticism of the Vedas. But as in ancient Greece, in time people became dissatisfied with an utterly mythological view of the world. And progress was made towards investigating it philosophically, towards the quest for an original unity behind and in all things: *tad ekam*, 'the one'. The creation hymn in the Rig Veda (X, 129,2) says of this that at the beginning of time there was neither non-being nor being, but only this One and nothing else.

So there was a paradigm shift. But it was a long way from the Brahmanas, with their esoteric sacrificial knowledge and tentative attempts to grasp this ultimate knowledge conceptually and make it concrete, to the first coherent philosophical conceptions of the early Upanishads. Composed between the eighth and the fourth centuries BC, these are regarded as the 'end of the Veda' (*vedanta*) and the completion of the revealed part (*shruti*) of the religious tradition of India.

Here is the foundation of a vision of unity which together with the belief in reincarnation and karma that gradually became established forms the new constellation of the religion of the time of the Upanishads. *Upa-ni-shad* means 'to sit near (*upa*) to someone or to put (*shad*) something down (*ni*)', in particular to sit as a pupil at the feet of a teacher as a sign of respect and with the aim of being initiated into a teaching, usually secret. The Upanishads themselves keep emphasizing the secret character of their teachings. And they offer neither something like a 'basic teaching' nor a coherent system of teaching. Rather, all the texts display very different literary styles and at the same time a broad spectrum of different doctrines and conceptions – beginning with the questions about the individual fate of human beings and extending to the relation of the human self to the absolute. But there is no mistaking the quest for unity.

**THE QUEST FOR UNITY**

In all religions there are epoch-making upheavals (paradigm shifts) in which a whole picture of the world is replaced by new, revolutionary ideas. That is also the case in India, where at a very early stage there were critical signs that the Vedic picture of the world could not be maintained as it was.
– There was criticism above all of the Brahmins. For these had increasingly become a kind of clergy, with ever more complicated

precepts and a whole science of sacrifice. The result was that they gained further privileges and an increase of power (they advised the rulers).

– But the gods were also criticized: after all, there were very many, very contradictory gods. The many gods of heaven (*devas*) and of the underworld (*asuras*), who governed the universe as beings of light and order or of darkness and confusion, behaved all too like human beings and made the dharma, the world order, seem unstable.

– Radical reformers emerged: the Buddha and Mahavira, the founder of Jainism, which rejected the authority of the Vedas and the Brahmins and parted company with the mainstream of Hinduism.

But precisely here something great and novel was in the making: is there then no unity behind the whole? So people asked. And that was the starting point for new questions and a very much deeper contemplation of things: the question of unity, a deep, eternal unity behind the colourful diversity of the phenomena of this world, all the gods and powers.

That is what took place there in India, almost a thousand years before the birth of Christ, in those philosophical writings which are called Upanishads. These now showed what the issue was: human beings must penetrate the visible surface of things and look into themselves. Then, if they so to speak shut their eyes and turn inwards, they will find in themselves the origin, the primal ground of being, the original One, Brahman. And they will experience that Brahman and Atman (the term given in India to the soul or spirit) are ultimately one.

That is not so far from what Christian mysticism discovered: that there is an ultimate unity somewhere in the depths of the human being. And from there they called on people to 'Seek God in all things – and above all in yourself.'

## THE MYSTERY OF THE FIG: THAT IS WHAT YOU ARE

Thus one of the doctrines of the Upanishads made history, and in the subsequent period left a lasting stamp on the religious thought of the Indians, namely that Atman and Brahman (not to be confused with the God Brahma) are 'fundamentally' one. This is a great mystical vision, formulated a good 500 years before Christ. At first it was clarified less by philosophical arguments than by didactic narratives.

Thus the pupil, eager to learn, asks the wise man how he can experience the deepest truth, the omnipresence and omni-activity of Brahman, the highest reality (according to Chandogya Upanishad 6.12.2–3). The pupil is to open a fig: there are many seeds inside it. He is now to open one of these seeds: but there is nothing in it. The wise man explains: 'My son, that subtle essence which you do not perceive there, of that very essence this fig tree exists. Believe it, my son. That which is the subtle essence, in it all that exists has its self. It is the truth; that is the self, your soul, that is what you are.'

So this is the great mystery of reality, which cannot be defined and yet is omnipresent, invisible and as effective as the apparently empty core of the fig. The Hindus say that the Brahman is the one, highest reality in all things, in which each individual being has a share and from whose life-force it receives. It is neither god nor goddess. It is an absolute without tangible form. Yet later a conceptual approximation to the indescribable was sought. The absolute is *satcitananda* – at the same time pure being (*sat*), knowing consciousness (*cit*) and all-fulfilling bliss (*ananda*).

It is indeed a highly speculative notion of the divine which appears in the Upanishads, removed both from anything that is in human form, anthropomorphic, and also from anything that is purposive and functional. But as ever, popular religion calls for living and concrete divine forms.

## RELIGION AND EROTICISM

In contrast to Christianity, which is in many ways hostile to sex and to women, from ancient times Indian religion, literature and art have everywhere contained elements of eroticism. These were inspired above all by the pre-Aryan fertility cults of the ancient East. The procreation of ancestors was an essential precondition for the safeguarding of food and the maintaining of the species. An Indian temple would be incomplete without erotic depictions, even of the loving couple (*mithuna*). Whether the depictions are of human beings or animals, they are meant in a magical way to ward off harm or bring good fortune. Thus from the beginning Indian religion, literature and art have shown an undisguised delight in sensuality, the body and sexuality. There are no inhibitions about depicting feminine charm and feminine nakedness.

The classic period of Hinduism was ushered in as early as under the Gupta dynasty in north India (300–500), in a heyday of Hindu art and Sanskrit literature. After the destruction of the Gupta kingdom around 500 (by the white Huns), however, lesser feudal rulers had come to power who encouraged new cults. Now erotic love between men and women, of the kind that is also celebrated in the biblical Song of Songs, developed widely and was illustrated with increasingly refined art. The elegant and

sensitive sculptures of Khajuraho near Bhopal in central India, formerly a
giant religious centre with 88 Hindu and Jain temples, are unsurpassed;
today 22 of these survive.

Europeans were often alienated and Indians tried to offer an explanation: was this pornography, or simply the illustration of that old guideline
of Indian eroticism, the Kama Sutra? It would be naive to assume a
spiritual mystical meaning everywhere. Meanwhile, historical research has
illuminated the social background: from the fifth century on, the feudal
rulers who had newly come to power ('rajputs': *raja-putra* – son of the
king) had forged their kingdoms in India with military means. To legitimate and consolidate their rule they made great gifts to the Brahmins and
gave powerful encouragement to temple building. In the following centuries sex and law were the main preoccupations of the Indian aristocracy.
And in both spheres people thought that they would have sure success
with the help of magical and superstitious practices.

The institution of the temple maidservants or Devadasi (literally maidservants of god) which also had its origin in the fertility cults was very
popular in India at the same time. The maidservants had to provide the
dancing, drama and music in the temples. In time, pieces which were
increasingly secularized and erotic were performed. And the bigger and
more splendid the temples became, the more room the artists had to depict
erotic themes. These became the great passion of medieval Indian art.
Whereas loving couples (*mithuna*) had been a universally accepted temple
decoration from the fifth to the ninth centuries, ostentatious sexual intercourse (*maithuna*) was a relatively new motif. However, it became increasingly established in the feudal period between 900 and 1400 (i.e. at
Khajuharo, 950–1150). The Kandriya temple with three friezes of erotic
depictions comes from 1050. Our question is: what drove these developments on?

## TANTRISM IN THE TWILIGHT

The sects associated with Shaktism, the worship of a female deity (*shakti*
= 'energy', 'primal force', and the name for this goddess), and especially
Tantric Shaktism (*tantra* = 'fabric', 'system'), exerted great influence. This
esoteric system of doctrine and ritual spread in India in the period from
600 to 900. At the latest in the ninth century Tantrism also reached
Khajuraho; a centre of the Tantric Yogini Kaula sect is attested for this
period. So it is not surprising that between the tenth and the twelfth
centuries ever more numerous depictions of dancing maidens in seductive
poses appear, and ever more frequently also sexual couples and orgiastic
groups. At the centre of Tantrism stand the five elements beginning with

m; *madaya* (wine), *matsya* (fish), *mamsa* (meat), *mudra* (roasted corn) and *maithuna* (sexual intercourse).

Tantrism certainly must not be vilified, but it must not be beautified either. On the one hand, in Tantrism, in contrast to orthodox Hinduism, women are undeniably thought more highly of and the restrictions of caste are done away with – even the 'untouchables' have a higher status. On the other hand, there is no disguising the fact that Tantrists often preached and practised a philosophy of sex. In original Tantrism the connection between yoga and sexuality may not have been aimed at the mere satisfaction of temporary 'needs' but at restraining the life-force, sublimating sexuality and being united with the Absolute. And the Tantric writings are certainly full of interesting speculations about the creation and destruction of the world, the veneration of deities and spiritual exercises. But they are also full of magic, abnormalities and obscenities. Priests led a life of lust and engaged in every possible sexual practice with their adepts. Even in Indian sources there was criticism that the sacred atmosphere of many temples had been destroyed by sexual extravagances. The practice of sexual intercourse with changing partners (and even with animals) as the way to union with the Absolute (*advaita* – 'not duality') can hardly be understood as a symbol of liberation.

It is not surprising that the temple girls were notorious for their promiscuity and corruption. This was in fact prostitution in the religious sphere. To put it pointedly: religion was abused for sexual purposes and sexuality was abused for religious purposes. Aristocrats in particular thought at that time that they could attain a long life, sexual potency and better control of women through alchemy, aphrodisiacs and magical practices. But the mass of people (who in Khajuraho were also influenced by Jains) increasingly rejected the Tantric practices, which moreover were often associated with macabre rites and bloody sacrifices. For a long time the temples in Khajuraho fell into disuse. And even now India's public life is characterized more by prudery than by libertinism. The institution of temple maidservants which became temple prostitution has long been banned.

## THE NEW HIGH GODS: VISHNU AND SHIVA

For the majority of Indians, abstract philosophical speculations have probably been of little importance at any time. What has been more important is the worship of gods, indeed of a particular deity, from whom promises and blessings were hoped for and who for believers represented an aspect or an incarnation of the divine. Therefore even the great philosophical conceptions of the Upanishads found only limited entry into the everyday religious practice of ordinary believers. Indeed, already in the Upanishads there are texts which bear witness to a reinforced theistic piety which is presented confidently: the salvation and redemption of the individual are made dependent on surrender in faith to a God who is thought of as personal. Between the third century BC and the third century AD this led to the classic Hindu religions as they are expressed in the great Hindu epics of the Mahabharata and the Ramayana.

For now new gods came into the foreground who had played little if any role in the Vedas. Often they had emerged from local cults. And more than Tantric Shaktism, in the period after the Vedas the new gods Vishnu and Shiva became established. Both Vishnu, who plays only a subordinate role in the Vedas as the consort of Indra, and Shiva, whose name appears in the Vedas only as an attribute of the ambivalent god Rudra, are highly complex figures. Their origin is largely obscure to historical research. In the course of time certainly various local gods and heroes were identified with them, so that now some of their individual features seem contradictory to us.

Vishnu ('Hari') is depicted with four arms, signs of divine power, and with four attributes: conch, discus, club and lotus. Between the creations of the world he rests on the snake Shesha with a thousand heads, who swims as milk on the broad endless ocean. His consort is Lakshmi, the goddess of wealth and happiness. His cult has a joyful and easy character for the many worshippers (the *vaishnavas*). They know that whenever the world order is in danger, Vishnu intervenes to protect it against the demons and to save the world. He (and only he) then assumes an earthly form, and incarnates himself as a human being or animal. Of ten such embodiments (incarnations) or avatars (descents) the most important are Rama and – as we saw in Haridwar – Krishna. However, the tenth is still to come: it will happen at the end of this age.

By contrast, Shiva is a god with two faces. With his terrible appearance he embodies the aspect of dissolution and destruction. As a great ascetic and model for all yogis, he sits meditating on the summit of a mountain in the Himalayas, the source of the Ganges, the embodiment of renunciation. At the same time, according to his name he is the 'one rich in blessing, gracious, benevolent', who through his infinite power of procreation brings everything into being and gives life. The embodiment of Shiva's 'feminine' energies, without which he would be powerless, is his partner Parvati (Shakti, Durga and Kali are also regarded as his partners), whose worship became independent in the cult of the goddess.

Shiva is often depicted only symbolically as linga (Sanskrit for 'phallus'), naturalistically or as a stumpy pillar: this is the expression of the divine power of procreation to which all life owes its origin. The linga is often associated with the yoni (vagina), the female counterpart, an expression of

Shiva's union with his consort but also of the complementarity of the sexes. There is a linga at the centre of every Shiva temple. The Shivaites (*shaivas*) give their god many names. However, in art he is popularly depicted as Shiva Natarja, 'king of the dancers', the dancing lord of the universe: his dance, the expression of his five activities (creating, sustaining, destroying, embodying and liberating), symbolizes the cycle of the cosmos, in which in an eternal rhythm millions of worlds are created every moment and millions more are created anew.

## THE CLASSICAL EPICS

Vishnu and Shiva are the great gods in the great classical epics which still live on at every level of the people. These epics are the most important collections of material for all genres of Indian literature.

The Ramayana (the oldest epic of Sanskrit literature, dating from perhaps as early as the fourth century BC) describes the 'Life of Rama', the prince Ramacandra and his wife Sita. It features numerous adventures: banishment from the royal court of Ayodhya, the abduction of Sita by the demon king, a victorious battle against the host of demons, the return to Ayodhya and finally Rama's enthronement and glorious reign as a just king. Thus Rama is venerated as the seventh incarnation of Vishnu.

The Mahabharata, the core of which originated between around 400 BC and AD 400, is the 'great' (*maha*) epic of the legendary 'Bharata' dynasty, from which modern India derives its official name ('Bharat'). It centres on the dispute between the families of the last two descendants of King Bharata (the Pandavas and the Karuvas) for rule over the western Yamuna Ganga valley. On the eve of the decisive battle it is Krishna, the eighth incarnation of Vishnu, who teaches the doubting hero Arjuna (as his charioteer) in eighteen 'songs', the Bhagavadgita, the 'Song of the Exalted One', about his duties as king and warrior and his real destiny as a human being.

## A HINDU TRINITY?

Whereas the cult of the god Brahma died out in the subsequent period (just a single temple is dedicated to him, in Puskar in Rajasthan), Vishnu and Shiva became the centre of a distinctive religion. Vishnu was now addressed as 'exalted' (*bhagavan*) and Shiva as 'Lord' (*ishvara*). Now they are at any rate exalted far above all the heavenly gods of the Vedas. They are almighty and omniscient; they create the world, sustain it and destroy it. Their functions often overlap.

Thus time and again the history of Hinduism is a continuous and sometimes discontinuous process of reinterpretation and reshaping. 'Paradigm shift' in fact means both

- continuity: an abiding religious substance of the Hindu religion; and
- discontinuity: a changing overall constellation of convictions, values and modes of behaviour: in a new era a new macro-model of society and religion.

Basically, classical Hinduism, with its understanding of the world of the gods, developed fully only in the eight great Puranas, written in verse (from the sixth century BC), which are dedicated to the three gods Brahma, Vishnu and Shiva. Only here do we find the doctrine of a Hindu trinity (trimurti) which is often compared with the Christian doctrine of the Trinity.

But what was the occasion for Christian speculation about the Trinity? Beyond question the relationship of the human Jesus of Nazareth, the 'son of God', to the one God and Father. In early Christianity there was the process of a speculative exaltation of the Christ figure and of a theological development which also included the Holy Spirit.

And what was the occasion for Hindu speculation about the Trinity? Here it was the highly confusing host of gods, almost too many to take in, which the Brahmans wanted to classify. So in medieval Hinduism there is a process of speculative unification and at the same time a differentiation of the various functions of the supreme Godhead, who is at the same time creator of the world (Brahma), sustainer of the world (Vishnu) and destroyer of the world (Shiva). The discussion here is only about three aspects (modes) of one and the same divine being. This has found its most significant artistic expression in the monolithic sculpture on the island of Elephanta near Bombay. The popes forbade this model to be used to depict the Christian Trinity (because it was heretical 'modalism').

## POLYTHEISM?

Travellers through India find many temples, great and small, as in Khajuraho, but also shrines and pictures of gods with much decoration and statues of gods which are well cared for. One can find little altars even in buses. No wonder that many people accuse the Hindus of being polytheists, of believing in many gods.

But that is not quite fair. Indian popular religion must not simply be compared with the Christian ideal religion. It would be fairer to compare one popular religion with another, say a Hindu temple with a Catholic baroque church. Then we might perhaps recognize:
- If by 'God' we mean all the divine beings that men and women venerate through invocations, through prayers, through hymns,

through offerings, then in fact many Christians too believe in several 'gods'. But they call these beings 'saints', 'angels', 'Mother of God' or whatever. The Indians call them 'devas', i.e. 'gods' of a subordinate rank.
– But if by 'God' we understand that which came first of all, the Absolute, the all-embracing God, then the Hindus too believe in one God, an Absolute. However, depending on the trend, they associate this figure with a quite specific revealer figure: Vishnu, Shiva or Shakti.

## HOW DOES GOD RELATE TO THE WORLD?
## THREE MODELS

But how does this divine One, Absolute, relate to the world? How did it come about that in the medieval schools of Hindu religion three fundamentally different answers were given more than a thousand years later to this basic question, which was already being asked in classical times, all referring to the same Upanishads? It was because on closer inspection there are already very different statements about Atman and Brahman in the Upanishads themselves. They were first brought together by the author (who has different names) of the Vedanta Sutra (also known as the Brahma Sutra), which is dated to the period between 400 BC and AD 200. The central difficulty of this synthesis, though, is that the author accepts two apparently contradictory views of Brahman at the same time without reconciling them. The Absolute is seen both as impersonal intelligence and as personal God (savidesha). That explains why since the Middle Ages in India there have been three different schools which are likewise called Vedanta, the end or conclusion of the Vedas. They all stand over against Buddhism, which declined in the classical age of Hinduism and was displaced by Islam at the beginning of the thirteenth century. They all maintain the authority of the Vedas, but interpret them in different ways. Their founders were philosophical thinkers, deeply religious mystics, reformers and founders of religious orders, all at the same time. None of them wants to engage solely in philosophical speculation and metaphysics but explicitly in theology, religion and the doctrine of salvation. They all usher in the great medieval Hindu syntheses (Paradigm IV) through which Hinduism took the normative shape that it still has today, so that some Indologists make Hinduism in its present form begin with the first of these thinkers, Shankara. These reformers offer the three following models of the relationship between the Absolute and the personal God and the relationship between God and the world.

Model 1: the Absolute and the world are completely one. That is what the 'philosophers of unity' or monists in India said and still say: they include a large number of intellectuals. By far the most famous Hindu thinker is Shankara, to whom we owe the restoration of Hindu religion in the face of Buddhism and Jainism in the ninth century AD.

This is his message. Basically there is only the One, the Brahman, which is identical with your soul, with Atman. The world is only a seeming reality, only Maya. To recognize this, however, you must transcend the level of naïve, ordinary truth where there is a multiplicity of things and selves. By meditation you will attain the level of the higher, mystical truths. There the different selves are one with the eternal, infinite divine Self, with the Absolute, which is being, consciousness and bliss in one: 'That is what you are.' So you do not gain redemption through lower knowledge or through ritual and moral works, but only through higher, mystical knowledge of the All-One. Does that resolve all the problems? No, contradictions arise from a counter-interpretation of the Vedanta.

Model 2: The Absolute and the world are completely separate. That is what the 'philosophers of division' or dualists said and still say. The most perceptive of them was Shankara's passionate opponent Madhva in the thirteenth century. He too organized a religious movement which still exists today, the Madhvas.

Certainly, he argues, bending the Upanishads, often rightly, the Brahman is being, consciousness and bliss in one, indeed is the one and only God, called Vishnu. But he tells his monistic opponents that they cannot go against all appearances and declare that the world is unreal. Precisely because it is incomplete, defective, evil, God cannot simply have changed himself into it. Rather it is created, sustained, ruled and also destroyed again by God. So the difference between God and the world, God and the soul, is quite real. That is why Madhva advocates a radical dualism, a duality = *dvaita* as opposed to Shankara's *a-dvaita* = non-duality. Isn't that convincing? But now there is a contradiction from a third side: earlier a middle way had been developed between these two extreme positions which avoids the manifest difficulties of both.

Model 3: the Absolute and the world are one in difference. That is what the differentiating monists said and say, led by Shankara's original follower Ramanuja in the twelfth century. Ramanuja had perhaps the most influence on the spirituality of India: he too was a brilliant mystical thinker and reformer, the founder of monasteries and an order for untouchables, which likewise still exists today.

Ramanuja firmly shared Shankara's basic intention – redemption through higher, mystical knowledge. But he rejected his undifferentiated monism: Brahman is indeed one, is two-less (*a-dvaitam*) but not impersonal, not without properties. On the contrary – and this is Ramanuja's decisive insight, which was eventually to win the most adherents among Hindus – the Absolute is identical with the personal God. That means that Brahman is none other than the personal God, who from eternity releases and sustains the world, guides it from within and takes it back again. Already in the Upanishads Ramanuja recognizes the veneration of a personal God and mystical union with him. So it makes good sense to offer trust, love, veneration, in short, devotion, 'bhakti', to the one infinite and at the same time personal God.

In this way Ramanuja developed theoretically an all-embracing, theistically 'qualified unity', so that his school is also called *vishishta-a-dvaita* = 'qualified non-duality'. At the same time Ramanuja laid the practical foundation for a movement with a strongly monotheistic piety, devoted to a single God – be this Vishnu, Shiva or a goddess. The future was to belong to it.

## VARANASI: THE MOST HOLY OF PILGRIMAGE CITIES

Like medieval Roman Catholicism, Hinduism too is unthinkable without the everyday piety which embraces the whole of daily life. Here secular and sacred are not separated. Saris and carpets are washed in the same holy river in which sacred baths are also taken. The rites (*pujas*) which recur regularly in the life of a Hindu are countless: not only the great temple festivals and processions in honour of the guardian deities of the village or city, but also fasts and above all rites performed before the image of the gods or the household altar. There is great freedom in the religious sphere as long as one follows the complex caste regulations, though mixing them up together is also very popular. Religious instruction and spiritual guidance are given by a guru, a teacher or spiritual guide, often for the whole family. In him the divine is directly present, and he is also the one who introduces the young Hindu to the religious tradition.

And like Roman Catholicism, Hinduism too is inconceivable without the pilgrimages (*yatra* – 'journeys') which interrupt everyday life, to places of divine presence and grace (*tirtha* – 'ford': originally probably the place where one crossed a river, and in a metaphorical sense places which help people to cross over the river of rebirths). They are rivers, temples, and also holy men, and a visit to them is expected to bring merit and salvation in worldly and spiritual matters. Pilgrimages are possible all through the year. But in many places there are times which are regarded as particularly meritorious, thus above all Kumbh Mela, which takes place about every four years, alternately in Haridwar and in three further cities. It attracts millions of visitors.

However, the most popular place, to which every Hindu wants to make a pilgrimage at least once, and which more than any other pilgrimage place makes it possible to encounter the different religious communities and tendencies, is Varanasi (which the English call Benares); with countless cult places it is the most holy and also the most turbulent of the pilgrim cities. What Jerusalem is for Jews, Rome for Catholics and Mecca for Muslims, Varanasi is for Hindus. All down the centuries this city and its temples have been destroyed several times. Most temples today date from the eighteenth century, when Varanasi was no longer under Muslim rule and not yet under British rule, but was under the Hindu rule of the Marathas.

Varanasi, today a city with 1,200,000 inhabitants, is perhaps the oldest settlement on the sub-continent to have been occupied without interruption. Its present-day name Varanasi derives from the two rivers which flow together here, Varuna and Asi, the Ganges. Whereas Haridwar in the upper Ganges valley is regarded above all as the city of Vishnu, Varanasi in the central Ganges valley is regarded as the city of Shiva. After his time in the Himalayas Shiva is said to have had a long stay in this city and therefore is especially venerated here. But this city is the scene of many other myths and epics. So here on special days the Ramayana is performed by heart, with the whole populace joining in, as a great piece of world theatre (ramlila = 'Rama play'). And even more important: it is believed that after many vain attempts at purification, only a bath in the Ganges was able to cleanse Shiva from the sin of murder. So the pilgrims hope that the river will bring about the same power of purification if they bathe in the Ganges.

## THE BATH OF PURIFICATION – NOT BAPTISM

As in Christianity, so also in Hinduism the bath of purification for the forgiveness of sin plays a great role. However, there are two decisive differences. The bath of Christian baptism (which today involves a complete immersion of the whole person only in the Eastern churches and among the Baptists) is performed by a baptizer – following the model of John the 'Baptist'. The person being baptized remains passive. And the baptism takes place once, on acceptance into the community, and cannot be repeated. By contrast, in Hinduism there is no baptizer and the bath of purification prescribed for sinners is a lifelong practice.

Today the bathing steps (ghats) in Varanasi, very much grander than those in Haridwar, also serve for bathing. For about four miles along the Ganges, from the mouth of the Varuna to the mouth of the Asi, there are perhaps seventy sets of stone steps leading down to the river. However, like all the great buildings by the Ganges, they have fallen into decay for lack of financial resources. In the monsoon season the Ganges can rise up to fifteen metres, and despite the Ganga Action Plan, far too little of the sewage from this city with its millions of inhabitants is treated.

For Hindu pilgrims, as for Christian pilgrims, there is a rich ritual repertoire in addition to the immersions: prayers, washings, cures by drinking water and a great variety of sacrificial gifts for the gods and their priests. The water of the Ganges is holy: it is drunk and taken home as holy water for household or temple rituals. Of course at this pilgrimage place, too, everywhere is very busy: there are stalls for flowers and votive offerings, for food and sweets to take to the temple. And above all there are souvenirs of all kinds, an abundance of which are bought after bathing.

The way in which men have their heads shaven is striking. In the history of culture, hair-style has always been dependent on social status or religious intentions: it is a sign of rank or of belonging to a religion. In Hinduism, traditionally the very first cutting of a boy's hair – after his first birthday and before his seventh – is performed at home in a solemn ceremony. The date is established precisely by a favourable constellation. Astrological practices have always played a major role, even for educated Indians. The planning of all important events – choosing a marriage partner, concluding business, the layout of temple buildings – is hardly ever done without astrological advice. However, the signs painted on the brows of priests and sadhus do not indicate astrological signs but the god whom an Indian takes as his preferred god. A Vishnavite usually has vertical stripes with or without a point, and often an extended V with straight lines of another colour in the centre. A Shivaite has two or three horizontal stripes, often with a point or an oval.

Here by the Ganges some people can be seen having all their hair cut off. Often this is done to perform a vow, but often it is also a sign of special mourning for a departed relative by the closest member of the family. Since ancient times it has been the custom to leave one tuft uncut; this has become an obligation for those 'born a second time'. Why? The tuft is meant to cover the suture or point by which the spirit entered the head at birth and from which it leaves it again at death. And no wonder that in Varanasi so many people have their hair cut off. For in this city of Shiva not only is life celebrated, but also death. This happens even at night.


## WHY BURN CORPSES IN VARANASI?

However, the nights are truly not all dark by the Ganges. By day believers often offer flowers (the fragrance of their personality) or fruit (their work) to the goddess Ganga. But once a year, at a festival in the night of the

November full moon, out of longing women whose husbands have gone abroad and not returned send lights floating down the Ganges: if the husband is still alive, he may return; if he is dead, he may receive a last greeting. This is a great theatre of lights.

Thousands come to Varanasi in their old age to die here; thousands come to sprinkle the ashes of their relatives in the Ganges; thousands come to burn a corpse at this particular spot. This cremation ceremony is expensive, because wood, which is scarce in India, is very dear (the sandalwood used by rich people costs an enormous amount) and around 300 kilograms of dry wood have to be bought for a single cremation. In addition an urn is needed for the ashes. From ancient times the clan of the dead person has been responsible for the whole ceremony.

But why burn corpses in an extremely expensive way here of all places? We already know the background. It is the doctrine of karma, which derives from the Middle Ages and explains why the situations, opportunities and fates of human beings are so unequal. Why? Because each has brought about his present existence in a former earthly life through good or evil deeds. Every deed is the cause of the things and actions which follow, and at the same time the effect of a previous cause. Thus people always live under quite specific conditions and restrictions, and this enables the Hindu to explain why things often go so badly for the good (because of former guilt) and well for the bad (because of former good deeds). Isn't that logical? Evil actions lead to rebirth in a worse existence – in a lower caste, as an animal or in hell (though this is not eternal); good actions lead to rebirth in a better existence – in a higher caste, even as a Brahmin or prince. However, the ultimate goal is to get out of the cycle of births, samsara, for ever.

For the ordinary Hindu, though, such speculations about former or future rebirths often play a subordinate role: for them sinful actions simply lead to hell, and good actions and merits to heaven. So dying or being cremated at a holy place can among other things represent a decisive step outside the circle of births. In Varanasi it is said to be Shiva himself who whispers a redeeming mantra into the ear of the dying person so that he goes directly to heaven without a further rebirth. Thus often between 30 and 50 bodies a night are turned to ashes in the open air at the famous cremation place of Manikarnika ghat. This happens, although for both hygienic and economic reasons the city runs a large electric crematorium by the Ganges. That is far cheaper, but it cannot give the decisive guarantee, that the soul goes directly to heaven.

When the corpse, which has previously been immersed in the waters of the Ganges, is put on the pyre – women covered with colourful cloths, men with white cloths – first of all the relatives surround the place. Then the husband or oldest son (always a male member of the family) is led forward to light the wood. For Hindus the cracking of the skull is the sure sign that the soul has departed. The soul is imagined as a very fine substance independent of the body which wanders from life to life; it leaves at the point in the head at which it entered the body at birth.

About three hours after the cremation the members of the family then go back to retrieve the ashes. Sometimes they remain several more days in Varanasi to mourn. Children and sadhus, however, are not cremated but buried; from this some scholars conclude that formerly burial was customary, and indeed this seems to be attested in the Vedas.

## PILGRIMS, BRAHMANS, SANNYASINS, PRIESTS

With Hindus, as with Christian pilgrims, the motives for a pilgrimage differ widely: people give thanks, they pray, and in particular they ask for healing from sickness or bodily ailments, for the blessing of children and for the aversion of disaster, private or public. They make vows, and above all they attain merits (*punya*), to reduce bad karma, their moral 'guilt'.

Countless Brahmans are at the service of the pilgrims and connect them with the deity. The vermilion spot which married women in particular usually have between their eyebrows is mere decoration. But the yellow spot made of sandalwood paste which the Brahmin presses on a person with his thumb or index finger is meant to open the 'third eye', the eye of wisdom, and to give knowledge.

Almsgiving is also part of the pilgrimage. Many of the countless beggars are content with a mere handful of rice. In the narrow streets of the old city there are numerous shops to cater for all needs and above all for sacrifice. As in Christian pilgrimage places here too religion is combined with commerce and kitsch.

And this Hindu pilgrimage place, too, is full of every possible kind of holy man, often strange. Some of them, in complete contrast to the Brahmans, think it important not to have their hair cut. Why? Not necessarily to allow organic growth. Since earliest times (one might think of the biblical Samson), the hair has been regarded as the vehicle of the soul and the power of life, which should not be wasted by constant cutting. Like other religious communities (for example the orthodox Christian clergy in the East), the Indian Sikhs refuse to cut their hair.

The sannyasins, the Brahmin ascetics, and the sadhus, the ascetics also of other castes, often monks, are highly respected. They have renounced all earthly joys and devoted their whole lives to their god. In India there are countless semi-naked or completely naked ascetics, yogis, who carry their few possessions around with them and are dependent on meagre gifts. In Varanasi, too, there are of course local priests; indeed, there is a real priestly Brahman establishment. This is responsible for looking after and guiding (*panda*) the thousands of pilgrims who speak quite different languages; it is responsible for pronouncing the prayer formulae necessary for the salvation of the soul (*mantras*) and for the correct performance of the rites (*pujari*), which differ depending on the religious community or temple. The liturgy can also be complicated in India.

## TEMPLE AND MOSQUE

The most important sanctuary in Varanasi is hidden in the busy streets of the old city. Today it is strictly guarded by a whole company of soldiers because of the tensions between Hindus (half the population) and Muslims (perhaps a third). This is the Vishvanath temple, which has been rebuilt several times, most recently at the end of the nineteenth century by a Sikh maharajah; the roof is decorated with 750 kilograms of gold.

This temple, too, which people usually visit after their bath of purification, is dedicated to the lord of this city, Shiva. For at this precise point Shiva is said to have shown all his power in battle with the gods Brahma and Vishnu: he is said to have appeared as a linga of pure light, as an endless pillar of light. Even if those who are not Hindus may not enter the temple, they know that the linga stands at the centre of this temple, too, as in any other Shiva temple. The holy precinct within the city of Varanasi takes its name, 'City of Light', from this light myth.

But there is no mistaking the fact that right next to this temple stands the great white Gyanvapi mosque of the last grand Muslim mogul Aurangzep, of unhappy memory. Unlike the first important grand mogul in the sixteenth century, Akbar the Great, who like his successor pursued a tolerant policy, the darkly puritanical Aurangzep had almost all the Hindu temples destroyed, even in Varanasi. This mosque reminds the Hindus daily that for a good three centuries (after 1194) Varanasi was under Muslim rule. As here, so too in Ayodhya, at the birthplace of Rama, rigorously monotheistic and moralistic Muslims have built a mosque in place of the temple. As we know from the recent massacres in Ayodhya, many Hindus have never become reconciled to that.

Normally Hindus could perform their manifold rites, pujas, unhindered, whether in the temple or more frequently in the family – hardly ever in great congregational services of the kind that are customary in Islam. However, throughout the whole of the Hindu Middle Ages Islam remained the great, at times extremely threatening, challenge. Moreover the hostility between Hindus and Muslims led to the splitting of the sub-continent in 1947, the year of Independence, into the secular republic of India and the Islamic state of Pakistan; in 1971 East Pakistan declared its independence as Bangladesh. A million refugees and hundreds of thousands of deaths were the terrible consequence. And still many Hindus see the Muslims of India and Pakistan as their main enemies. Here it becomes dramatically clear that there can be no peace among the nations without peace among the religions.

## RENEWAL INSTEAD OF RIGIDITY OR LOSS OF MEANING

When I thought of the metre-high barbed wire here in Varanasi which I had just passed, between the main Hindu temple and the adjacent mosque; when I noted all the soldiers here and the potential for conflict which they represented; and when on the other hand I observed the sheer overpopulation of the city, the traffic jams and all the misery, it was clear to me that the real challenge to Hinduism today is more than Islam. The real challenge to Hinduism and Islam is the European process of modernization, which now has India completely in its grasp.

Hence the question, how will Hinduism cope with modernization? – Now of course there are many people who have come to the Ganges from all over the country and think that religion should remain as it is. Nothing must be changed. Above all they are opposed to 'progress'. But such encapsulation makes religion rigid.

– On the other hand there are many people all over the country who at least secretly say that it is religion which has kept Indians away from modernity for so long, and who now think that India should go along with progress totally. However, such total modernization of course means that religion loses its meaning.

So I think, and many Indians will doubtless agree with me, that something else is needed: neither rigidity nor a loss of meaning but a renewal of religion. That means that there must be a fight against its negative aspects. The crass superstition, the discrimination against women everywhere, the often ruinous demands over dowries for girls, and often the murder of girls – all that just cannot be tolerated. But on the other hand the humane content of Hinduism, laid down in the great religious documents, should be preserved. A renewal of Hinduism is needed.

## INDIA: THE MODEL OF A DEMOCRATIC CONSTITUTION

A tremendous bridge over the Ganges is a landmark in Calcutta and a symbol of India's entry into the modern age. It lies almost 1200 miles from the sources of the Ganges, on its branch, the Hoogli, west of the delta in the city which from 1858 to 1911 was the seat of the British colonial government. Calcutta, the old trading centre and cultural metropolis in India, is now the largest city and industrial agglomeration in the country, with a population of 12,000,000.

The imposing colonial buildings from the second half of the nineteenth century, which have been smartened up, are today the witnesses to a vanished pomp. They recall the two faces of the colonialism of British merchants, civil servants, military and missionaries: St John's Cathedral, the Governor's palace, the administrative buildings and the Queen Victoria memorial.

For a long time in India the often harsh political oppression of the British and the economic exploitation of the country which made Great Britain rich stood at the forefront of critical attention. But at the celebrations for the fiftieth anniversary of Independence in 1997 many Indians also put the British achievements in modernizing India in the foreground:
– With the formation of an English-speaking élite for the civil service, science, business and the army a modern infrastructure was built up by means of Western technology (bridges, streets, canals, railways) and new institutions were established: the press, the postal service, the telegraph. India is now a unified sphere of business and administration.
– Along with this, the extremely heterogeneous Indian subcontinent, with its fifteen main languages and all the different religions and confessions, was unified politically for the first time. Structures were created which were to prove themselves in the construction of what is now the largest democracy in the world after Independence. Despite all the breakdowns and scandals about corruption there is a parliamentary democratic system in which it is taken for granted that power may change in elections (which with this degree of freedom and fairness are rare in Asia and even rarer in Africa). In contrast to China, freedom of speech and of the press are allowed, and basic rights are observed and effectively protected by an independent judiciary. At least politically and culturally, Indian democracy is more successful than Chinese dictatorship.
– Prohibitions of cruel religious practices have brought about a humanization of Hinduism: these include the prohibition of the voluntary self-immolation of high-caste widows (1829); the ritual murders which were still customary in the cult of Kali (1831); the sacrifice of children and

especially girls (1823); and slavery (1849). Widows are allowed to remarry (1856) and the principle of equality of persons before the law has been introduced. As well as embodying the principles of democracy and federalism (federal states), the constitution of the Indian republic is a secular one. This is not secularism in the sense of a total absence of religion but a separation of state and religion and a tolerance of all religions.

Thus as a constitutional democracy India is a model for Asia. However, there is a big but: economically and socially the opposite is the case. Does that perhaps have something to do with religion?

## INDIA: ECONOMICALLY BACKWARD AND SOCIALLY SPLIT

One central problem of India has not been solved either in the around 200 years of British colonial administration or by the democratic government of the last 50 years: the poverty, which is still terrible, and, associated with it, the illiteracy and fatalism of the masses. The main cause of this is the population increase which no government has been able to cope with: in the 50 years since Independence the population has increased by more than half a billion. Granted, there are no longer any great famines, and alongside the rich and powerful upper class a prosperous urban class is also developing (around 15 per cent). But over against it stands a poor, illiterate, neglected lower class (about 30 per cent of them below the poverty level), above all in rural areas, but also in the city slums. The pollution of the atmosphere and the destruction of the forests and rivers are becoming an increasing threat everywhere.

Why have all these problems hardly been tackled so far in India? Is religion really to blame for this? Certainly not in the first instance. Nor is Indian democracy itself to blame, but rather its leaders, who think above all of their own interests and neglect the needs and concerns of the people. It is paradoxical that the intelligent leading class, who think in terms of all India and speak English, and who have done India the undeniable service of holding together a multi-lingual and multi-cultural nation by a firm central leadership, are also to blame for India's poverty and backwardness. The lazy elephant of South Asia has completely neglected the compulsory universal schooling and fundamental land reform which the East Asian 'tigers' introduced as the basis of their at least initial economic boom (doubtless not without the influence of the Confucian work ethic). After all, as long as half the population is illiterate, as long as great landowners withhold land from large parts of the population, and as long as the state often remains inefficient because of corruption, economic and cultural progress will remain limited to a minority.

The process of modernization, and the urbanization, industrialization and democratization bound up with it, which have already long since broken up the class structure in Europe, have of course also shaken the caste structure in India. The very first government of India after its independence in 1947 decreed the equality of all under the law. It abolished the legal discrimination that existed under the caste order and granted everyone at least in principle free access to all institutions of the nation. In 1997 it even proved possible for a person of no caste to be elected as the Indian state president – something that formerly would have been quite unthinkable.

But the gulf between the legal situation and social reality is still great. Indeed, with its more than 1500 languages and dialects India is socially and culturally perhaps the most complex land on earth. There are no simple solutions to problems there. A large proportion of Indians still live in the country: here the Brahmins and upper classes live in the middle of the village, the Shudras around them, and those outside the caste system on the periphery or in their own settlements. A total abolition of the castes would also result in the abolition of an economic system of mutual dependence, help and solidarity which so far is just about functioning; this can hardly be changed overnight.

In the cities, too, to which more and more people are flocking, the boundaries between castes are becoming increasingly blurred because of ever closer contact in the working world. However, there too people still think in terms of the traditional superiority and subordination which seem to give each member of society his due. But today even a Brahman can live in poverty and earn his living as a cook or a tour guide, whereas lower classes have become rich, perhaps in business life. It is not the Brahmans but the Vaishyas, the merchants, who are generally best placed economically. But only in our day have those outside the caste system, the Dalits, the oppressed, slowly but effectively organized themselves under their own political leadership, and now the other parties must take note of them.

Is perhaps a future 'development dictatorship' needed? No. Indira Gandhi's emergency regime in 1975–7 clearly failed. But even economic liberalization and deregulation are not enough in the face of so many uneducated and unemployed people. What are urgently needed are serious educational and social reforms to reduce the tremendous gulf between the English-speaking élite and the Indian masses and to improve the scandalous living conditions of the lower classes. That is the only way to stop the parties with a religious orientation, which exploit Hinduism for their political purposes, from getting more and more members. These parties are striving for a Hindu state (Hindu-Rashtra) and threaten to undermine the democratic system. Films and comics with often mythical or religious themes are of little use as 'antidotes'.

No, in the face of the frequent threat of a lack of moral orientation and a spiritual void, the leading classes in particular will hardly gain critical insight into themselves without strong ethical motivation from the religious tradition of India. They need such ethical motivation to overcome the frequent selfishness and corruption, to set themselves realistic limits, and to engage in a common national effort. Even leading Indians are complaining that the old élite of politicians, bureaucrats, soldiers and intellectuals have not succeeded in establishing universally binding ethical standards. And unfortunately today India has hardly any national spiritual leaders of the stature of the poet Rabindranath Tagore, the religious philosophers Sri Aurobindo or Radhakrishnan, or Mahatma Gandhi, the social reformer and passionate seeker after truth. The Western education of the intellectual and religious élite of the country would not in itself be an intrinsically bad presupposition for a fundamental change, along with a progressive urbanization and globalization that largely undermine the separation of professional groups, the foundation of the caste system, which is usual in the villages. But there is a danger that the young business élite of the new middle classes have only one thing in mind: money.

Still, it is a sign of hope that in August 1997, the fiftieth anniversary of Independence, the 'untouchable' (with a Christian wife) who was elected state president with an overwhelming majority, K. R. Narayanan, appealed to the great religious and ethical tradition of India: 'India had the unique honour to show the world that human beings do not live by bread alone. Cultural, moral and spiritual values have always been the fundamental supports of our society. And it is precisely here that the greatest challenge to India is posed: it comes from the weakening of this basic moral and spiritual structure in our public life. The evils of communalism, of caste thinking, of violence and particularly of corruption are damaging present-day Indian society.'

## HINDU ETHICS

Critics of Hinduism inside and outside India claim that it has been an essential factor in the poverty and misery of the Indian masses. They argue that its other-worldliness, fatalism and resignation in the face of social injustices, and above all its caste system, favour political irresponsibility, social passivity and indifference to growing corruption. There is certainly much truth in that.

But aren't these critics overlooking something to which State President K. R. Narayanan made a positive allusion, namely that right from the beginnings of Hinduism and even more since the nineteenth-century renewal movement there has been a strong tradition of ethics, ethical values, standards and attitudes? And if we can find among the Aborigines in Australia a primal ethic that goes back to the prehistoric beginnings of humankind, we can find such an ethic even more in the great Indian written culture of the Vedas, which displays numerous elements of an ethic (values, norms, virtues), though these are scattered throughout the works.

However, there is no precise word for 'ethics' in Sanskrit (the nearest is probably *achara* = 'well-going'). That means that there are only a few systematic treatises on ethics. But already in the second century BC we find a first systematization of ethics. It comes from Patanjali, the founder of the philosophy of yoga, which has a quite practical orientation. He teaches the liberation of the spirit (*atman* or *purusha*) from matter by methodical efforts to control both the physical and the psychological elements of human nature.

The eight stages of his yoga sutras begin at the first stage with 'yama' – self-control. Here he requires five ethical exercises to be performed in thoughts, words and actions. These can be described as elements of a basic ethic (similar to the second table of the Decalogue):
- non-violence, not hurting (*a-himsa*),
- truthfulness (*satya*),
- not stealing (*a-steya*)
- chastity, a pure way of life (*bramachaya*),
- a lack of desire, not possessing (*a-parigraha*).

But even more than Patanjali, the Bhagavadgita provides stimuli towards the ethicizing of Hinduism, in the 700 verses of the religious and philosophical didactic poem from the Mahabharata epic (Book 6), the earliest strata of which might come from the third century BC. The Bhagavadgita is the best known and most influential holy scripture of India, often called the 'gospel' of Hinduism; and at the same time it is one of the great ethical documents of humankind. For:
- It is open dogmatically. It allows different philosophical views (monism–dualism, theism–pantheism, sacrifice–the rejection of rituals) to stand side by side in juxtaposition. Thus different schools and religious communities can appeal to it and find here the basis for their (often contradictory) expositions.
- It has a realistic starting point: it is not an ashram in the forests or a life in segregation, but the battlefield of life with all its conflicts, external and internal. Answers are given to quite concrete problems in this context.
- It presents a markedly secular ethos: this is not an ethics in the sense of an ethical system but an ethos in the sense of a moral attitude. Here neither asceticism nor a monastic renunciation of the world is called for as a way of liberating oneself from the cycle of births, but rather an active life associated with detachment from the world of the kind that could largely

also be affirmed by a Jew, Christian or Muslim, a Buddhist or a Confucian: do your duty in the world but do not succumb to it. So this is a commitment without greed and possessiveness.

Already in the Bhagavadgita there are three classical ways to salvation, all of which are recognized. However, they culminate in the third:

- the way of knowledge (*jnana-marga*), to overcome ignorance (through meditation, yoga and philosophy);
- the way of works (*karma-marga*), not only ritual and Brahmanistic works but also social and religious action;
- the way of the love of God (*bhakti-marga*), increasingly popular because the lower castes, indeed those outside the caste system, can also follow this way without restrictions. Moreover the Bhagavadgita culminates in love of God with the famous sentences: 'Remembering me, honouring me, sacrificing to me, bow before me. Then you will come to me' (18.65).

## SPIRITUAL RENEWAL: RAMAKRISHNA

In the nineteenth century a renewal movement with an ethical orientation developed. A national Indian culture and national independence would hardly have come about without it. It was the first of all the many movements for social reform, especially in Bengal, which – beginning with Rajah Rammohun Roy – attempted to respond to the modernity which had erupted under British rule. But without the contemporaneous spiritual renewal it would not have had such depth or such a power of endurance. The Hindu Renaissance led in the nineteenth century to modern Reform Hinduism.

In it appeared an uncouth, barely educated, childlike peasant boy from a poor village Brahmin family who finally after some resistance became a priest in a quite new temple in Calcutta. In time he began to show even the intelligentsia with a modern English upbringing that Hinduism was not dying out, that it was by no means finished. Rather, once again it could become an inexhaustible source of spiritual renewal. From his youth Ramakrishna, as his name now was, had had trance-like experiences and visions, the expression of an excessive longing and love of God.

In the great temple precinct of Dakshineshvara, founded in 1855 by a rich widow who nevertheless came from one of the lowest castes, Ramakrishna experienced Kali, whose image is of an ugly and terrifying black figure, as a young, beautiful and graceful 'mother' (*ma*). This was an experience not unlike Christians designating the mother of Jesus 'Queen of Heaven' or 'Mother of the Universe'. Later he even identified Kali with the Brahman, the Absolute. However, he abhorred Tantrism, and did not consummate his marriage to a wife who was betrothed to him at the age of four, and whom he later identified mystically with the mother goddess.

There is no doubt that Ramakrishna (1836–86) was a completely traditional Hindu, and yet he was an essential inspiration for all the 'Neo-Hindus' who were everywhere striving for modernization. He was not a social reformer, and yet he inspired many social reformers. These included the founder of the Neo-Hindu association Brahmo Samaj, Keshab Chandra Sen, who attacked with rational arguments idolatry, superstitious practices and social evils like the burning of widows and compulsory dowries. For Ramakrishna and his disciples, who became increasingly numerous, meditation, praise of the name of God and emotional love of a personal God (whether revered as Kali or whoever) were decisive: this was bhakti-marga, the 'way of dedication'.

Thus Ramakrishna became convinced that all religions are true, even if they are not free from errors. Whether it is a primitive veneration of images which does not in fact venerate the image but the deity, or the contemplation of Brahman without images, which certainly represents a higher form of religion, they are all different ways to the one all-embracing deity.

Certainly it is impossible for Christians to recognize Ramakrishna as an incarnation of God, as an avatara on the same level as Rama, Krishna, Buddha and even Jesus Christ, as was propagated by his disciples. Nor is that acceptable to some Hindus. But it should not be difficult even for Christians to recognize this extraordinary man as a saint of Hinduism and as an embodiment of a being mystically filled with the deity.

## THE ENCOUNTER BETWEEN THE RELIGIONS OF EAST AND WEST: VIVEKANANDA

Ramakrishna's most prominent disciple was Swami Vivekananda, born in 1863 in Calcutta, which takes its name from the goddess Kali. Here, where he also died in 1902, he founded a centre for spiritual energies and the culture of knowledge named Belur Math, by the Ganges. It is the headquarters of Vivekananda's international Ramakrishna movement, and Vivekananda's study in it is still held in the highest honour. He was the one who introduced the legacy of Ramakrishna into the national movement that was now developing.

Brought up in a Christian school, like many of the young men who had had a modern education he had lost faith in traditional Hinduism and had become a rationalistic sceptic. But the law student was increasingly attracted by Ramakrishna and was finally appointed his spiritual heir. In the year after Ramakrishna's death, Vivekananda took monastic vows along with eight or ten companions and made an intensive study of the religious Sanskrit literature. Then he wandered laboriously for almost three years as a begging monk all through India, from east to west and from the foot of the Himalayas to the southern tip. However, neither the blind rigidity of the orthodox Hindus nor the one-sided rationalism of the social reformers of the Brahmo Samaj could satisfy him.

More by chance than anything, he heard of a Parliament of the World's Religions which was to be held in September 1893 in the framework of the World Exposition in Chicago. He quickly decided to travel to Chicago, an obscure and unknown Hindu monk who had some difficulties in gaining admission as a delegate. But on the very first day of the congress he put all the other speakers in the shade with an inspiring speech, given without notes and in perfect English. And he remained the most powerful figure in this Parliament, which was the first formal meeting between Christianity and the Eastern religions. It was far ahead of its time in calling for harmony between the religions of East and West instead of the previous conflicts and confrontations.

According to Vivekananda, the presupposition for ethics is an orientation on the divine. This is possible in many ways: 'Every soul is potentially divine. The goal is to manifest this deity within by controlling nature both outwardly and inwardly. Do this by works or by worship or by psychological control or by philosophy – by one or all of these – and be free. That is the whole of religion; doctrines or dogmas or rituals or books or temples or forms are only secondary details.' Here Vivekananda, as a good Hindu, not only opposed the over-estimation of doctrine, dogma and rites but at the same time argued that the three or four practical Hindu ways to salvation could supplement one another (in compatibility and complementarity): the way of meditation (*yoga*), the way of knowledge (*jnana*), the way of works (*karma*) and the way of the love of good (*bhakti*) all lead to the one goal, to the one God.

This view now also governed Vivekananda's attitude to the other religions: 'I am proud to belong to a religion,' Vivekananda declared to the delegates, 'which has taught the world tolerance and universal acceptance. We not only believe in universal tolerance, but we accept that all religions are true.'

Here, however, he was understanding Hinduism from his very personal inner perspective as the highest form, the embodiment, of all true religion, as the ideal of a religion. Of course, Christians would claim the same thing in their own way and from their own inner perspective for Christianity (or Muslims for Islam). However, would Vivekananda and Ramakrishna have wanted the divinization which is given them in Belur Math and which has features which are also painful for some Indians? Still, for me there is a more important question.

## THE 1993 PARLIAMENT OF THE WORLD'S RELIGIONS

On 4 September 1993, precisely a century after the first Parliament of the World's Religions, the delegates of the world religions met once again in the same large room. There they certainly did not pass a declaration on a universal ideal religion for all humankind, as Swami Vivekananda would have wanted. But they did pass a Declaration toward a Global Ethic, i.e. for a shared ethic for men and women of all religions and philosophies. Swami Vivekananda would certainly have approved of that.

This did not mean that the dogmatic differences which exist between the religions were done away with. Today the issue is not the unity of all religions. The issue is peace between the religions, which is an essential presupposition of peace among the nations.

But it is of fundamental importance in particular for this peace among the religions that the ethical imperatives which human beings are to observe are essentially the same in all these religions. As we have already seen, they can be discerned in the founder of yoga and the Bhagavadgita. They appear in the Hebrew Bible, the New Testament, the Qur'an and all the great philosophical and religious traditions of humankind. The 1993 Parliament of the World's Religions attempted to translate these great imperatives for today and to make them quite specifically understandable for men and women of our time.

## THE GANGES OF RIGHTS RISES IN THE HIMALAYAS OF RESPONSIBILITIES

We have reached the end of our long journey from the source of the Ganges to its mouth, a round trip which used to take pilgrims about six years. The island of Gangasagar in the Ganges Delta (a little more than 40 miles south of Calcutta) is regarded as the mouth of the Ganges, and so the temple there is especially holy. But it reminds me not so much of the legend of this place as of the 'great soul', 'Mahatma' Gandhi, who with exemplary fearlessness drove on the social, political and religious renewal of India initiated by his predecessors: by his political agitation, with which he mobilized the masses, without violence and often practising civil disobedience.

But what about Gandhi today? Has he been made a saint and thus forgotten? Gandhi himself did not want to be a saint but a seeker after truth. He was not concerned with a dogmatic or moral system; he sought to hold firm (*agraha*) to the truth (*satya*) and in this way maintain an ethical attitude. In particular he wanted an India in which all religions lived peacefully together, where the god of the Hindus (Ram) was not played off against the God of the Muslims (Rahin), but was just one God: Ram-Rahin. He wanted an India in which Hindus and Muslims were brothers and sisters and all fought together against the social inequality, economic exploitation and omnipresent corruption.

Gandhi did not orientate his ethical principles only on the Bhagavadgita but also on Jesus' Sermon on the Mount. He attacked the seven modern social sins, and in so doing pointed forward to a postmodern Hinduism. These sins were, according to him:

1. Politics without principles
2. Business without morality
3. Wealth without work
4. Upbringing without character
5. Science without humanity
6. Enjoyment without conscience
7. Religion without sacrifice.

And he reminded a time which seemed to him, as a great champion of human rights, to speak all too one-sidedly of human rights and too little of human responsibilities, even in the United Nations Universal Declaration of Human Rights, that 'The Ganges of rights rises in the Himalayas of responsibilities.'

But the destination even of the Ganges is the sea, into which all rivers flow. And the destination of all religions is the God to whom they all lead in different ways. Thus already as schoolchildren many Indians learn the verse:

Just as different rivers which have their sources in different places all pour their waters into the sea, so, O Lord, the different paths which people with their different tendencies take, varied though they are, crooked or straight, all lead to you.

# III

# *Chinese Religion*

## LION DANCE

The lion dance could be taking place anywhere in China. There have been lion dances since the time of the Han emperors at the beginning of our era. Originally, however, there were hardly any real lions in China: the first were sent to the Chinese emperors as gifts by the rulers of the territories of present-day Iran and Afghanistan.

A fable circulates among the people that in ancient times a monster (*nian*) which devoured human beings and animals burst into China. Neither the fox nor the tiger had been able to help. Only a lion wounded and drove out the monster, but it threatened to come back after a year. At that time the lion was busy guarding the door to the imperial palace. People had to fend for themselves. So they made a model lion out of bamboo and fabric and drove out the monster for ever.

Since that time the lions have danced, especially on the eve of the Chinese new year, the most important festival for the Chinese. They are meant to keep evil away for a year and bring good fortune, which is often symbolized by a large pearl, with which the lion plays.

## SINGAPORE: MODERN AND TRADITIONAL CHINESE

But our lions are dancing in the lion city, in 'Singa Pura', though there are no real lions here either. However, the mighty lion which is today enthroned as a landmark above Singapore harbour, the second largest harbour in the world, is a symbol of economic strength and political power: in a strategically favourable situation, as is well known this island state is the crossroads of South East Asia. Only just over thirteen miles wide (north to south) and twenty-five miles long (west to east), with some islands facing it, Singapore has achieved an unprecedented economic miracle: in a single generation a poor, dirty and chaotic city, plagued with malaria, has become a modern, prosperous, clean and green metropolis.

The 3,000,000 inhabitants earn one of the highest gross national products in the world and have the seventh largest airport.

Singapore did not become an independent sovereign state until 1965. But only 30 years afterwards it was reckoned by the Organization for Economic Cooperation and Development to be in the top group of high-tech states. Here there is a more resolute fight against corruption, drug-dealing and neglect than in the USA or the EU, though there are severe restrictions on democracy and political involvement. Under a strict government, supported by the population, Singapore is an Asian metropolis without poverty, slums, criminality or street children.

Here on the periphery of the South Chinese Sea, Chinese show what they are capable of. For of the 3,000,000 inhabitants, almost four-fifths are Chinese. The city state of Singapore appears to be a state which is Chinese but at the same time truly modern: Chinese culture and Western modernity are closely connected.

## MEN AND WOMEN OF DIFFERENT CULTURES AND RELIGIONS LIVE TOGETHER

However, unlike Hong Kong or Taipei, Singapore is not an exclusively Chinese city. Singapore seeks emphatically to be a multi-racial and multi-lingual city. For 17 per cent of its inhabitants are Malays and 7 per cent Indians. Therefore Chinese, English, Malay and Tamil are all official languages of this city state.

Great demands are made of all pupils in the schools. An examination after the third year at school decides what type of school a child may choose. This is of crucial importance for further education at a university or another school. Singapore quite deliberately encourages élites. And here, because of their number and language, the Chinese inhabitants of Singapore are clearly at an advantage.

Simply because of the tremendous economic, political and cultural significance of China, people are very interested in the roots of the vast majority of the population in Chinese culture and upbringing. Indeed, for the sake of good relations with its big Chinese brother, the government is propagating Mandarin Chinese instead of the South China dialect which is spoken by many immigrants into Singapore. However, these immigrants have maintained their age-old customs.

## ANCESTOR WORSHIP AT THE CENTRE OF
## POPULAR RELIGION

It is paradoxical yet typical of Singapore that quite traditional Chinese celebrations for the dead take place under the arcades of the high apartment blocks in which most people have to live here. For the Chinese, everything is by no means over with death. Death is a transition to another life, and relations between the living and the dead continue.

For the Chinese the concept of the family essentially extends also to ancestors and to prehistory. The childlike piety (*xiao*) which is focused on mutuality extends beyond death. Thus since earliest times the veneration of ancestors has been at the centre of Chinese piety. No longer to be able to communicate with the ancestors was and is for many Chinese the main reason not to convert to Christianity.

Depending on the social position and wealth of the dead person, the burial is celebrated more or less expensively. Here the precise location is important. This is the only way in which the spirit of the dead person can find the family's sacrificial offerings when it returns. The location can be the occasion for a dispute between families which belong to different religions. If, for example, a Malay family has already reserved a place for a marriage festival and now the Chinese want to hold their celebration for the dead there, there is not only the problem of the date but also a ritual problem: the place would be unclean for the Malays and quite unsuitable for a wedding. But in Singapore the city administration has attempted to introduce rules for such conflicts between cultures.

## GIFTS FOR THE DEAD

Chinese funerals are family festivals. For close members of the family, white is the colour of mourning. The solemn Daoist liturgy of the dead is particularly popular; it is held with sacrificial offerings and joss sticks, with much music to drive off evil spirits, and solemn invocations of Daoist deities. The lantern in the middle symbolizes the soul which is to ascend on high. According to traditional Chinese belief the soul is to attain the 'Western heaven', and the rituals are intended to help it here. So they give the dead person directions for the way to the other world.

However, since all human beings have their failings, the ancestor spirits usually go to 'hell', which corresponds to 'purgatory' for Catholics. There they must be provided by members of the family with the things that they also need in earthly life. Up to the Chinese Middle Ages (the end of the Sui period in AD 617) real objects were burned. Now the symbolic gifts are made out of paper: consumer goods of all kinds, from televisions to watches. There is also a good deal of money for the bank of hell in gold and silver currency, and even a car.

If the ancestor spirit does not receive enough, it does not bring good fortune to the living, indeed it shows its displeasure by causing misfortune for the living. Some people therefore feel the need after a certain time to burn yet more such objects for the ancestor spirits. And this can be very costly. Therefore people are deterred from burning objects that are excessively expensive.

The coffin is finally taken away, and the relatives accompany it for some of the distance. The burial or cremation takes place at the Chinese cemetery. Significantly there is no mixing of the religions at the last resting place. Since they are Muslims, in any case the Malays do not use a coffin. They simply wrap the dead bodies in white cloths and bury them if possible on the same day, whereas the Chinese often bury their dead only after funeral celebrations lasting for days.

After the burial the picture of the dead person is put on the household altar alongside the household gods. In this way the dead person is appointed a family ancestor. Ancestors and gods are honoured and venerated with joss sticks, gestures and invocations. After all, in the end the achievements of the present generation are to some degree grounded in the good deeds of former generations. The veneration of ancestors is also characteristic of other religions, though not in the intense form it takes among the Chinese. Here there are often problems in adapting the traditional forms to modern living conditions.

## THE TWO SIDES OF POPULAR RELIGION

Of course, traditional Chinese piety does not just relate to the end of life. The birth of a child and marriage are also special occasions at which the family meets to share a meal and venerate the household gods and ancestors, in order to share the event with them. This popular piety functions without any priesthood, dogma or magisterium. It is certainly not without its problems, and other ethnic groups regard some Chinese customs as crude superstition. Moreover the well-educated and highly sophisticated younger generation in Singapore is hardly prepared to accept all the customs, festivals and rites, which are grounded in superstition. However, more important than the often remarkable form of the rituals is the moral disposition which often underlies them.

Of course, Chinese pious observances often also take place in temples. A Buddhist temple in Singapore is dedicated to the Guanyin, the goddess of mercy (originally the male Bodhisattva Avalokiteshvara). But today it serves as a typical Chinese temple of three religions, which is also open to Confucians and Daoists and in a quite practical way depends on their gifts. People of all classes come here every day, even crowds of them on particular festivals, in order to ask gods or ancestors for advice about particular problems: marriage, an illness, a job, a career. The little stick which finally falls out of the container when rattled bears a number, but it must be additionally confirmed by a red yin-yang symbol. The number refers to a text: this gives the believer an answer which can be favourable, unfavourable or indefinite, depending on the category.

This popular religion seems to be less about a great search for meaning than about the direct attainment of proofs of grace (in the succinct Latin phrase, *do ut des*: I give so that you give). In this temple with its great wealth of gods and figures – and with the Buddha at the top – people seem to be less interested in ethical standards than quite practically in a successful life: how to remain healthy, how to overcome sicknesses, how to eat properly, how to build good houses and how to use the mysterious forces and energies of the cosmos to drive out or trick the evil spirits everywhere and make the good gods gracious. Moreover soothsayers are used for every possible occasion, for example to identify a favourable site for a house or tomb, or the day for a wedding or funeral.

However, over-hasty judgements are out of place here. For popular religion with all its customs, usages, rights and festivals satisfies deep emotional and religious human needs, and not just the longing for riches, health and a long life. It can help people to be in harmony with themselves, with the human world, nature, the world of spirits. Indeed, in popular belief we can see how open present-day Chinese are to the transcendent-divine dimension. Still, their approach is pragmatic: if a God does not prove effective (*ling*), they turn to another.

## THE QUESTION OF ETHICAL STANDARDS

For a long time the more than two million Chinese in Singapore have boasted that they have the best of both worlds: the traditional Chinese world, culture and education, and at the same time Western modernity with all its tremendous technical achievements and great possibilities. But many people are now asking what will be left of Chinese culture if the headlong Americanization goes on so intensively.

At any rate the hard-working and satisfied generation which built up Singapore is far from happy about the materialistic attitude of the present generation. Convenient integration into society without moral integrity can easily lead to social disintegration. Yuppies and hedge funds hardly guarantee a state's prosperity.

Moreover some responsible people are warning about a 'materialism without morality'. They say that the real problems of Singapore are ethical standards. Shortly before he retired as Prime Minister in 1990, Lee Kuan Yew, who led Singapore in 1959 to autonomy from England and in 1965 to become an independent republic which enjoyed a sensational economic boom, remarked that power and responsibility should not be regarded merely as a favourable opportunity but as something that is entrusted to faithful hands.

## CONFUCIANISM OR COMMON VALUES?

The self-discipline, diligence, adaptability, contentment, saving, cleanliness and order that are called for all over Singapore are said to be specifically Confucian virtues, the expression of a Confucian work ethic. And in fact in this society family, school, business and state generally seem to have a hierarchical order: people define themselves by their social relations to others. Each individual has his or her quite specific place and the social order is guaranteed by all meeting the demands of their social roles.

To ensure that modernization did not lead to a total Westernization with extreme individualism and moral permissiveness, in 1984 Singapore resolved to introduce Confucianism into the school curriculum. But this experiment was stopped with the arguments, first, that it sanctioned authoritarianism, and secondly, that it put the non-Chinese at a disadvantage: the Christian charismatic groups with their missionary claims should be accorded the same rights.

This criticism was taken seriously, so in 1991 the Singapore parliament issued a white paper on shared values: these did not need *a priori* to be regarded as Confucian values. There was even criticism of particular dangers in Confucianism like nepotism or hierarchical family relationships. But on the other hand it was emphasized that specifically Confucian ideals were quite relevant for Singapore, for example the concept of a government by 'honourable men' (*junzi*), who would be responsible for doing what was right for the people and who would have to enjoy their trust and respect.

## WESTERN CRITICISM AND THE EASTERN REPLY

In the West people are all too ready to criticize Singapore. They are fond of talking about a Confucian 'state religion' which encourages only passivity, submissiveness and conservative politics. In the face of such Western critics people in Singapore point to facts: Singapore has the least corruption of all the threshold countries – it comes seventh after the Scandinavian countries, New Zealand and Canada, and before Switzerland (tenth), Germany (fifteenth) and Italy (thirty-ninth). This information was provided by Transparency International in September 1998.

And indeed we can ask: In the last 50 years would Singapore have done better with unrestricted Western individualism? And conversely, is Confucianism really a kind of collectivism, as a Western cliché would have it? Is it really Confucian teaching that the needs of the individual must be sacrificed completely to the demands of the community, the state, society? No. Confucianism, too, knows an autonomy of the individual conscience. A Confucian interest in harmonious human relations and a concern to save 'face' and maintain a social role can certainly prevent change and encourage crony capitalism. But the Confucian delight in learning, which includes learning from the successes and failures of others, can encourage reforms.

Moreover the economic crisis in East Asia, which tangibly interrupted Singapore's fantastic economic boom, has sparked off some self-critical reflections. Many of Singapore's present leaders recognize the limits of the previous purely economic ('economistic') model (the old formula). So far a relative harmony has prevailed in this multi-cultural society under Chinese leadership. But it was guaranteed by a state in which all the economic, social and political impulses came from the top.

Today, though, it is recognized that harmony calls not only for incorporation and subordination, but above all for participation: the right for families, schools and communities and businesses to have a say and play a part. As for education and training, there has recently been an emphasis:

- not only on respect for teachers, but also on a capacity to discuss with them;
- not only on dry learning by heart but also on constructive criticism and the formulation of independent positions;
- not only on early specialization in education but on flexibility and the widest possible horizon;
- not only on conformity and predictability, but on innovative and creative thought which cannot then be limited to the economic sphere.

All this shows that those who regard people in this super-modern trading metropolis only from an economic, technological and political perspective reduce the reality. These people also want their cultural, philosophical, ethical and religious side to be understood. The Yue Hai Qing temple in the middle of the Singapore Business Centre is a sign of this.

## ETHNIC AND RELIGIOUS HARMONY INSTEAD OF CONFRONTATION

In so many countries of Asia there are ethnic and religious tensions, conflicts and fights. But in the small, constricted city state of Singapore many people from the most varied cultures and religions live peacefully together: Chinese, Malays, Indians, Westerners – in the same apartment block, in the same office. No ghettos are tolerated here. This is an indication that a clash of civilizations is by no means inevitable.

But how is such peaceful co-existence possible? Since the foundation of the state in 1965 the government has followed a programme of multi-cultural exchange and religious harmony. The different religions have equal rights, and by law incitements to hatred and disunity are strictly punished.

Critics say that the praesidial system of Singapore is not sufficiently democratic. But Singapore is not a totalitarian state, nor is it the government that holds this society together. What holds it together are the common basic values which have even been laid down by a parliamentary decree, but which most people take for granted here as so-called 'Asian values':
- The community comes before the individual.
- But the community respects and supports the individual.
- The family is the basic unit of society.
- Problems are to be solved by consensus and not by confrontation.
- Ethnic and religious harmony is to be encouraged.

It is clear that these basic values were not invented at the foundation of the state. Rather, for the most part they come from the great Chinese tradition. And we must go back a long way into the history of China if we want to understand the many different levels in Singapore and China today

## CHINA: A CONTINENT IN ITSELF

Guilin in the southern region of Guangxi is one of the most beautiful river landscapes on earth. Three hundred million years ago a broad sea extended here. It deposited mussel chalk. Millennia of erosion finally created these absurdly shaped mountains, with countless caves. Sub-tropical rain brought greenery to them.

All these mountains have long given rise to many legends and have for ages inspired Chinese painters. There is 'Elephant Trunk Mountain' (*xiangbi shan*), or the 'Mountain of Extraordinary Beauty' (*duxiufeng*) in the middle of the town or 'Wavebreaker Mountain' (*fubo shan*) to the north. Guilin's beauty is praised on countless scrolls and in countless verses. Some regard this spectacular landscape as typically Chinese. But it is quite different from the usual mountain landscapes and is far away from the fertile plains and metropolises of the east, 1400 miles from the political centre of Beijing – the same distance as, say, Naples is from Copenhagen.

China is so to speak a continent in itself: a giant land mass almost 30 times as big as Germany, two-thirds of which is mountainous country. Largely isolated by deserts, steppes and mountains, China saw itself quite naturally as the 'Middle Kingdom' (*zhongguo*), as 'everything under heaven' (*tianxia*), as the centre of the world. To the west lies the mighty barrier of the Himalayas, to the north a broad belt of desert, to the east and south the Pacific Ocean. Three rivers flowing from west to east divide the land:
- the Yellow River with the north China of wheat and millet;
- the Yangzi with the central China of rice and the lakes;
- the Xiang with the southern China of mines and metals.

## A STATE OF MANY PEOPLES WITH A COMMON SCRIPT

China is a state of many peoples. For Sun Zhongshan (Sun Yat-sen), the founder of republican China, the Chinese nation consisted of Manchurians, Mongols, Tibetans, Muslims and of course the Han. In the European Enlightenment, under the impact of the writings of the Jesuits, and of Leibniz and Voltaire, China was idealized. But then, in particular under the influence of Rousseau and Hegel, it came to be depicted as a land of economic and cultural stagnation. Today we know that the Chinese are a people with a history and culture going back for millennia, who have succeeded in finally 'Sinifing' all the conquering peoples, especially those nomads from the Mongolian steppes who have liked to settle here.

The giant land, with now 1.2 billion inhabitants, 90 per cent of whom live in the eastern provinces, is held together, despite different dialects, by the same script. The same characters (logograms or ideograms) are present everywhere. These are symbols which indicate the meaning rather than the sound of a word; the syllables can have a quite different meaning depending on the tone of the word or sentence, but can be understood in different parts of China and also in Korea, Vietnam and Japan, though they are read differently.

Meagre graphic signs from which the Chinese script developed already appear on pottery of the Late Stone Age between 5000 and 4000 BC. They include the sign 'tian' for heaven, interestingly a large man with two legs – thus in the Shang dynasty of the second millennium BC. We find the same sign with only a few changes in the classical era of the Han emperors, who ruled around the time of the Roman empire. The same characters can be rendered by the different peoples with very different words. Thus even today Chinese characters are comprehensible which were written down 2000 years ago. For they also have the same meaning in present-day writing.

Thus with the help of Chinese script, which has changed little in the last 2000 years, a giant 'Sinified' sphere developed from Pyongyang to Taipei and from Turfan to Tokyo. In contrast to alphabetical script, their signs express ideas of meaning, order and value which have been governed by the Confucian tradition, substantially more than 2000 years old.

At a very early stage the Chinese regard the art of writing as a sign of higher education, not rhetoric, as did the Greeks and Romans; as an art form it rated well above painting. Since the spirit and character of a person are expressed directly in his writing, they saw calligraphy as the highest form of all arts.

## EARLY CHINESE SOCIETY HAD A RELIGIOUS ORIENTATION

At the beginning of the twentieth century, in Chinese medicine substances from what were alleged to be dragons' bones still played a role in the healing of malaria and skin diseases. They were sold in shops in Beijing, and in 1934 led to the discovery of the primal Asian human being, Beijing man (*Sinanthropus pekinensis*), in Zhoukhoudian near Beijing. The Chinese already had an ambivalent attitude to the dragon, the mythical beast associated with ancestors: one of both love and fear. Dragons could give rain and life, but they could also spread death and destruction.

It is a long time now since this Beijing man who lived around 500,000 years ago was regarded as the earliest man; Africa has a vast chronological priority. That has been most recently confirmed by the international team of Chinese and other geneticists who have been working on the Chinese Human Genome Diversity Project: the original inhabitants of the Yellow River and the Yangzi valley immigrated from the south-west and probably came from Africa.

But unlike African history, the early history of China can be followed very well on the basis of new written discoveries from the Early Stone Age (*c.* 5000 BC) on. Whatever may be conjectured about the influence of ancient eastern and particularly Indo-European peoples (in connection with the forging of bronze, the breeding of horses and the introduction of chariots), it is certain that both script and bronze objects (cultic utensils and weapons) display typically Chinese forms and motifs from the start.

Earlier Western scholarship had assumed that ancient Chinese society was not really religious. But the China of the Sinologists often did not correspond to the China of the Chinese. First, earlier scholarship put the history of China far too late, and secondly, it restricted the Chinese tradition in an all too rationalistic way to specific philosophical writings. More recent research offers us a more differentiated picture of China:

– Chinese culture by no means entered history 'adult' 5000 years ago, as was long assumed, but underwent a 'childhood' (we might recall the native inhabitants of Australia and Africa). This was a mythical phase of dreams, heroes and heroic acts.

– The notion of an almost timelessly static, 'eternal China' fails to take account of the revolutions, the paradigm shifts that took place even in Chinese society, often with several dynasties and capitals at the same time, with shifting frontiers and abiding zones of conflict. In an earlier period scholars relied one-sidedly on Chinese historiography, which began amazingly early, 3000 years ago. But they failed to note that at a very early stage this had been monopolized by the imperial court, made official and indeed bureaucratized (by a state office for historiography), and served to present a moralistic evaluation. In this way Chinese history took on a traditionalistic, conformist and stereotyped colouring.

Beyond question early Chinese history had a religious character. However, only fragments of its mythology have been preserved (for example, the myth of the world egg from which heaven and earth were created). But its soothsaying and its sacrificial cult, which lasted until the deposition of the last emperor, are well documented. If we go back 5000 years to the beginning of Chinese history we find a society in which shamans, soothsaying and ancestor worship, and with them the transcendent spiritual dimension, permeated daily life. At the centre stood religious ritual rather than the training of a firmly defined state apparatus. Thus early Chinese culture was a shamanistic culture with a marked religious stamp at the centre of which lay the veneration of ancestors and rites.

## SHAMANS AND SOOTHSAYING

But what is a shaman? 'Shaman' is a word used by the Tungus, the peoples of central and eastern Siberia and north-east China who are classified as the Manchu-Tungusic language group. 'Shaman' denotes someone who is excited, moved or elevated. Thus the shaman is a person, a man or a woman, who is seized by the divine; who, though possessed by the spirits, at the same time controls them, indeed in some circumstances can fall into a controlled trance. Shamans can function as simple spirit mediums, healers, exorcists, interpreters of dreams or rainmakers. It is said that they can recall the souls of the sick or the dead and even travel through the air. In China such shamanism is by no means just a phenomenon of the past. It still lives on in the gods and practices of religious Daoism, in certain forms of Buddhism, and in the more recent Chinese folk religion which has arisen out of a fusion of the two.

There has been soothsaying in China since earliest times, and today it can often be found on the streets. Everyone wants to know what the future holds, even if it is simply read off the palm of one's hand. The earliest inscriptions to be found in China, which are frequently very short, often contained predictions. These inscriptions – unlike those in Mesopotamia – are less economic than sacral, and are often magical; they are used for intensive dealings with spirits, ancestors and gods, for messages to go with sacrifices to ancestors and for lists of presents on tombs. In China, from the beginning human beings have been regarded as spirit beings or beings filled with spirits.

How was soothsaying done in ancient China? Less with astrology than with the help of oracular bones made of tortoise shells and the shoulder blades of oxen. We have evidence of this above all from the early Shang dynasty (c. 1766–1045 BC) with its capital Anyang; no temples and palaces survive, but – and here we are at the height of the Bronze Age – cultic utensils, weapons and musical instruments, especially glockenspiels. Above all, however, around 200,000 fragments of inscribed bone have been found. From the Stone Age on, in north China such bones were exposed to the fire and heated until cracks and fractures appeared; these were then interpreted. How are we to understand this?

The animal bones were skilfully prepared: it was assumed that the dead animals had special powers which could lead to contact with ancestors, spirits and gods in the other world. The question addressed to ancestor spirits or gods – about war, hunting, the weather, the harvest, a journey or the family – was inscribed on the front side. Holes were bored in the other side and then glowing points of wood, horn or metal were pressed in, to produce the cracks and breaks. Now the king or the interpreter of the oracle could read the answer on the front. These were often scratched into the bones. Between 2000 and 3000 different written signs have been found.

## NO SEPARATION BETWEEN MONARCHY
## AND PRIESTHOOD

The study of oracles, like astrology, was not a private matter but the concern of the ruler. The ritual normally took place at court, often in

connection with animal sacrifices. It evidently also involved music, dancing, trances and a great deal of wine: there are numerous artistic bronze
ritual vessels. The king (*wang*), the political ruler and military leader, often
functioned as the supreme shaman (*wu*) and priest (*zhou*), the highest
mediator between the divine and the human.

The early kings were already called 'sons of Heaven'. But unlike the
rulers of Egypt or Japan they never claimed to have a divine nature, to be
gods themselves. However, they too possessed unlimited power. At any
rate, already in ancient China there was no separation of kingship from the
priesthood, no dualism of politics and religion, no 'church' over against
the state. This heralded the absolutizing of imperial power. There was *a
priori* little need here of a developed theory of the state, of a senate to share
in government, or of an independent judiciary.

Sacrificial rituals and soothsaying dominated life: kings and the nobility
did not want to make important decisions on state matters or in their
personal lives until they had enquired of the soothsayers, the ancestor
spirits or the gods. They expected protection and blessing from Heaven.
Presumably soothsaying books were used at a very early stage; some of
them have come down to us, like the *Book of Changes* (*Yijing*), which was
already interpreted philosophically at an early stage; present-day soothsayers and geomantics still consult its 64 oracular signs.

The discovery which dates from the Shang dynasty is confirmed by rather
later ritual bronze inscriptions from the beginning of the Zhou dynasty,
which followed (1045–249 BC). Chinese historians regard the Zhou as
having been more humane than the Shang: under them prophecy with the
aid of yarrrow stems became popular. The Xia dynasty, the first dynasty of
all (between around the twenty-first and the eighteenth centuries BC), may
also have had the same religious background; in contrast to the five mythical
primal emperors this dynasty is now thought likewise to have been historical
(on the basis of discoveries made at Erlitou). But in fact at any rate in the
early period we must reckon with a number of cultures with a regional stamp.

## THE ANCIENT CHINESE WORLD-VIEW

For the Chinese, human beings and the cosmos belong together. Their
picture of the world has always comprised three levels: the kingdom of the
dead below, the earth as the abode of the living, and finally the heaven
above, the place of the ancestors and God. It is assumed that at death the
three higher souls (*hun*) rise to heaven. The seven lower souls (*po*) sink
down into the earthly kingdom. The ancestors, especially the royal ancestors, are imagined as being somewhere above – as demigods in proximity
to the countless nature gods.

However, these nature gods are subject to a supreme deity called 'Lord' (*di*) or 'Lord in the Heights' (*shangdi*). He is understood anthropomorphically (i.e. in human form) as a remote transcendent being (perhaps the creator God) and receives no sacrifices. However, it has to be pointed out that in addition to the usual animal sacrifices there were also a large number of human sacrifices; beheaded skeletons above all of prisoners of war attest this. These were destined above all for the ancestor spirits, who were to be propitiated by a readiness to sacrifice the living.

After the conquest of the Shang by the Zhou the name 'Heaven' (*tian*) comes into the foreground. 'Heaven' is now understood less and less anthropomorphically, but rather as an invisible cosmic and moral power and order which has intelligence and will and impartially guides the fates of all human beings; the physical blue heaven above us is only a symbol of this. From heaven, gods and ancestors can protect and bless or punish and curse. From heaven, the rulers were entrusted with their office and could only exercise this 'heavenly mandate' as long as they remained virtuous.

## ARCHAIC ELEMENTS LIVE ON IN PRESENT-DAY POPULAR RELIGION

Nowhere is one closer to heaven than on a holy mountain (*shan*). And no mountain is more holy to the Chinese than the mythical Taishan, which is connected with the creation of the world. Most emperors climbed this holy mountain at least once in their lives, there to sacrifice to Heaven and thus to do justice to their name as 'son of Heaven'. With the imperial palace in Beijing, the mighty temple precinct – which in the course of time came to contain more than 800 sacral buildings – counts as one of the most important building complexes of classical architecture. Today it is easy to climb Taishan, and thousands do it every day.

Little red bands tied to bushes are petitions for happiness. Stones put on branches are meant to bring freedom from worry. Such customs can be found in all cultures on earth and should not be over-hastily dismissed as the obsolete practices of an outdated civilization.

The urge of people to know what fate has in store for them has not died down even today; they want to know about the future, about the meaning of their own life, about some hidden circumstances, for example the unknown causes of a sickness or culprits who cannot be discovered. There have been a great many ways of so to speak sharing in the knowledge of the gods: whether in ancient China from shoulder blades, tortoise shells or yarrow stems and coins; in ancient Rome from the flight of birds and the entrails of sacrificial animals; or as everywhere today simply from the palm of the hand or from the constellations of stars or cards. All this has little to do with the rational and logical laws of science, and much to do with the pre-scientific 'logic' in the heart of the 'believers'. Believers readily and willingly accept the possibility of extra-sensory knowledge about the future and hidden connections and are ready to accept certain rules of the game.

There are also sacrificial offerings and miraculous healings in Christianity, particularly in that form of it which is called popular religion, a form which has grown up more or less organically. However, that does not mean that as enlightened men and women we have to accept everything in this bizarre world of popular belief.

Rather, for the sake of the credibility of the religion itself a rational discerning of the 'spirits' (not a rationalistic scepticism) is called for. It is important to make a distinction between the veneration of ancestors and the ancestor cult (manism), or between material and spiritual sacrifices, and even in principle between religion and superstition.

### THE DISTINCTION BETWEEN RELIGION AND SUPERSTITION

The Chinese used to think that all religions were good for people because they taught them to do good. Of course, that was not always the case. The Marxist critique of religion was not completely wrong in claiming that religion was a pernicious superstition.

In 1979, when I was the first Western theologian to have the opportunity to speak in the Chinese Academy of Social Sciences in Beijing, on 'Science and Belief in God', the first statement that I made was: 'We have to distinguish between religion and superstition.'

It is superstition if I attribute absolute divine force or power to something that is earthly and relative, in other words if I divinize a human person (as also happens in modern personality cults), or make salvation or doom dependent on an object, an amulet or a picture. It is superstition if I attribute magical power to a particular number (in China three, five, eight or nine), or if I want to indicate the only favourable place for a piece of furniture, a house or even a bank according to the complicated rules of the so-called 'science of wind and water' (feng shui, geomantics and astrology), as being the place on which good fortune or misfortune, profit or bankruptcy, absolutely depends.

All that is superstition. But it is not superstition for me to feel indebted for my life to a divine, absolute power, authority, order. And it is not superstition if a Chinese like Confucius feels reverence for Heaven as the symbol of the clear, the bright, the incomprehensible and the powerful, and because of this reverence wants to follow the 'will of Heaven' or the great order of the 'Dao'.

## CONFLICT INSTEAD OF HARMONY

According to tradition, the early Zhou kings were humane leaders. They seem conscientiously to have done their duty to Heaven, the ancestors and the people. That cannot be claimed for their successors. They lacked the political wisdom of their ancestors. The result was a period of political instability: barbarian invasions shook the kingdom. The capital was therefore moved eastwards, to Luoyang. But these 'Eastern Zhou' had only a nominal imperial supremacy. Feudal leaders began to fight for supremacy and to destroy the unity of China. What cannot be directly documented is vividly depicted in scenes from Chinese shadow theatre and the Beijing Opera (the best known of more than 300 forms of Chinese theatre).

People had reason to complain. And we can hear their complaints in the eighth-century BC *Book of Songs*:

> Parents, have you borne me
> to suffer this pain?
>
> The innocent among the people are
> condemned with me to slavery.
> Woe on us!
> Where will help come from?
>
> There is the great God:
> Does he hate everyone?

Here we can hear complaints similar to those of Job in the Old Testament: God is silent about human suffering; he seems to be an enemy to human beings. In China, too, religious doubts spread among the thinkers of the time. In the sixth century BC these contributed to a kind of enlightenment. Two questions were particularly urgent. What is the status of human beings in the universe? And, how do human beings find a social order and harmony?

Human destiny was now connected more with human action than with the authority of spirits and demons. Granted, the worship of the gods was not abandoned, and soothsaying, sacrifices and shamanistic seances continued. But for many people they became incidental. Their significance seemed to have been relativized. There was criticism of the magical priests (*wu*) and their magical practices, and of magic. A new time dawned, with social transformations and a spiritual reorientation. It is associated with the name of Confucius, who as a Chinese wise man is so different from any Indian guru that we should already be warned against simply contrasting 'East' and 'West'.

## A THIRD RELIGIOUS RIVER SYSTEM

Only in China could there be a father and a son, the seventy-sixth and seventy-seventh generation of the same family, the most famous in the land, 2500 years old. Such was the family of Confucius, the Chinese sage; his simple tomb in Qufu, 60 miles south of Jinan (Shantung), the place where he was born and died, is now again being visited by countless people.

The wise man is the basic type of the Far Eastern wisdom religions. In a quite different way the mystic is the basic type of the Indian religions, Hinduism and Buddhism. And the prophet is yet another quite different basic type of the three prophetic religions from the Near East, Judaism, Christianity and Islam.

With its around 5000 years of ascertainable history, China has by far the longest surviving high culture on our planet. What remains of the cultures and religions of Mesopotamia, of the Sumerians, the Babylonians and the Assyrians? They have disappeared, as have those of the Egyptians, Greeks and Romans. But despite all the upheavals, Chinese culture has endured. Indeed, the Chinese religions form a third independent religious river system, of the same value in cultural history as the religions of Near Eastern and Indian origin. This system finally extended to Korea and Japan, to Vietnam and Taiwan. So talk of 'East and West' is as superficial and sweeping as talk of 'Western and Asian values'. Any traveller can quickly establish that India and China, South Asia and East Asia, are two different worlds – beginning with script and literature, and extending through art, dance and dress to people's mentalities. By comparison with widespread Indian mysticism and mythologies, Chinese culture is far more stamped by sober rationality and historical thought.

That must not be confused with rationalism and historicism. Rather, we do better to say that the Chinese religions have a wisdom ('sapiental') character. And though ethnologists and those who study religions have always had difficulties in defining what is 'typically Chinese', there is no mistaking the fact that a high esteem for age and its wisdom is a constant of Chinese culture.

In the classical texts, the word 'Sheng' denotes a wise and virtuous person, usually a ruler in the mists of time. The character written on the oracle bones consists of a large ear and a small mouth and indicates an acute sense of hearing, possibly also for the voices of spirits, and the transmission of what has been heard. The heroes in China's mythical era were regarded as wise men: the 'Three Exalted Ones' and the 'Five Divine Emperors', the cultural heroes or primal inventors like the Great Yu, the Yellow Emperor, Yao or Shun. The old kings of the Shang and early Zhou dynasties along with their ministers were also regarded as wise men. And now the wisdom teacher in the strict sense came to stand out as a wise man.

## ETHICAL HUMANISM

These wisdom teachers appear as early as the middle of the turbulent time of the 'spring and autumn period' after the sixth century BC; they usher in a first epoch-making paradigm shift in Chinese culture and religion. It is amazing that almost at the same time as the Greek Pre-Socratics, a shift also took place in China from mythology to philosophy, to a new human self-awareness. However, in view of the difference and chronological distinctions in the religious and spiritual river systems I would prefer not to follow Karl Jaspers in speaking of an 'axial period'.

The era of Chinese humanism began, the mature stage of ancient Chinese culture, in which a transition took place from magical religion to rationality; in which human beings and their reason were accorded priority over the spirits and gods, and finally a great interest developed in history, art and literature.

Now the scholars, men of letters and intellectuals (*shi*) became numerous and formed the top level of society. After them came the peasants, then the craftsmen, and lastly the merchants. Education and learning brought more respect than did wealth. A delight in learning entered Chinese society. The time of political conflicts was also a time of spiritual new beginnings.

## CONFUCIUS: ONE WISE MAN AMONG MANY

The most successful among the 'hundred schools of thinkers' in the new educated class was someone who was later to advance to become *the* Chinese wise man. He is buried in Qufu, in the quiet family forest cemetery, enclosed by a wall six miles long: his name is Kong Fuzi (c. 551–479 BC), Master Kong, known in the West in a Latinized form as Confucius.

The contours of his appearance as handed down in statues and monuments may not be historical. But the characteristic basic features and outlines of his life and teaching are: coming from poor circumstances and an impoverished noble family, this man travelled a great deal through the then feudal states. However, he looked in vain for a ruler who could make use of his counsel. By the age of 40 he had held an official position only for a year, as something like a 'minister', probably a supervisor. But from

then on he devoted himself completely to teaching his pupils and occasionally had conversations with rulers or ministers. He did not concern himself
with soothsaying and magic, but with music, poetry and the study of
venerable writings.

His teaching remained alive. For him, oracular decisions were less
important than the ethical decisions made by human beings themselves.
He did not want to arouse the magical forces of nature but the moral
forces in human beings.

The spiritual profile of Confucius is unmistakable, and we can recognize
it from the *Analects* (*lun yu*: 'collected sayings'), which were written down
by his disciples. This is a relatively small collection of aphorisms, anecdotes
and conversations which (unlike the Pre-Socratics) are not a speculative
explanation of the world, but give quite practical wisdom related to
experience. A very realistic, vivid method of argument and an antipathy to
abstract deductions characterize Chinese philosophizing from the beginning. All this also recalls another 'master'.


## COMPARISON WITH ANOTHER 'MASTER'

Like Jesus of Nazareth 500 years later, Confucius lived in a time of social
crisis for his people. As an itinerant teacher and 'master', he too attempted
to respond to this crisis through his message. He too collected disciples
and pupils around him, and his family did not become involved. The social
origin of his followers did not matter. They were to contribute to his
insights.

There are many further parallels to Jesus. Confucius, too, is neither an
ascetic not a monk who withdraws from the world; rather, he works in the
midst of this life. He too is no mystic, practising psychological self-analysis
and teaching stages of meditation: he does not strive for ecstasy or Nirvana.
No more is he a metaphysician who speculates about God, the ground of
being and last question. Nor did he ever call himself 'God' or 'son of
God'. From his disciples he called for practical discipleship rather than
veneration. On the other hand, he was not a sceptic or a rationalist, who
reduces all thought to rationality. He shared in the traditional religious
ideas, some of which are strange to us today: belief in spirits, signs and
sacrifices. More importantly, though, he too lived what he taught.

Confucius was confronted with the traditional order in a quite practical
way. And contrary to external conformism and hypocrisy, he interpreted it
critically in terms of an inner attitude and personal responsibility. Confucius, too, is by no means a naïve teacher of virtue, whose piety revolves
around order, as is often claimed, someone who simply preaches harmony
and a readiness to classify, and is thus a systematician. Rather, he advocates

a very individual, personal ethic, expressed in clear moral demands. 'Where everyone finds fault one must examine; where everyone praises one must also examine' (*Analects* 15.27). It is necessary to oppose even those in power, and in some circumstances even to renounce office where the authorities diverge from the right way (*dao*).

## CONFUCIUS HIMSELF

Despite all the parallels, Confucius' own profile is unmistakable. Confucius is not a prophetic figure like Jesus. He does not proclaim passionately the dawn of a future kingdom of Heaven or kingdom of God which already has consequences in the present. Confucius is and remains an enlightened teacher of wisdom, and despite his gaze forwards towards a better future, his orientation is backwards, towards a better past, towards the humane rule of the early Zhou rulers. His model for the future is thus that of an idealized golden age. Hence he argues for a moral and political ethic based on the family, an ethic which sees a connection between personal virtue and the good of the state. Faced with the new kingdoms that had come into being, all the wars and rebellions, the revenge and murder, the harshness and heedlessness of the civil war, Confucius is thus concerned to restore the original social order, based on moral principles.

For Confucius, the questions of external form are extremely important for a more peaceful, more just, more stable, more effective society. It is important to observe the old 'rites', customs and moral norms (*li*), which come from within, the original religious and civil rules of behaviour: 'I transmit and do not create. I believe in and love antiquity,' he also remarks in the *Analects* (7.1). Men and women should not be anxious about gods and spirits but bow to the great old tradition. In this way he finds harmony with himself and the world. This is an ethic which tries to reconcile a universal moral claim with the traditions of Chinese culture.

Wandering through the residence of the Kong family in Qufu, which has been rebuilt and extended time and again, one asks oneself: Did Confucius want to replace religion with morality? Did he have a religious horizon? Certainly, but it is extremely different from that of the Jew Jesus of Nazareth. Confucius displaced the original divine figures of ancient China, which were full of life; the 'Lord in the Heights' (*shangdi*) is mentioned only once in the *Analects*. Rather, what is present for him is 'Heaven' (*tian*), and he understands that as an effective power, as order, law and being. It is this Heaven, set over all, that human beings, and especially the ruler, have to understand and fulfil: 'If one has sinned against Heaven there is no one to pray to' (*Analects* 3.13).

'Tian' occurs eighteen times in the *Analects*, always in connection with will, action and emotion. A quite personal remark by the wise man, who at that time was still unknown, has come down to us: 'Nobody will ever understand me. I neither resent Heaven nor blame men. I learnt lower things and perceive higher things. The only one who understands me is perhaps Heaven' (14.37).

## THE CENTRAL TEACHING: HUMANITY

Otherwise, all Confucius' reflection is on human behaviour with all its natural basic family and social relationships. Human beings are not to be saints, but they are to become 'honourable'. This is not a reference to the nobility, but to 'moral nobility'. A man is to be open to all that is good and true and beautiful; music, in which reason and feeling fuse, is particularly important for Confucius. But at the same time such a 'wise man' should also be engaged in politics.

Human beings should strive for a harmonious relationship with one another and with nature and show all men and women inner humanity (*ren*) in the framework of outward forms of behaviour (*li*): human goodness, concern, benevolence (but justice instead of love for the wicked). 'If a man is not humane, what can he do with the rituals? If a man is not humane, what can he do with music?' (3.3). *Ren* is used more frequently in the *Analects* than *li*, external norms, which was previously dominant.

Thus for the Chinese, Confucius has become the comprehensively educated teacher and guide who reflects practically on ethics and politics in the spirit of humanistic wisdom, though his teaching became established only long after his death. His is a rational world-view which is concentrated on this world. When asked what wisdom was, Master Kong replied: 'To apply oneself to the duties of man and, while revering the spirits and gods, to keep away from them – this may be called wisdom' (6.22). So the fabulous beings on the roof may remain. But interpersonal relations are more important. Classical Chinese architecture also expresses harmonious moderation in human beings: nothing presses upwards; no building stands in the centre; the whole layout should strive for harmony.

So with reverence for Heaven, but with distance and restraint towards gods and spirits, Confucius calls both for a renewal of the inner constitution of the individual and as a consequence of this for a renewal of the outward constitution of the state. In practice this renewal focuses on the re-establishment and consolidation of a benevolent government and a true social order and harmony in the family and in the state: 'If you govern them by decrees and regulate them with punishments, the people will evade them but have no sense of shame. If you govern them with virtue and regulate them with the rituals, they will have a sense of shame and flock to you' (2.3).

## EXPLICATION OF HUMANITY: THE GOLDEN RULE

Confucius was asked: 'Is there one single word that one can practise throughout one's life?' His answer was: 'It is perhaps "reciprocal care of others" (*shu*).' 'Reciprocal care of others' means taking heed of one another in practice and being tolerant: for Confucius, *shu* is shorthand for that Golden Rule which he adds immediately afterwards: 'What you do not wish for yourself, do not impose on others' (15.24). So 500 years before Jesus' Sermon on the Mount Confucius preached that universal norm of behaviour which in the Sermon on the Mount is formulated in a positive way: 'Whatever you want people to do, do also to them' (Matt. 7.12).

It is amazing that in Confucianism, as in Christianity, the humanitarian ethic culminates in love of one's fellow human beings. For Confucius, 'humanity' (*ren*) means 'loving people' (12.22). Granted, for him love of others remains a quite natural feeling and is orientated on ties of family and nation, ordered by social proximity (the scholar Mo Di differs; he all too tactically calls for a 'universal love' on grounds of expediency – it pays).

For Confucius, the neighbour is first of all the member of the family. And Confucius also has no inhibitions about claiming domination of the Chinese (= the Zhou) over the 'barbarians' and allowing these only the Chinese way of life. But even for Confucius, love of neighbour extends beyond the family in the narrower sense, from one's own children to those of others, to parents and the old: 'All men within the four seas are brothers' (12.5). In former times the earth was thought of as being rectangular and bordered by seas, with a round, nine-storey heaven above it.

## BASIC HUMAN RELATIONSHIPS

Confucianism is primarily concerned with the outside of Chinese life: shaping family life and politics. It regards the whole of human society as a system of personal relationships which are to be ordered in a harmonious way, starting with the family.

If we look at an average Chinese family, we find that in China respect for age is taken for granted: the grandmother has no need to fear for her status in the family. Typical Chinese cooking has found its way into many European families. But there has been less discussion about the way in which family relationships are ordered in China. The strong cohesion of the family, even the wider family, is fundamental for the Chinese and binds closely together even members of the family who live on different continents. People support and help one another, both in private and in business.

To the present day, five basic relationships are important in the Chinese family: those between the superior and the inferior, between father and son, between husband and wife, between older and younger brother, and between friends. The strong cohesion between the members of the family is meant to be the basis of social stability and to encourage it. These five relationships are all orientated on reciprocity, but of course they can easily be exploited hierarchically.

At the beginning of the fifth century Confucius with his wisdom school – which called itself 'the School of the Meek' (*rujia*) – laid the foundation for Chinese ethics and politics for more than 2000 years. As well as the *Analects*, five other classics, formerly also attributed to Confucius, are of fundamental importance for Confucianism (which is a Western term):

- *The Book of Changes* (*yi jing*);
- *The Book of Documents* (*shu jing*);
- *The Book of Songs* (*shi jing*);
- *The Book of Rites* (*li jing*);
- *The Annals of Spring and Autumn* (*chung qiu*);

A sixth classic, *The Book of Music*, has not survived.

Numerous thinkers developed the teachings of Confucius. Foremost among them comes Mencius (Mengzi), who was born in Zuxian, not far from Qufu (332–289 BC). He was a contemporary of the Greek Aristotle, and like him spoke positively about private property but wanted to see business carried on and supplemented with ethical rules. First of all the human being is to be a *homo ethicus* and only secondarily a *homo oeconomicus*, concerned for his own advantage.

### HUMANITY: THE BASIS FOR A SHARED FUNDAMENTAL ETHIC

In former days hardly anyone went to the tomb of this great Chinese sage. Now, though, thousands come. We must remember that the core of his teaching is not authoritarian and patriarchal but is truly humane. In the *Analects* of Confucius, humanity, *ren*, in the sense of concern, goodness, benevolence, is the ethical term most frequently used.

Humanity could very well also be the basis for a fundamental ethic today – not only in China but for humankind as a whole. Humanity, according to Confucius, is to be understood as 'reciprocal care of others' (*shu*), mutual respect. As he explains in the Golden Rule, 'What you do not wish for yourself, do not impose on others.'

According to the basic norm of true humanity, good and evil can be distinguished in a quite elementary way, which is valid for all. For the Chinese there is nothing 'beyond good and evil'. Confucius is said to have stated that there are only two ways: humanity and inhumanity.

So one finds much assent among Chinese if one formulates as a universal basic criterion for a global ethic that whatever helps a person to be truly human is fundamentally good. That means that:

- Human beings, both as individuals and as a society, should not behave in an inhuman, anti-human or bestial way, as happens time and again.
- Rather, as individuals and communities, human beings should behave in a truly human, humane way: towards themselves, towards society and also towards nature.

## A SINGLE CHINESE STATE: THE FIRST EMPEROR

A small memorial to Confucius was erected in Beijing in 478 BC, in the second year after his death. However, a temple to Confucius (*kongmiao*) was built only under the Han dynasty in 195 BC. This development is to be seen in the context of an epoch-making paradigm shift after the period of the 'Warring States' – to the single Chinese state with Confucianism as the state religion. Statehood in China had always been bound up with one person, the ruler. But now the foundations were laid for what amounted to 'bureaucratic' state centralism.

Paradoxically this unified state was founded by a king who was not at all Confucian. This was Yongzheng, king of the state of Qin, which for a long time had been well organized and which was expanding. He was a highly purposeful despot who conquered the other seven great kingdoms and achieved the first unification of China. At the same time he carried through important reforms: he abolished the feudal system and replaced the nobility with imperial officials and kinsmen. He introduced a system of prefectures and provinces. He unified the laws and the script (which was essential for the functioning of the bureaucracy and the state), and then went on to unify weights, measures and currency. He also regulated the breadth of wagons, developed roads, and linked the frontier fortifications (initially clay walls) with a great wall almost 1500 miles in length. Of course, all this had to be done with hordes of forced labour: prisoners of war, criminals, peasants in debt . . . A million people are said to have perished in this period, building the wall.

Zheng gave himself the title of First (*shi*) Emperor (*huang di* = 'divine ruler', the title of the highly revered Yellow Emperor) in order to announce an unending chain of imperial successors. His family name Qin (formerly Ch'in) gives the whole of China its name. This Qin Shi Huangdi (259–210 BC) felt that he was more god than man. In the West he has become known through the recently excavated giant tomb site with its army of terracotta figures, numbering many thousands. In his reign this first emperor suppressed all free thought. In 213 BC he had all books which did not correspond with his political line burned (except those on medicine, agriculture and soothsaying). He is alleged to have had 460 scholars opposed to his regime (probably Confucians) buried alive.

The emperor was supported by the anti-Confucian, 'realistic' legalists who had become influential in Qin at an early stage; their theorist was Han Fei. They did not want to shape the people 'idealistically', through education and morality, but through techniques of domination and penal law. There was a strict system of rewards and punishments without regard for person. The laws, not ethics, were to bring about order. This legalism made it possible to pursue self-interest and gave full scope to the *homo oeconomicus* with no responsibility, intent on his own advantage. Whatever served the power and order of the state was good, and military strength was the most important goal of the state. Unconditional obedience to the government apparatus was the necessary precondition.

## CHINA'S CLASSICAL PERIOD: THE HAN DYNASTY

Qin's son survived his brilliant and violent father – who for Confucian historians is the embodiment of the tyrant – by only four years. Then the storm burst everywhere against this legalistic rule of force which 'rationally' despised all traditions. Finally the rural war-lord Liu Bang came out on top in the civil war. This peasant's son took the title emperor, but personally remained modest. With good advisers he founded the famed Han dynasty, which now ruled for 400 years (206 BC–AD 220). He wanted to maintain the single state, but without the totalitarianism of the first emperor. Now the people could breathe again. Salt and iron industries were developed. And the Confucian ethical framework was in fact to guarantee a stable state structure internally for centuries.

The ban on books was lifted and the writings which had survived in hiding began to be collected and checked carefully. Copying was regarded as a meritorious work. China's classical period now began. This was the conclusion and at the same time the consummation of Chinese antiquity.

Contemporaneously with the Roman empire in the West, the Han organized and led an empire which was by no means inferior in extent and population and was commercially linked with it by the 'Silk Road', the trade route over the Taklamakan desert. The ethnic Chinese still call themselves 'Han Chinese'.

It was above all Emperor Wu, the most important Han ruler, who created the new frontiers and the new structures of the kingdom within them. An important feature was that the state cult was not performed by a special priestly class but by the emperor in person – as 'son of Heaven' he was endowed with secular and sacral power. The state cult was later wholly concentrated on the grandiose capital Chang'an (present-day Xi'an). At a local level the emperor was represented by his officials. The real political power of the emperor was in fact controlled by the civil service, which grew increasingly powerful; often the emperor's political power seemed secondary to his symbolic and ritual function. The heavenly mandate did not make the emperor God.

## CONFUCIAN STATE RELIGION: CONFUCIUS – *THE* MASTER

The Chinese lifestyle, which was to last for 2000 years, was decisively shaped in the Han period. And in the course of this paradigm shift Confucius, who in feudal China at the end of the Zhou era was regarded as just one teacher among others, now became *the* master. The Confucian classics became the official philosophy and Confucianism the state doctrine. More and more temples to Confucius were built. Confucius may not have been deified, but he was celebrated as the symbol of Chinese culture and the figure with which it identified.

The five classics mentioned earlier became the basis of examinations for officials in 125 BC. Centuries later the classics, comprising more than 600,000 characters, were engraved on 190 stone tablets and erected in the temple of Confucius in Beijing. In the forecourt there are also 198 stone pillars with the name of 51,624 officials from the various dynasties who passed their examinations.

Human beings remained central: the educational ideal of the officialdom trained in Confucian schools, carefully examined, given an adequate salary and thus independent – in the Han period there was a minimum of officials and laws – was humanity, piety and integrity. They aimed to maintain a firm moral attitude which also made independent decisions possible: an ethic of shrewdness (*zhi*) replaced many laws. The élite of these educated officials thus formed a select aristocracy which was supplemented and renewed time and again by selection from below. Its sole credentials were knowledge and mastery of the writings of Confucius. Thus it proved itself capable of ensuring that the communities in the centralized state administered themselves, and this kept Chinese society alive even when dynasties changed.

These élites, governed by Confucian values, at the same time produced powerful philological and historical works. These include the monumental history, the *Sima Qian*, based on careful study, which gives a systematic and comprehensive account in 130 chapters of the period from the very beginnings to its own time (87 BC). What the oracle archive is for the Shang period and the bronze inscriptions are for the Zhou period, the state handbooks are for the Han period: a unique source for historians.

The Confucian officials now saw the emperor as the highest teacher in the land, who had to teach what was in the classical books, if possible uninfluenced by religious magicians (*wu*). But in a later Han era fights between cliques, the domination of eunuchs, and intrigues involving the harem and the empress were a heavy burden on the officials, and endangered the ongoing existence of the Han dynasty. And by now a countercurrent to Confucianism had become increasingly strong, Daoism.


## ACUPUNCTURE: PARADIGM SHIFT IN MEDICINE

What one cannot see on an X-ray one can often feel. Most of us know the word 'acupuncture', the method used in China for about 4000 years to fight pain, above all in rheumatism, neuralgia and migraine. But very few people know that this word comes from the Beijing Jesuits of the seventeenth century, who formed it from *acus*, needle (originally gold and silver needles) and *punctura*, 'point'. In fact it denotes a means of healing by putting needles in particular parts of the skin, which in turn are connected with particular internal organs, in order to diagnose and to heal diseases of breathing, circulation and digestion, the nervous system and the blood. And fewest of all know that this Chinese science and art of healing is a by-product of Daoism.

In contrast to Confucianism, which is primarily concerned with the external harmony of Chinese social life – the formation of the family system and politics – Daoism concentrates on inner harmony, on the health and healing of the individual. It promises not only redemption from guilt and sin but also a long life and immortality. In particular in the great classical era of China under the Han (from the third century BC to the third century AD), Chinese medicine moved away from the medicine of oracles and demons and turned towards new methods of healing, connected with a particular cosmology and anthropology. A paradigm shift also took place in medicine.

## A HOLISTIC VIEW OF HUMAN BEINGS

Medicine from the Daoist tradition attempts to see human beings holistically: the sickness is not just to be localized as the disease of an organ which needs to be repaired, but is also to be seen as a disturbance to the whole equilibrium of the forces in the human organism as a consequence of a lack of harmony. According to Daoism, human beings are embedded in a universal system of relationships, correspondences and streams of energy. It is above all important to observe the law of the correspondence between macrocosm and microcosm. Human lifestyle is to accord with the regularities in the macrocosm. At the same time it is important to observe the law of the rhythm of the two cosmic primal forces, and in the case of sickness to restore the equilibrium that has been disturbed. The passive feminine dark yin and the active male bright yang govern everything in the world and in human beings, from the rhythm of day and night to the rhythm of the heart and breathing. Life energy flows over the fourteen invisible meridians of the body. Thus the inner organs and their functions can be influenced from the around 360 acupuncture points.

Whatever one may think of these Daoistic correspondences and regularities, it is indisputable that this medicine, acupuncture, moxibustion (burning of moxa cones on the skin) and other old therapeutic methods, special breathing exercises, massages and aerobics have some success. The alternative classification of illnesses (nosology), their comprehensive diagnosis by touch and a diagnosis of the pulse, and finally the comprehensive range of medicines which can be seen in any traditional dispensary even in modern Chinese hospitals, for example in Beijing, are also illuminating. The classical work on acupuncture and moxibustion was written by Huangfu Mi (215–82).

All this beyond doubt presents a challenge to modern Western medicine to rethink the indissoluble connection between healing and wholeness in medicine. Bodily and moral hygiene are connected. The individual, nature and society, physical, spiritual and social well-being, cannot be separated. It is noteworthy that the earliest Chinese textbook of medicine and acupuncture, *Nei Jing* ('The Inner Teaching'), the first compilers of which lived 500 years before Christ, and which is inspired by Dao, prescribes a clear order of priorities for therapeutic interventions: before acupuncture come medicines, before medicines comes a correct diet, but before a correct diet comes treatment of the spirit. So it is the Daoist religion of healing and wholeness that takes us into the middle of that 'Chinese wisdom' which has to do with the Dao, that primal law of all events in humankind and in the cosmos to which human beings are to adapt their way of life.

## WHAT DOES 'DAO' MEAN?

In Chinese there is a dao, literally a way ('law', 'teaching', 'principle of order') for everything: a dao of nature, of culture, of the spirit, a dao of the beginning, the middle and the end . . . This already shows that dao is understood to be incomprehensible yet at the same time all-pervasive. Before Confucius dao was still a symbol for human ideas, and even Confucius himself never used it in a comprehensive sense. It was always concretely the dao of something, the way of something.

But later dao was universalized to become the way that includes everything. That, at any rate, is how dao is already understood in the most famous Chinese wisdom writing, *Daodejing*, which has been translated more frequently than any other wisdom book. A fragment of it was found in 1997 in Guodian (in Hubei province) which presumably comes from the fourth century BC. This work is attributed to the legendary sage Laozi (= 'old master'), though it is not known whether he ever lived. According to legend he was born white-haired, after 81 (9 × 9) years in his mother's womb. He became an archivist, but it is said that he forsook civilized China and went westwards to convert the barbarians. His parting from Confucius as portrayed in pictures is certainly not historical but symbolic.

Laozi left only the slim book *Daodejing*, the 'Way and Power Classic'. What does it teach?

– Dao – 'way' – is here understood comprehensively as the first and last principle, which cannot be defined, named or described. It is not a personal deity but the primal ground of the whole world, existing before heaven and earth. It is the mother of all things, and makes all things originate in rest, without acting. Therefore this dao is at the same time

– De – 'power' (also 'virtue'). De is at work as the power of the dao in all the bringing forth, unfolding and preservation of the world and is in all phenomena, making them what they are. Yet the dao and its power cannot be grasped directly or controlled anywhere. The dao is 'empty', without properties that can be grasped by the senses. And only if human beings are freed in 'emptiness' (*wu*) from passion and desires, only if they make the cosmic order, the dao, their own as the law of their lives and allow themselves to be filled by the dao; only in this way, in action which has no purpose or in non-action (*wu-wei*), do they sense the silent working of nature. Then they live in harmony with nature, indeed they can attain unity with the dao.

Tai-ji (t'ai chi) meditation is meant to help here: the gentle, flowing, slow exercises are meant to co-ordinate consciousness, breath and movement and relieve the tensions in the body and the blockages in the energy meridians. But these exercises can also be performed with sword, spear or knife, which reminds us that tai-ji was originally a technique of self-defence. How are the two connected?


## DAOISM: THE ANTI-CONFUCIAN
## OPPOSITION MOVEMENT

'Non-action' entails as few laws and regulations as possible. Thus the wisdom teaching of Daoism – along with Laozi, mention should be made of Zhuangzi, allegedly the author of the classic *From the Southern Land of the Blossoms* – became an anti-legalistic and anti-Confucian opposition movement. Already in the Han period it developed; it was taken up by hermits and recluses, but later often also by political protesters, indeed rebels and revolutionaries.

The Daoists rejected political involvement as being typically 'masculine'. They thought that legalists and Confucians attempted to guide and direct human beings all too harshly. That would only make the state of the world even more chaotic. And indeed in the Han empire, as in the Roman empire, class conflicts and impoverishment exacerbated by large-scale capitalism and great estates had consequences which finally made a decisive contribution to the collapse of both empires.

The Daoists bluntly declared that the Confucian ideals of wisdom, ritual and government were often ridiculous. Above all they criticized the Confucian scholars or officials, who adapted their private and social life to conform to the political system. Instead of the existing ordinances, rituals and conventions and the levelling down brought about by public institutions, the Daoist way recommended leaving people as they were and nature as it was. Then and only then would harmony prevail. Why? Because the detachment of human beings from nature is the root of evil.

So in the face of legalistic social organization and the Confucian activism and moralism, the Daoists propagated a return to nature in which human beings were harmoniously bound up with prehistory. In the face of the traditional opposition between human beings and nature, Daoism sought the unity of human beings and nature. However, this could only be realized by individuals in their solitude or by mystical immersion: by a persistent passive, 'non-action' or non-intervention (*wu-wei*) which strives for harmony with the great nature, the dao, that is perfect harmony.

A longing for simplicity and originality (*retour à la nature*) which was not unknown later in Europe was expressed in Daoism at a very early stage. Intuition, inspiration, the unfathomable nature of artistic creativity, can doubtless be grasped more in images and words against a Daoist background. But already at that time such an attitude on the part of the individual could easily either be commandeered by those in power or be transformed into a barbarian cultural revolution.

## DAOISM: A RELIGION

Daoism was very much more than a philosophy. It became a truly religious movement. This movement adopted many of the elements of the old Chinese religion of the shamans and soothsayers. But on the other hand it created a tremendous corpus of writings: allegedly these were all divine experiences transmitted to the Daoists in a state of trance, but without the name of the author or the time of the composition. Finally they were collected in a Daoist canon (*daozang*). The philosophical treatises of Laozi and zhuangzi are only two of the 1120 volumes. Alongside cults of purity (yoga exercises, dietetics, gymnastics, the quest for elixirs), above all cults for lengthening life were integrated into Daoism. So the Daoist religion became popular among both ordinary people and the aristocracy, above all as a religion of immortality. Its great promise was that when Daoists died they would enter one of the paradises or go to the islands of bliss outside China.

The beginning of the Daoist religion is usually put in Sichuan, where in the late Han period the hermit Zhang Daoling received a revelation of the 'Most High Lord Lao' in AD 142. It accused the people of a lack of respect for the true and the good; they were said to offer more veneration to the demons who brought corruption. In this revelation Zhang is named by the god Lao as the 'Heavenly Master' (*tianshi*) who has the task of abolishing demonic practices and introducing the true faith.

By what means is this to be done? The new Sect of the Heavenly Master rejected the bloody sacrifices at that time offered to the spirits of the dead and replaced them with joss sticks, incense and boiled vegetables. It introduced the confession of sins into the healing of sicknesses: the sick persons wrote down their sins in locked rooms at certain times of the year and priests prayed for them. To attain forgiveness and salvation these lists of sins were then offered to Heaven on the tops of mountains or in the depths of the earth by being buried or cast on the rivers to sink.

## THE DAOIST 'CHURCH'

Zhang gathered together his followers in communities made up of men and women; these had priests and priestesses which represented dao on earth. This in fact gave rise to a kind of Daoist 'church' with married priests (exorcists, magicians, geomantics, soothsayers) and unmarried monks and nuns who strove for perfection as hermits or together in monasteries – only the actual living quarters were separated. On the holy mountain of the Daoists, Qincheng Shan near Chengdu, the capital of Sichuan, one can witness a women's liturgy of the 'Three Pure Ones', the Daoist trinity, exclusively performed by women but intended for both women and men in a very collected and dignified way, with singing, music and offerings of incense.

The Daoist 'church' is the main heir of ancient Chinese popular religion, which is celebrating a resurrection today among the Chinese rural population (75 per cent of the 1.2 billion), unoppressed by 50 years of the Communist critique of religion and with hundreds of temples. For the people there are holy water and incense, feasts based on the rhythm of the year (the Chinese new year festival with lion or dragon dances to drive out the demons) and pomp in worship. For believers there are ceremonies of purification and renewal, forms of confession and penitential exercises on particular days, fasts and legends about the saints, magic and superstition.

All this is dominated by an earthly and a heavenly hierarchy. On earth there is a kind of Daoist 'pope' at the head of this church (alongside it, of course, there are many other Daoist sects), but without a supreme teaching authority: he is the 'Heavenly Master' as a representative of the supreme God.

However, in heaven there are countless divine or quasi-divine figures, indeed well up in the hierarchy of gods there is even a kind of madonna. And at the highest level there are the 'Three Pure Ones': alongside the 'Lord of the Heavenly Jewel' and the 'Lord of Dao' there is the 'Supreme Lord Lao'. Laozi, the human founder figure, here appears completely divinized as the third person in a trinitarian belief which in fact amounts to belief in three gods. So far, conjectures that Daoist belief in a trinity, which seems first to have been fully established under the Buddhist Tang dynasty (618–907), was influenced at a very early stage by Christian Nestorian (or Gnostic) thought present in the capital Chang'an have not been verified.

On the basis of internal and external practices, with mediation and elixirs, believers could hope for immortality: to belong to the 'earthly immortals' or even to the 'heavenly immortals', to those 'geniuses' (*xian*) with godlike traits (namely the capacity to fly). But through their experimentation they made some discoveries in the spheres of chemistry, medicine and pharmacology. Traditionally, Chinese science seeks less for causal connections in the sense of a rationalistic and objective contemplation of nature and more for those general connections, say between microcosm and macrocosm, into which, according to Daoist teachings, human beings are incorporated in their actions.

But alchemy is one thing, morality is another. As a precondition for immortality, in Daoism, too, a moral life is called for: not to cheat or deceive others, to do good actions and repent for one's own transgressions, to aim at progress in meditation and in daily life. So for Daoism, mystical experience and the practice of an ethic belong together.

The Sect of the Heavenly Master still exists today: the sixty-third Heavenly Master fled in 1949 to Taiwan, where the sixty-fourth at present holds office. However, the 'Way of the Highest Peace' (*taiping dao*), which arose at the same time and was then highly politicized, and which in the later Han period sparked off the first mass peasant revolt with a religious motivation, could not survive. Above all the hundreds of thousands of 'Yellow Turbans' operating in the most varied parts of the land, along with the 'Five Bushels of Rice' sect, brought about the downfall of the Han dynasty. Its empire collapsed into three kingdoms, all under soldier emperors (220–80). This resulted in around 400 years of divisions. The situation was the same as that in Europe at the same period, in the transition from antiquity to the Middle Ages, with shifts in population, migrations of peoples and threats from horse-mounted peoples from the steppes.

## YIN AND YANG: TO INTERVENE OR
## NOT TO INTERVENE?

China had always been a land of gigantic floods with thousands of victims, but at a very much earlier stage it had also been a land of canals, dams and locks. With good reason the legendary founder of the first, Xia, dynasty, the 'Great Yu', was regarded as the king who succeeded in taming the floods. So China with its Confucian stamp may by no means be dismissed as reactionary and hostile to science. In many respects China was technically far ahead of the rest of the world: some inventions like paper, porcelain, gunpowder, wheelbarrows, rudders, seismographs, magnetic needles, conveyor systems, threshing flails, armour and much else were made here, some of them a thousand years before they were introduced into Europe. It is amazing that as early as the third millennium BC, in the last years of the 'Warring States', the provincial governor Li Bing had the course of the Min Yiang divided at Chengdu to avert floods: a monumental technical achievement. The 'outer river' flowed on to Qincheng Shan. The 'inner river', however, was split and an ingenious system of canals was built. To the present day these canals distribute the masses of water over the land, which in this way has become one of the most fertile areas of Sichuan.

Two things become clear here. Human intervention (by diverting the river into canals) can have positive consequences: the Confucians attached great importance to that. But so too can non-intervention: letting things flow naturally (the 'outer river'), in a way which does not change nature unnecessarily. This is important to the Daoists. The devastating floods of 1998 in China which drove millions from their homes were caused by cutting down forests (85 per cent of the original forest in the Yangzi river basin), intensive industrialization, massive overbuilding and more recently climate warming. These have prompted new reflections in China, too, about the problems of human intervention. To intervene in nature or not to intervene? To respect the natural rhythm as far as possible, to correct and direct only where it is really necessary?

## DAOISM AND CONFUCIANISM PERMEATE EACH OTHER

Even in the Han era there was a growing interpenetration of Daoism and Confucianism. Yin and yang thought, which became influential after the first century BC, gave decisive help here. Already in the *Book of Changes* (*Yijing*) we find the idea that all things and situations arise out of a combination of cosmic primal potencies, yin and yang. The primal forces of yin and yang are the two polar powers which create and permeate the whole universe through their interplay. Like every great mountain, everything in the world has two sides (that is possibly where the idea of yin and yang comes from): a northern, shady, cold, rough, feminine side (yin) and a southern, sunny, warm, bright, male side (yang).

So the whole of reality is caught up in the tension between bright and dark, active and passive, creative and receptive, hard and soft, male and female. That explains the change in nature between warm and cold, day and night, summer and winter, and also sun and moon or sun and earth. These principles, which are not least gender-related, unmistakably indicate that here the woman, as the passive dark side, is portrayed as being undeniably worse than the man.

The harmony of yin and yang finds its most apt expression in the yin-yang symbol, that circular symbol with its complementary light and dark surfaces and the dark and light points. It shows that each element bears within itself the core of its opposite and at the climax of its development begins to turn into its polar opposite. Daoism and Confucianism can also supplement and support each other in the complementarity of yin and yang.

– Yin-yang Daoism can be cultivated above all in the private sphere, and largely remains decisive for the inner spiritual life of the individual and individual groups. It is more the religion of the people, but also offers the educated a kind of philosophical comfort in times of chaos and political division.

– Yin-yang Confucianism, however, which takes up much of the Daoist understanding of nature, dominates the ideology of the state, learned officialdom, official morality and public life. It is primarily the religion of the intellectual upper class, and is predominant in times of law and order.

Thus the two basic attitudes can be reconciled in practice: to put it simply, men and women are Confucians in action and Daoists in contemplation. And at the same time there is a new comprehensive theoretical synthesis: yin and yang are identified with heaven and earth, both of which proceed from the ultimate reality (which is largely understood in Daoist terms), the Great Ultimate (*taiji*). On both a large and a small scale, by interaction they produce all the things of this world, above all the five elements or 'phases of transformation': fire, water, earth, wood, metal. The phases alternate without interruption in an endless cycle: from rest (yin) to movement (yang) and from movement to rest. Thus the regularities of the macrocosm and the microcosm correspond in a quite natural harmony and hierarchy. For human nature is good: it needs only moral education. But precisely at this point Chinese culture was confronted with a great challenge.

## THE ADVANCE OF BUDDHISM

To Chinese thought, which whether Confucian or Daoist is complementary, on the whole extremes are unpleasant, a fascination with evil is alien and the drama of redemption is unnecessary. But the invasion of the barbarians in the fourth century already shook the Confucian state ideology of natural harmony and morality, as it did the 'romantic' escapism of individualistic Daoists.

It is no coincidence that particularly after the end of the Han era, Indian Buddhism made massive progress. It offered an acute analysis of human blindness and entanglement in the world. Thus it went into a question which was seriously neglected in both Confucianism and Daoism, that of the negative in human life, and proclaimed a way to redemption from suffering. The delegations of Chinese monks to India were followed by more and more foundations of monasteries in China itself. And here, simply because of the adoption of many Chinese terms, there was often a coalition with Daoist natural religion, especially at the imperial court. Buddhist elements found their way into the popular cult in particular.

## CHINA'S GOLDEN AGE: THE TANG DYNASTY

Something like a Chinese 'early Middle Ages' now began. After three centuries of divisions, fighting and waves of migration, in the sixth century there was a second unification: this was achieved by the Sui dynasty, which came from Inner Mongolia and had risen to power through a *coup d'état*. However, it remained in power for only three decades. Nevertheless, its reforms (which included state examinations for officials) prepared for the coming era. Nor should we forget the building of the Grand Canal, which links north and south, the Yellow River and the Yangzi, and finally was to attain a length of over 1300 miles.

With the Tang dynasty which followed (618–907), China again achieved world status: it became a powerful empire, no less important than the contemporary empire of Charlemagne in Europe and the Umayyad caliphs of Damascus. An expansionist foreign policy created security against the Turks and brought control of the Silk Road. At times China's power extended from the Korean peninsula in the east to Central Asia, to Pamir and to the Aral Sea in the west.

The state capital was again cosmopolitan Chang'an (Xi'an), with a population of more than a million and open to the world. From 635 on, not only Buddhists but also Nestorian Christians were hospitably received there (the famous stone pillars of Xi'an, dating from 781, written in Syriac and Chinese, give the most important information about the spread of Nestorian Christianity). A long period of peace and prosperity led to a heyday in Chinese culture. It is called 'China's golden age'. That applies to historiography as well as the law, administration and the army and extends to science, literature and art. These became the great models for the whole of East Asia as far as Japan. After the Tang era, despite all its own roots and characteristics, Japan became part of the 'Sinified' world of culture.

## RELIGION FROM OUTSIDE

Under the rule of the cosmopolitan Tang, which lasted for nearly three centuries, the Buddhism which had already found an entry into China in the persons of non-Chinese who came along the Silk Road of Central Asia and the southern sea route became a decisive influence. That happened not least as a result of printing, which was invented by Buddhists. With a gigantic number of translated texts and a wealth of alien forms of religion which came into being in South and Central Asia, it sparked off completely new impulses and helped to reintegrate the kingdom.

The consequence was a third paradigm shift in Chinese religion and culture, which even influenced wall painting, sculpture and court ceremonial: a specifically Chinese Buddhism produced new schools. The novel Chinese meditative Buddhism adopted from Daoism the experience of nature; faith Buddhism developed a distinctive Buddhist liturgy with the solemn invocation of Buddha.

The grandiose Buddhist art of the Tang period radiated all over East Asia: sculptures, wall paintings, stone grottoes and cave temples (in Datong, for example, there are 53 caves and around 51,000 sculptures). But of course there was also opposition. Already under the first Tang, partly through the influence of Daoist court circles, there were vigorous persecutions of Buddhists: thousands of temples and monasteries which had become rich were secularized. Tens of thousands of works of art were destroyed. Hundreds of thousands of monks who had bought credentials for monastic ordination were demoted to the status of tax-paying laity. But that by no means put an end to Buddhism.

## BUDDHISM SINIFIED

Buddhism is the only Chinese religion to have come to China from outside; indeed, to the present day, with Confucianism and Daoism, it is the third form of Chinese religion. Meditative Buddhism, Japanese Zen, and also faith or Pure Land Buddhism all arose in China, so that to the Japanese later Buddhism appeared less an Indian than a Chinese religion.

However, on the basis of their veneration of ancestors and their historical thought the Chinese had no time for Indian cyclical thought and the idea of a constant rebirth. It seemed intolerable to most Chinese that an ancestor could return in a lower status, possibly even as an animal. And in the end the Buddhist monasteries, at first popular and exempt from tax, but then increasingly numerous and prosperous, largely fell victim to secularization.

Nevertheless, because of their Daoist natural religion the Chinese were open to the idea of a Buddha nature hidden in every human being, of which one can become conscious through illumination. They also liked the notion of enlightened saints and heavenly helpers and the notion of different heavens and hells.

And so it came about that Buddhism, which perished in its homeland of India, found a new and lasting home in China. However, it did so on condition that it 'Sinified' itself, made itself Chinese. Of course, we may ask why Christianity could not be established in China in a similar way to Buddhism.

## A RENEWED CONFUCIANISM OF THE 'HIGH MIDDLE AGES'

The brilliant Tang kingdom gave rise to increasingly dangerous social tensions: the great landowners swallowed up the small ones, and corruption, moral decay and the domination of eunuchs was omnipresent. The kingdom collapsed under a rebellion by military governors (907). Only after a time of divisions and collapse ('the Five Dynasties') was there a new unification of China at the end of the tenth century: under the Song dynasty, which was to last 320 years (960–1279). This was a time of reforms (*xinfa* – 'new politics'), which generally speaking brought external peace, social stability, a growth in the economy and a new heyday in art and science. Now the foundations of a popular culture were laid, to replace the culture of the nobility which flourished in the Tang dynasty. The capital of the Northern Song was Kaifeng, and after it was conquered by the Jurchen in 1127, Hangzhou became the capital of the Southern Song. Here we have no less than a fourth paradigm shift, which begins with a renewed court Confucianism (the 'Academy of the Princes'): now the ideal was no longer the monk but the person with a comprehensive education. This was a 'high medieval' renaissance of Confucianism, known today as neo-Confucianism.

Just as Christianity was rethought in the high Middle Ages in response to the newly discovered Greek philosophy of Aristotle, so in China in the Song period the classical heritage was rethought in response to the Buddhist challenge. Here the rational morality of Confucianism was organically bound up with the cosmological and ontological ideas of Buddhism and some rituals of Daoism. Now people spoke of a unity of the three ways. It is significant that in Chinese culture too the usual distinctions between statesman, thinker, poet, painter and calligrapher hardly exist. Something like a Chinese scholasticism also developed in this period.

Great speculative systems, like that of the statesman, historian and philosopher Zhou Xi in the twelfth century, can be compared with the systems of Latin scholasticism, for example that of Thomas Aquinas in the thirteenth century. All things come forth from, take part in and return in a cycle to the unlimited supreme reality of the 'Taiji', the 'Great Ultimate', sometimes also called 'Taiyi', the 'Supreme One'. A principle of order (*li*) with an ethical orientation can be found in the inner and outer worlds. Human beings have to correspond to these by learning from the Confucian tradition and dealing with concrete reality. Against this background Zhou Xi developed a normative system of ethical rules and practical modes of social behaviour.

Later, in the fifteenth and sixteenth centuries, the philosopher, statesmen and general Wang Yangming (a contemporary of Martin Luther), as the heir of Zhou Xi, developed so to speak a modern, 'idealistic' view of the ultimate reality. All knowledge and moral progress can be attained by looking into one's own 'heart'. The Ultimate Reality is thus understood not only as an objective principle but subjectively as my spirit, which contains all things and is identical with the spirit of the universe. This is a spirit which manifests itself as a universal moral law through the knowledge innate in human beings. In human beings there is an innate sense of justice and injustice, to which they need only to remain loyal.

## THE END OF THE CHINESE MIDDLE AGES: MONGOL RULE

But back to the medieval Chinese emperors, who now became barbarian. The Mongolian tribes from the steppes of Central Asia had long had a fascination for the plains of northern China with their wealth and their vast human resources. Under the leadership of Genghis Khan they were united and given a military organization and now strove to rule the world.

In the thirteenth century Genghis Khan's grandson Khubilai Khan in fact succeeded in conquering the whole of China (1276). Fascinated by Chinese culture, he also moved his residence and all the central authorities from Karakorum to Beijing (*khan-balik* – ruler city), which was now developed in all its splendour. Here he founded the Mongolian Yuan dynasty (1279–1368) with its Mongolian-Chinese (dual) administration.

Never before had the whole of Chinese territory been conquered and occupied by a 'barbarian' people. And China was only part, though perhaps also the 'heartland', of the giant Mongolian empire. This now stretched from the East China Sea to the Black Sea and from Siberia to the Himalayas, and was to last for almost a century The Mongols were relatively tolerant of the religions. Indeed, under the *pax mongolica*, for the first time it was possible to travel from Europe to Beijing. Marco Polo, who made the most important journey to Asia in the Middle Ages, took this opportunity under Khubilai Khan. During the Mongol rule the Italian Franciscan Giovanni di Montecorvino became the first Roman Catholic missionary to go to Beijing.

## CONFRONTATION WITH MODERNITY

After different rebel movements against the Mongol oppression, some with a strong religious motivation, the Ming Dynasty, the last national and 'Chinese' dynasty of this millennium, created an impressive nationalist

Chinese restoration (1368–1644): the economy was rebuilt and the examination for officials was totally revised according to the Confucian teaching of Zhou Xi; the penal order was reformed and the arts and sciences were renewed. Above all there was a strictly centralized civil administration which controlled the military. The newly united empires made a time of peace and prosperity possible. The grandiose architecture and the blue and white porcelain of the Ming era are still admired.

However, the greatest danger now threatened not from the northern steppes but from the South Seas. European modernity announced itself in China at a very early stage: the first Portuguese ship entered Chinese waters in 1514, and soon the Portuguese had a footing in Canton and other ports. They were given official permission to settle on the uninhabited island of Macao, facing Canton. The oldest European colony in China was also the starting point for the European Christian mission.

We saw that Syrian-Persian (Nestorian) Christianity had already penetrated to China a millennium earlier – as an ethnic minority with no direct missionary intentions. The first missionary was the Franciscan Giovanni di Montecorvino (1294), whom I mentioned earlier. But Christian mission also ended with the Mongol dynasty. One reason for that was that throughout the whole period not a single Chinese could be ordained priest. By contrast, the Jesuit mission at the beginning of European modernity was a more hopeful undertaking, with a well thought out and bold plan.

## THE STRATEGY OF AN INDIRECT MISSION FROM ABOVE

The central figure was a 50-year-old religious from Macerata in Italy, Matteo Ricci (accompanied by Michele Ruggieri). He finally landed in Macao after a difficult voyage and from there began a mission in South China from 1583 onwards. This Jesuit could write and speak Chinese. He skilfully presented himself more as a philosopher and moralist, a mathematician and astronomer, than as a Christian missionary. Equipped with scholarly books, with new instruments, with a realistic map of the world which was much admired, and with telescopes, prisms, clocks and also religious paintings, he and his followers linked up with the ideal of Confucian learning, which was well-calculated for Christianizing China. They assimilated even in their dress.

They sent news to an astounded Europe of the mighty realm of the Ming emperors with an incomparable high culture going back over five millennia which, as we have seen, had developed printing, gunpowder, porcelain, the compass, flying dragons, chain bridges and many other things far ahead of Europe. To the Chinese, the Italians appeared as the first much-admired representatives of a still pre-modern (pre-Copernican and pre-Cartesian) European science, though in the next century this science was to make very rapid progress and overtake China.

There is no question that Ricci and his followers were utterly intent on mission. However, for them mission was in no way identical with confrontation. On the contrary, assimilating themselves diplomatically to the milieu of Chinese scholars, they familiarized themselves both with the difficult forms of Chinese courtesy and with the Chinese classics. In this way they could better proclaim in Chinese conceptuality their message of the one true God, the 'Lord on High' or the 'Lord of Heaven'. They did not want to win over to Christianity so much the masses as the élite, the political and social leading class of educated officials, the mandarins, and if possible the emperor himself.

From 1601 the emperor allowed Ricci (whose Chinese name was Li Madou) to live in Beijing. Renewed Confucianism with its undogmatic openness, its lofty individual and social ethic, its high esteem of parents and ancestors and its reverence for a supreme being (without gods in heaven and fables about gods) seemed to him to be a far better ally for Christianity than that popular Buddhism, with its belief in idols, which was first developed in South China and its basically quite un-Chinese doctrine of the transmigration of souls.

Deliberately a 'scholar from the West', at first Ricci did not build a church but taught in a 'private academy', as was quite customary in China. In 1605 the emperor gave him permission to build a chapel at the place where his successor Adam Schall von Bell was to be allowed to build the first church. A church still stands there today; it was rebuilt in 1904, having twice been burned down.

## A PEDAGOGICAL-DIPLOMATIC ADAPTATION

In his missionary work Ricci did not at first introduce the 'mysteries' of Christian faith which went beyond reason (the Trinity and the Incarnation) but the rational 'foundation' of Christian faith: God, the Creator of heaven and earth, the immortality of the soul, the rewarding of the good and the punishment of the bad. Should not such teaching be acceptable to the Chinese?

European critics today have interpreted the method adopted by Ricci and his followers as Jesuitical dishonesty. But this is wrong. I studied philosophy at the Gregorian Pontifical University in Rome for six semesters, during which the name of Jesus was hardly mentioned, before being allowed to study theology for eight semesters, and I know personally that Ricci was simply practising what had become possible in Catholic theology since Thomas Aquinas. A strict systematic and didactic distinction was drawn between 'natural theology' and 'revealed theology'. Here, though, Ricci rightly referred, not to Aristotle, but to the original Confucius.

In his famous work *The True Idea of God*, Ricci demonstrated how in their original form the Confucian texts, not yet influenced by Buddhism and anti-Buddhism, already contain analogous concepts to a God understood in Christian terms (*shangdi* – 'Lord on High', or *tian* – 'Heaven').

It is a pity that Ricci did not know what to make of the Neo-Confucian 'Great Ultimate' (*taiji*) and that his notions of the Trinity and Jesus Christ were stamped through and through with Hellenistic and scholastic ideas. Otherwise he could, for example, have also used the messianic Chinese ideas of a 'heavenly man', 'divine man', 'true man'.

Here was Thomistic hierarchical thinking with all its problems: in Ricci's catechism the name of Jesus of Nazareth is mentioned only once, on the periphery. When some Chinese – and Ricci was able to win over as converts some important scholars – later discovered that the Christians regarded a man called Jesus from the time of the Han emperor as that 'Lord on High' whom the Chinese venerate as the supreme being, they found this comic, indeed incredible. And they were no less agitated to find that when it came to baptism, Ricci, who was so tolerant on the 'natural' level, was as intolerant as any Counter-Reformation Catholic: he called for a complete break with the Confucian, Daoist or Buddhist past, to the point of burning figures of Buddha and tablets of ancestors. Chinese just could not do that.

So is it surprising that in time resistance developed to this pedagogical-diplomatic adaptation of Christianity to the Chinese reality, which was done with such boldness? There was resistance on all sides:
- first from Buddhists who defended Buddhism;
- then also from Confucians who doubted the Christian interpretation of their classical writings;
- and finally from Ricci's own Christian ranks, caused by the all too clear rivalry between the different colonial powers and missionary orders (the Franciscans and Dominicans against the Jesuits).

## THE TRAGEDY OF CHRISTIAN MISSION IN CHINA

Even during the lifetime of Ricci, who was highly respected in China, other missionaries began to preach to the people in a simple but crude way. To the Chinese this inevitably appeared increasingly as a malicious double game: to the educated, the Christians – in accord with Confucianism – offered philosophy, morality and science. But to the primitive people – in contradiction to Confucian rationality – they offered the most remarkable dogmas and miracle stories. When the Chinese authorities, who were in any case mistrustful of the numerous religious groups, saw how illegal Christian associations of the 'Teaching of the Lord of Heaven' were forming under foreign leadership, some of them engaging in secret activities, in 1617 (seven years after Ricci's death and state funeral) the first expulsion of missionaries took place. However, these either remained in hiding or returned in even greater numbers.

The decisive confrontation took place only later, when the Ming dynasty, like others before it, had already come to grief through social conflicts, extravagance and corruption, a system of court concubines and intrigues among the eunuchs. However, its policy was largely continued by the subsequent alien dynasty of the Manchu emperors from the Tungu language group with the dynastic name of Qing (1644–1912). They too encouraged Confucianism in Chinese society. First of all a period of social stability, national strength and progress in science and culture followed, under the important emperors Kangxi and Qianlong.

But the Christian missionaries now spoke out against the use of Chinese names for God which had been customary hitherto and introduced Latinized terms for 'God', 'Holy Spirit', 'person' and many other things. The message of the Christian God now inevitably seemed to the Asians to be a completely alien, European import and Christianity a religion that had been grafted on to their own. But despite the dispute over Chinese names for God and rites (above all the veneration of ancestors), initially the Christian mission in China still made progress (in 1670 – a good century after Ricci's beginnings – it was reckoned that there were around 275,000 Catholics there).

In 1692 the emperor of the new Manchu dynasty, the great Confucian statesman Kangxi, who was also famous in Europe for his education, generosity and spiritual flexibility, allowed the preaching of the gospel throughout China under a new edict of tolerance. The Jesuits at the imperial court hoped for the conversion of this enlightened monarch, whom the philosopher, ecumenist and diplomat Leibniz also regarded as the greatest ruler in the world. Under this emperor, who ruled for 60 years, the Jesuits Johann Adam Schall von Bell and then Ferdinand Verbiest (both imperial mandarins of honour first class) became heads of the astronomical office which was responsible for the calculation of the calendar and the fixing of the festivals, both of which were very important. Between 1708 and 1717 Jesuits even carried out a major land survey.

However, the Christian missions failed above all because of Rome: the fate of the Jesuits in China was sealed by the Roman Inquisition, nowadays called the 'Congregation of the Doctrine of the Faith'. In 1704 Pope Clement XI forbade Chinese Christians to practise their rites under threat of excommunication; this included the veneration of ancestors and Confucius and the use of the two traditional names 'Lord on High' and 'Heaven'. This was one of the colossal errors of an authority which with an appeal to God's Spirit likes to claim to be infallible. The Chinese reaction followed in 1717 in a judgment by the nine highest courts: the missionaries were expelled, Christianity was banned, the churches were destroyed and Christians were compelled to abjure their faith. The life work of Ricci and the Jesuits was obliterated – by their own church government. However, Christian missionaries were to return 120 years later, though in a quite different context.

## REACTION AGAINST THE MISSIONARIES

The Manchurian Qings ruled the land until immediately before the First World War. In the seventeenth and eighteenth centuries China was still powerful and prosperous; indeed now it reached its greatest extent – to the south-west (1681) and Outer Mongolia (1697), even to Taiwan (1683) and Tibet (1759), which present-day China claims in its territorial demands. But the empire seemed to have been increasingly weakened: by population growth and by the enormous expansion of this state of many peoples, and also by luxury in the cities, corruption in the administration and poverty in the country. Popular rebellions and civil wars were the result. In addition there was now a constantly growing threat from outside by the European colonial powers. Dominated by an orthodox neo-Confucianism which had become rigid, in the nineteenth century the giant empire slowly fell victim to a paralysing and repressive traditionalism, against which the numerous progressive Chinese thinkers could not make much headway. Often vacillating between despotism and liberality, the regime stubbornly held firm to the dogma of the cultural superiority of the 'Middle Kingdom'.

Thus despite numerous modernizations, China as a whole proved incapable of achieving a creative encounter with Europe, which was making rapid progress in science, technology, economics and military developments, and of producing a truly modern Chinese paradigm. Now China began to feel the effect of never having undergone either a Reformation or an Enlightenment in the modern sense. So it was not in a position to modernize its pre-industrial bureaucratic agricultural economy or to democratize its pre-modern economic system and government. The long-term consequences were inner decay and impotence in foreign policy.

In the first half of the nineteenth century, at the high point of European nationalism, colonialism and imperialism, there was another missionary wave in China. Now Protestant missionaries from Germany, England,

Holland and the United States were also at work, all of whom came from the revival movement. They hoped to win over China in order to prepare for the imminent return of the Lord by a rapid evangelization of whole areas, prepared for by the Holy Spirit.

The political breakthrough for the European powers followed in 1842, which for the Chinese was a year of national shame: after the scandalous British opium war (which was also clearly criticized by the missionaries) to support the highly profitable British opium exports from India to China, the Chinese government capitulated – faced with 80 British warships on the Yangzi before Nanjing: China had to cede Hong Kong 'in perpetuity' and open up five harbours to the British, and it was successively torn to pieces by the Western powers.

In the further notorious 'unequal treaties' which were then concluded two stipulations were juxtaposed: foreign merchants might sell opium throughout China and missionaries might preach the gospel throughout China. Rome played along with this, since the mission, whether Protestant or Catholic, was thus wholly aligned with the imperialistic calculations of the European great powers. Their 'bases' were spread all over the land. Colonization meant Christianization and vice versa.


## FIVE GREAT REVOLUTIONARY MOVEMENTS

In the first half of the nineteenth century, unlike the merchants and diplomats, the missionaries were in direct contact with ordinary people. They provided the most comprehensive information about China to Europe and the United States (only now is the Chinese part of the archive of the American Board of Missions being evaluated in Harvard). They also supported the religious and social revolutionary liberation movement against the political despotism of the foreign Manchu regime and the spiritual oppression from a traditionalist Confucianism.

So we can understand how the Chinese who reacted to European colonialism and imperialism first of all regarded the Christian missionaries as their allies. Within a century they now produced five great revolutionary movements which in China were finally to lead violently to an epoch-making paradigm shift to modernity. Only in the second half of the nineteenth century did they also have an anti-missionary, anti-Christian character. These were:

1. The Taiping movement, supported both spiritually and financially by the missionaries and their home communities, for a Christian 'Heavenly Kingdom of Supreme Peace', 1851–64: this was a peasants' revolt with a Christian religious and political nationalist ideology, seeking equal education for men and women, a system to produce a balance between rich

and poor regions, and a 'communist' abolition of private property. It gained almost all South and South East China and the capital Nanjing. Finally it was defeated by troops from eight 'Christian' lands on the orders of the Chinese government. All in all, 20,000,000 people died.

2. The Boxer uprising under the banner of the 'fists of justice and harmony', 1900: this was first against the 'alien' Manchu rule, then against the Western foreign powers, and finally also against the missionaries, who in the second half of the nineteenth century were less orientated on the imminent kingdom of Heaven than on the establishment of colonial churches. The Beijing embassy district was besieged and the German ambassador and other diplomats were killed, along with 250 missionaries and around 30,000 Chinese converts. The uprising was finally put down by an expeditionary force from Germany, France, England, Japan and the United States. Beijing had to pay high reparations.

3. The national revolution of Young China for Democracy, Nationalism and Popular Welfare (agricultural reform), led by the doctor Sun Zhongshan (Sun Yat-sen). On 12 February 1912 the last Qing emperor Puyi, still a child, abdicated. The monarchy was abolished. This marked the end of the 2200-year empire and the establishment of a republic. In 1919 the 4 May Movement, started by Beijing students, turned against Confucian values (obedience, respect for the elderly, forms of courtesy and rites). After Sun Zhongshan's death in 1925, Jiang Jieshi (Chiang Kaishek) became leader of the revolutionary party, the Guomindang. In 1927 he attempted to liquidate the Communists, who had previously been his allies, and dragged out the land reform.

4. The rise of the Chinese Communist Party, 1924–34, 1947–49. This had a nationalistic tendency (it was against the Japanese) and also a social tendency (it sought to mobilize the peasants); it was also radically opposed to Christianity, the 'imperialistic foreign legion'. China was unified by force, and on 1 October 1949 the Chinese People's Republic was proclaimed by Mao Zedong (Mao Tse-tung): 'The Chinese people has risen!' Immediately all foreign missionaries were expelled and the church press was banned; all schools, hospitals, charitable institutions and all church property were confiscated. A three-self movement was required and encouraged by the party: the Chinese churches were to be self-supporting, self-administrating and self-propagating.

5. The Great Proletarian Cultural Revolution, 1966–76: this was Mao's wife, the 'Gang of Four' and the Red Guards against the 'four old things': old customs, old morals, old ideas, old culture and thus of course also against anything religious and Western. Numerous sanctuaries were either damaged or destroyed. Only after Mao's death in 1976 did a change take place in the state and party in the direction of a more pragmatic religious policy. However, this now showed that, like other religions, so too Chinese

Christianity had remained alive by means of smaller groups and 'house meetings' and could now develop within narrow, purely religious limits (churches, seminars for priests, Bible translations). That raises the question:

## IS THERE STILL CHRISTIANITY IN CHINA?

How will Christianity in China continue after this dramatic history of revolutions? A historical retrospect teaches us that there can be no longer any question of an external harmonization (model 1, Nestorianism) or even a syncretistic mixing (model 2, Manichaeism). But missionary confrontation (model 4, seventeenth/eighteenth centuries) or even imperialistic alienation (model 5, nineteenth/twentieth centuries) are finally things of the past. However, the anti-missionary reaction of the Chinese state (model 6, twentieth century) has also proved to have little future.

If anything has a future, it can only be a true rooting of Christianity in China. However, such roots would have to go beyond even the complementary synthesis of the Jesuits (model 3, Ricci in the sixteenth century), in the direction of an authentic 'indigenization' or inculturation of Christianity on Chinese soil (model 7, contextual inculturation).

That means that there can be no 'mission' or 'church' with a colonialist imperialist intention, no Westernization of Chinese culture, no more missionary importation of Christianity from outside, no simple translation of Western theology into Chinese thought forms. Rather, Christian faith needs to be reflected on and realized from within, and Christian values need to be 'diffused' for the people's well-being – all in the social and cultural climate of present-day China and in the framework of an independent church which sustains itself, administers itself and even propagates itself. At any rate, despite all the terrifying revolutionary excesses in China, no one wants to go back to pre-revolutionary China.

Today there are again also two Catholic churches in Beijing, communities with priests: the southern church is near to the place where Ricci worked. Today people preach, pray and sing in Chinese, and in contrast to former days want a completely indigenous clergy. But this official church has no connection with the pope. There can hardly be any agreement with Rome without the appointment of bishops in the country itself. And without Rome's acceptance of the three 'selfs' – self-support, self-administration and self-propagation of the church – there will be no reconciliation between the official church and the underground church.

The Protestant churches, whose organization is less centralized, find it easier to accept the 'three-self movement' for themselves. The religious policy of the Communist government called for an alliance of the churches that appeal to the Reformation (Presbyterians, Anglicans and Methodists) in a single 'Protestant' church. This status is described as 'post-denominational'. At any rate the confessional differences between the Reformation churches imported from outside have been overcome, and a new Chinese identity of this church is beginning to develop. In this way it has also been possible to avoid the split into an official church and an underground church.

## A FUTURE FOR CHINESE RELIGION?

The state cult perished with the last emperor. Bernardo Bertolucci's grandiose film about the last emperor of China, the child Puyi, has once again given us a powerful visual reminder of this state cult with its colourful splendour and ritual symbolism. The imperial cult at the centre of China, the centre of the world, performed at the beginning of the spring and the autumn, time and again brought home the religious and cultural unity of the kingdom in a powerful way to thousands of participants all down the centuries. What is important for the validity of the state ritual is not the quantity of sacrifices or the religious enthusiasm of the participants but its correct performance. Only through ceremonies prescribed in scrupulous detail are effective sacrifices offered to the great powers of nature and the ancestors. Down to the twentieth century people were to be given the impression that the state authority, with the emperor as the link between earth and heaven, along with his officials, had control of the cycle of nature, which is so important for an agricultural society. All that is long past. The rulers never lacked warnings. As early as the fourth/third century BC Mencius had developed the doctrine that the emperor can forfeit his rule if he does not correspond to the mandate of Heaven. Bad governments may be deposed. Since then the doctrine of removing the mandate (*geming*) has applied, and time and again it has served to justify rebellions and revolutions.

However, the Communist revolution completely abolished the mandate of Heaven. Still, the more time went on, the less it could be overlooked that the atheistic Communist Mao Zedong had in fact put himself in the place of the 'son of Heaven' and had assumed the position of a 'red emperor'. This was a divinizing personality cult in the style of Stalin (and often also on Daoist domestic altars), though it was in turn removed by the 'Cultural Revolution', which ended up in a lack of culture. The consequence was a massive destruction of trust and standards, and often a cynical attitude to life and a moral nihilism.

The 1989 democratic movement showed that the more time went on, the less the people were prepared to put up with the rule of the 'red emperor', the new 'son of Heaven'. Hundreds of thousands of people throughout the land demonstrated for weeks for freedom and democratic rights, until in the night of 3/4 June the government had the protest put down with tanks on the 'Square of Heavenly Peace'. This did not solve the problems, but only repressed them. At any rate since then, the state and the party have withdrawn from many areas of life. An economic reform is under way, from a state economy to more private economy. That means that both individuals and families have to rely on themselves in a new way. Still, the question what kind of political regime and what world-view will finally become established in the new China is an open one.

## DOMINATION OF THE MARKET?

Where a few years ago one saw almost only bicycles and people in uniform dress, now one sees car after car and people in Western dress. The market is changing China. What is developing in Singapore so to speak from the perspective of Western capitalism is happening in Beijing, Shanghai, Canton, Sichuan and also in smaller Chinese cities against the background of an Eastern socialism that is attempting to modernize itself only in economic terms. But the dangers are similar: recklessness, a greed for profit, a belief in the omnipotence of money, speculations on real estate and the stock market.

Imperceptibly a new and hardly more benevolent materialism with a Western stamp is also spreading in China: a consumerism which makes all values available. And with all the rising prosperity (especially for a small stratum of rich and super-rich), many people are threatened by new impoverishment, unemployment and massive migration to the cities, and at the same time by a rise in meaninglessness, lack of commitment, moral permissiveness, criminality, corruption and drug addiction coupled with a crisis in the family. All in all there is a loss of both a social and a spiritual home.

But this decay in tradition, which is of unprecedented magnitude, also makes many people long for non-material, spiritual values and standards. Contrary to all 'scientific' prophecies that religion will die out, at any rate in the new secular context, the power of the great religions to survive which has kept them going down the centuries is manifesting itself. They have a proven power to adapt, a capacity for assimilation and integration. And even Chinese Marxists today recognize that the religions are not just 'opium for the people' but highly complex, long-lived phenomena. With both deep ethnic roots and an international dissemination, the religions manifestly form an indispensable ingredient also of Chinese culture, which in turn cannot be understood without Confucianism, Daoism and Buddhism.

## LATENT RELIGION BREAKS THROUGH

The religious sensitivity of the Chinese has remained; however, their perception of the holy has at all times been bound up with this world. And in the face of the moral vacuum left behind by Communism it is understandable that people are again concerning themselves with the most varied forms of traditional Chinese religion, indeed that something like a 'religious fever' has broken out in China. People are flocking to the Christian churches, both the official church and the 'underground' church. The veneration of ancestors is still alive, and it would be illuminating to investigate how far in China, as in Singapore, the rites and customs have tacitly adapted to modern conditions instead of disappearing.

In some places people are rebuilding the Daoist or Buddhist temples destroyed by the Cultural Revolution, or are building new ones. And if no popular religion is practised every day in China, as it is in Singapore, Hong Kong or Taiwan, in the People's Republic, too, thousands upon thousands of people are making pilgrimages to the famous pilgrimage places. And even if they are indifferent or sceptical tourists, there they are confronted with the old religious traditions. Religious objects and of course a good deal of kitsch are on sale along long stretches of the main roads, like those leading to Taishan.

Can this popular religion, which is again making itself felt, along with a good deal of superstition, and which so often has prompted people to impotence, resignation and a longing for consolation, have the liberating effect which is still also urgently needed today (and not enslave people again)? That is questionable. There are doubts whether it can offer a new quality of spiritual life for educated Marxists in particular.

People's longing for meaning in life, morality, spiritual and physical health are satisfied by other movements which are also becoming relevant to society and politics. I watched the police in Beijing on an April Sunday in 1999 apparently helpless when more than 10,000 members of the Falun Gong or 'Buddhist Law' sect (*falun* = wheel of dharma, *gong* = breathing technique), people from all over China dressed in ordinary clothes, gathered illegally and sat down in front of the Beijing headquarters of the party and government in the Square of Heavenly Peace. Only in the evening did they disappear without a trace. This was the biggest demonstration since June 1989, a silent sit-in by this Buddhist-Daoist movement. They practised Qigong, that traditional Chinese teaching which with meditation, yoga-like exercises and traditional Chinese medicine arouses invisible energies for the health of one's own body and the healing of others. It was inspired by Li Hongzhi, who in 1998 escaped to America. Even according to a government estimate, this organization numbers around 70,000,000 members (10,000,000 more than the Communist Party of China). The movement is concerned (as Buddhists) for the 'law' (*fa*) or (as Daoists) for the way (*dao*) and stands for truth, tolerance and courtesy. However, it has often been attacked by local or regional authorities and therefore needs protection from the law. Moreover further demonstrations in July 1999 were treated harshly: in a very short time thousands of demonstrators were arrested, and the organization was banned as superstition.

If we keep the history of the revolutionary movements in China in view, we can well understand the anxiety of the Communist regime, which 50 years after seizing power hardly still believes its own ideology. Since political opposition was hardly ever possible in China, the revolutionary movements often attacked discredited regimes 'from below'. There were movements of peasants and ordinary people which had a religious colouring, like the Daoist Yellow Turbans who overthrew the Han dynasty under the banner of 'Taiping'; the 'Supreme Peace' or Taiping movement in the middle of the nineteenth century; and 50 years later the Boxer uprising against the Manchu emperor. Disappointed and frustrated, in the present spiritual vacuum many people are finding a spiritual home in sects like Falun Gong, which promise salvation and healing by spiritual means. Such sects can easily become radical in times of political oppression; the Internet in particular is offering new possibilities of communicating information, networking, indeed of mobilization.

Since the 4 May Movement, traditional Confucianism has been rightly accused of being a pre-modern religious ideology without a future. Relations between men and women, indeed between people generally, are seen in a purely patriarchal, authoritarian and ritualistic light. And in fact the question arises whether Confucianism can be rid of authoritarian and ritualistic patriarchalism to such a degree that the genuine and central impulses of Confucius himself again take effect.

Modernity has established itself in China, comparatively late, but all the more rapidly and radically. Such a grandiose building as the Temple of Heaven in Beijing seems to come from a time which is now long past. The rectangular three-step terrace on which it rests symbolizes the earth, nature, the human world. The three-step roof with its blue tiles and the crowning golden pearl denotes Heaven, supported by pillars which stand for the seasons, months and days. This is the ideal of an artistically balanced shape which unites content and form, reason and feeling.

### THE TEMPLE OF HEAVEN: HARMONY BETWEEN HEAVEN AND EARTH

Today there is no longer an emperor. There is no 'son of Heaven' who could be a mediator here in the centre of the cosmos, the land, the city, with prayers and sacrifices between earth and heaven. That is no longer possible. But does that also mean the end, for all times, of the 'Heaven' over Beijing, China, the world?

I do not believe so. Religion has not died out even in China, and for most Chinese, Heaven still remains a great primal symbol.

– Ordinary people see natural catastrophes like floods as a 'sign of Heaven', an indication that human beings have destroyed the harmony between heaven and earth.

– But as always, many educated people also see the visible heaven as a sign of the invisible, the mysterious, the holy, the divine.

For the whole philosophical tradition of China was once a quest for the unity of heaven and earth. And even today, people in China still seek harmony between heaven and earth: between heaven and threatened nature, between heaven and endangered human beings. They seek harmony in society and in human beings themselves.

I am convinced that this spirit of great harmony expressed by the Temple of Heaven can be of great importance for the future of China. For China's most recent past has shown that it is not easy to maintain the horizontal, the elemental commands for humanity, in society, without this vertical which points to heaven.

## THE CONTRIBUTION OF CHINESE RELIGION
## TO A GLOBAL ETHIC

A conventional Confucianism which sees itself as a backward-looking ideology, which engages only in sterile studies and which favours a society of hierarchical relationships with no reciprocity is not much help to a global ethic. A permanent domination of children by parents and of women by men, and a patriarchal social order generally, have no future. But an 'ethic of social assimilation' also goes against the importance of the self, of goodness and the integrity of the moral person as these are expressed in the *Analects* of Confucius.

What is helpful towards a global ethic is an original Confucianism, rid of the emperor cult and officialdom, which rediscovers the value of human beings and strengthens their will to assert themselves, their sense of reality, their moral qualities and their powers of perseverance:

- which maintains humanity, true humanity, as the central value;
- which *a priori* regards people as part of a community and not as isolated individuals;
- which thus grounds the fundamental relationships to others in society on universally valid ethical values that do not depend on any particular interests.

In the framework of a new world order, what Confucianism has always emphasized will have to be taken note of: the priority of ethics over economics and politics and the priority of the ethical person over all institutions. But so too will

- an economic order which for all its recognition of self-interest orientates people on moral obligations and social responsibility;
- a political order which is not to be simply governed by the power of the stronger but ultimately by the Golden Rule;
- a harmony of human beings with nature and its natural cycles, which combines economy with ecology;
- an interpretation of reality which remains open to the breath of 'Heaven', the dimension of transcendence.


## THE GREAT WALL

Two thousand, two hundred years have now passed since the unification of China and the building of the Great Wall under the first emperor.

China's Great Wall no longer protects people.

But China's Great Wall no longer divides people either.

People in China, too, no longer want to shut themselves off, but to be open: they want to take part in the one world and to join in shaping the future of humankind.

The great humane tradition of China will help here: the sense of humanity, mutuality and harmony.

# IV

# *Buddhism*

## ARCHERY: AN EXERCISE IN ATTENTIVENESS

Who first taught the art of withdrawing the self, forgetting the self? It was not a psychologist of our time but the Buddha, 2500 years ago. He taught 'the art of attentive life' for which the archer has become the symbol.

In this context archery is not a sport, nor a military exercise, nor even a source of aesthetic satisfaction. Rather, it is used to train the mind, to attain a clear consciousness. In archery it is important to test oneself, one's body, one's emotions: to calm one's mind, to pay attention to all that one does, says and thinks. Archers have to learn to devote themselves wholly to the matter in hand and to forget themselves. They have to remain without a purpose until 'it' shoots. Recollection, extreme effort, inner calm and concentrated presence of mind are needed.

For the Buddha, right effort and right attention (*sati*) are the presupposition for that meditative recollection (*samadhi*) which leads to perfect enlightenment (*bodhi*).

## THE BUDDHA: ONE OF THE GREAT
## GUIDES FOR HUMANKIND

Hinduism, too, grew up organically: a river flowing lazily like the Ganges. But there are moments in the religious history of humankind when a powerful figure steps into the river of a religion and guides it in a new direction – by word, action and fate. Then there is a spiritual revolution. It leads not only to a new constellation, a new paradigm within one and the same religion, but also to a new religion, in this case in the sign of the lotus.

Gautama, named the Buddha, i.e. the one who has been 'awoken', 'enlightened', is such an epoch-making guide – there are only half a dozen of them in the long history of humankind. Venerated by countless people throughout the world, alongside Christ he is the figure on this earth who is most frequently represented in art. He emanates calm, sovereignty, superiority and peace. The arch at the top of the head (*ushnisha*), at the point where according to the Indian view the soul enters and leaves, indicates the enlightenment; the 'third eye' (*urna*) in the middle of the forehead symbolizes the spiritual insight; and the extended ear lobes (originally probably his princely earrings) symbolize the wisdom of the Buddha.

## THE BUDDHIST CREED

For a long time there was no statue of Buddha in Bodh-Gaya as there was in other places where he was commemorated. All that was venerated here was a stone footprint of the Buddha, in markedly stylized form. In the beginning the person of the Buddha was not depicted but only hinted at in symbols. In his teaching he himself had in fact directed people away from him.

So to the present day the creed of the Buddhists is:
'I take my refuge in the Buddha,
I take my refuge in the teaching (the dharma),
I take my refuge in the Order (the sangha).'
One could also express the Christian Creed in a very similar way:
'I take my refuge in (or better, I believe in) Christ,
I take my refuge in his teaching (the gospel),
  I take my refuge in the fellowship of believers (the church).'

It was the Buddha Gautama who, from the heights of the Himalayas and the Hindu Kush down to Indonesia and into China and Japan, showed the way of salvation to hundreds of millions of people in a manner which is still unsurpassed: it is a way that can be followed.

So it is not surprising that the very first note about Buddha in Christianity, written around 200 in Alexandria, remarks that 'in India there are people who follow the commandments of the Buddha' and 'because of his extreme holiness venerate him as a God' (Clement of Alexandria, *Stromateis* 1.15). However, the Buddha himself would have rejected anything like this in his lifetime, as would Jesus of Nazareth.

## GAUTAMA'S WAY TO ENLIGHTENMENT

Buddhism did not originally involve lofty speculations but rather was about coping with the realities of life. And the rich prince Siddharta Gautama, who was married at an early age, experienced these realities when –

according to the legend – for the first time he went out into the countryside from the luxurious precincts of the palace.

Here he was confronted with all the suffering of the world to which men and women are exposed. There was no avoiding it. Everyone will grow old one day. Everyone will fall sick one day. Everyone will die one day. Old age, sickness and death are three signs of transitoriness. That is the basic problem of all human existence. Nothing in life is stable. Everything is dependent on something else. Everything is changeable and transitory. Everything ultimately involves suffering.

The turning point in Gautama's life came when he encountered a begging monk. All at once his privileged life seemed to him to be meaningless: it became intolerable to him. One day, shortly after the birth of his son, Siddhartha told his young wife that he was leaving his family. He abdicated. Indeed, he went away from his homeland, the noble republic of his family, the Shakyas, on the frontier between India and Nepal. He would later be called Shakyamuni, 'the sage of the Shakya family'.

By that time he was 29 years old. In the garb of an ascetic he embarked in poverty on a life of homelessness, finally to find redemption from suffering as a monk. In succession he joined various itinerant ascetics, yogis, but without success. Then all alone he engaged in quite dangerous practices of breath control, fasting and renunciation – again in vain.

After six years he gave up the excessive asceticism, and as a result lost his pupils. He withdrew to a river and practised meditation. There he was refreshed and under a tree, after a long period sunk in deep meditation, he at last experienced the enlightenment (*bodhi*) that he longed for, redemption, liberation. In this way Siddharta became the Buddha, the 'awakened one', the 'enlightened one'. Now he had answers to the four basic questions: what suffering is, how it arises, how it can be overcome and the way to achieve this. From then on this was to be his message. Everything is summed up in these 'Four Noble Truths'.

## THE TREE OF ENLIGHTENMENT

Something like this happened around 2500 years ago in what is now the northern Indian federal state of Bihar near the small town of Uruvela. That is why the tree here, a descendant of the original fig tree, is called the bodhi tree, the tree of enlightenment. And the town of Uruvela is simply known as Bodh-Gaya. It is the second greatest memorial to Buddha after Siddhartha's birthplace, Lumbini.

This was indeed a new religion. It rejected the foundations of the old Indian religion, the authority of the Vedas and with it the domination of the Brahmins and bloody sacrifice. This was replaced by the spirit, inwardness and meditation. The Buddha took this course independently in his own strength. And yet this awakening was no redemption of himself by himself: it could not be brought about by human beings. However, it was not a gift of God either: for the Buddha there was no such thing as an almighty creator God.

In gratitude Buddhists later set aside this place where Buddhism originated as a holy precinct and called it the 'diamond throne'. At a very early stage a temple was also built here, the Mahabodhi temple, the temple of the 'great awakening'. In the course of the centuries it has undergone some alterations and was not restored until just over a century ago, in 1881, by a Burmese king, by which time it was in a state of complete neglect.

Other older sanctuaries were destroyed. That was because for a time Bodh-Gaya had become utterly Hindu. And for the Hindus the Buddha is merely the ninth embodiment (avatara) of the god Vishnu, who has been succeeded by the tenth. The other small temples and monasteries all date from the twentieth century. At any rate, here at the place where Buddhism originated they make it quite clear how far this religion has extended over the years. There is a Tibetan temple and a Chinese temple, a Thai temple and a Japanese temple. The monastic movement has become a world religion.

## THE WHEEL OF TEACHING

The Buddha himself attached very little importance to temples, rituals and ceremonies, and not much to gods and demons. He wanted to leave the question of an ultimate primal ground of the world unanswered, referring to more important things. His famous answer was that anyone hit by a poisoned arrow should not first ask who shot it, but immediately have his wound treated by a capable doctor.

In the Deer Park of Sarnath, before the gates of Varanasi, the Buddha met five itinerant ascetics who had left him earlier but now became his first followers. They formed the core of the monastic community, the Sangha. First there were five; soon there were 500. According to the reports of Chinese pilgrims, between the fifth and seventh centuries 1500 lived and taught in Sarnath alone. So this is the third great memorial to Buddha: it was here that the Buddha set the dharma, the wheel of teaching, in motion.

The Buddha travelled around with his monks teaching for another 45 years, through Bihar and Uttar Pradesh. According to an ancient tradition dating from 368 BC, he died at the age of 80 in Kushingara (present-day Kasia) in Nepal from food poisoning. This is the fourth great memorial to Buddha. In this way the Buddha had entered the final redemption, Parinirvana, without rebirth. He did not appoint a successor or representative. His disciples were to observe the dharma, but not to anyone.

## AN ETHIC OF UNSELFISHNESS

It has often been asserted that Buddhism is not really a religion but a philosophy. However, Buddhism is certainly not a philosophy. It does not set out to offer any explanation of the world. It is a religion, a doctrine of salvation and a way of salvation.

And indeed the Buddha understood himself as something like a doctor who wants to help sufferers to find liberation and redemption. However, he does so with a remedy that everyone must try out for themselves. To this degree he is something like a present-day psychotherapist who helps people to overcome the crises in life, to cope with suffering, to be content with their limitations, finitude and mortality.

But the Buddha is more than a psychotherapist. He is more radical. In his enlightenment he himself experienced that when human beings see through everything they can recognize that everything that they see is unstable. Nothing in the world has stability, all is changeable; indeed even one's own self, to which one clings so tightly, essentially has no abiding substance, but is likewise transitory.

So the suffering from which human beings are to be cured is this clinging to their own selves. They are to learn through the Buddha's therapy to free themselves from their own selves. They are to find the way from being concerned for themselves and entangled in themselves to an unselfishness that then makes them free for an all-embracing compassion. That is something which should really not be so remote for Christians as well.

Thus this 'not-I' doctrine of the Buddha does not set out to be a metaphysical doctrine. The Buddha resolutely rejected such a doctrine. It seeks to offer quite ethical and practical help to human experience. Human beings are to turn from their imprisonment in greed, hatred and blindness towards unselfishness, away from the egocentricity of the self which has no lasting existence. Moreover there is also a dispute among Buddhists as to whether the self is not only not fixed, unchangeable and substantial but even quite unreal. In the end of the day unselfishness in the ethical sense is not alien to Christianity either. After all, the Bible says, 'Whoever loses his life will gain it' (Luke 17.33). This is a key statement for the dialogue between Buddhists and Christians.

## AN ANSWER TO PRIMAL QUESTIONS: FOUR NOBLE TRUTHS

Christians often understand the message of Buddha wrongly: it is not pessimistic or resigned, nor does it seek to provide the consolation of another world. It sets out to show a way in this world, indeed in everyday life. Its existential Four Noble Truths are meant as help in answering the primal human questions and in seeing through and coping with both the world and one's own life:

- The first question is: What is suffering? The answer: Life itself is suffering: birth, work, separation, age, sickness, death. All that is suffering.
- The second question is: How does suffering arise? The answer: Through a thirst for life, through clinging to things, through greed, hatred and blindness. But that results in rebirth after rebirth.
- The third question is: How can suffering be overcome? The answer: By giving up desire. Only in this way will new karma, the consequence of deeds both good and evil, be avoided; and only in this way will a return to the cycle of births be prevented.
- The fourth question is: By what way is this to be achieved? The answer: By the way of the reasonable mean – neither the quest for enjoyment nor self-chastisement. The famous Eightfold Path to Nirvana is:

> right knowledge and right disposition: knowledge (*panna*),
> right speech, right action and right life: morality, ethics (*sila*),
> right effort, right attentiveness (*sati*) and right concentration (*samadhi*).

Knowledge is the presupposition for moral conduct, for an ethic in which the lay disciples usually remain, even if then they are subjected to a new rebirth – hopefully a better one! But by training the mind the monks attempt to get beyond meditative concentration in order finally to be redeemed from the cycle of births and to enter Nirvana, 'extinction', the ending of greed, hatred and blindness. So this is the Buddhist way of salvation which lasts a lifetime; it is very different from the Christian way. But again, after all, it is not so fundamentally different that one could not draw parallels, especially if one does not look at later developments but at the founder figures themselves, at Gautama and Jesus of Nazareth.

## STRIKING PARALLELS

Their whole conduct already shows similarities: in their preaching neither Gautama nor Jesus used a sacral language (Sanskrit or Hebrew) which has become incomprehensible but the vernacular (the middle Indo-Aryan dialect or Aramaic, the language of the people). They did not arrange either a codification or even a record of their teachings. Both Gautama and Jesus appeal to human reason and the capacity for knowledge. They may not engage in systematic and reflective lectures and dialogues, but they use generally understandable, clear, proverbs, short stories, parables which are taken from unadorned everyday life and are accessible to everyone, without laying down formulae, dogmas or mysteries.

For both Gautama and Jesus, greed, power and blindness are the great temptation. Neither Gautama nor Jesus is legitimated by any office: they are in opposition to the religious tradition and its guardians, to the formalistic ritualistic caste of the priests and scribes, who show no sensitivity to the suffering of the people. Both Gautama and Jesus soon have very close friends around them, their circle of disciples and a wider following.

So there is a basic similarity not only in their conduct but also in their preaching:

– Both Gautama and Jesus present themselves as teachers. For both, their authority lies less in their scholastic training than in the extraordinary experience of a quite other reality.

– Both Gautama and Jesus have an urgent, joyful message (the 'dharma', the 'gospel') to deliver which requires people to rethink ('go down into the river', *metanoia*) and to trust (*shraddha*, 'faith'). This is not orthodoxy but orthopraxy.

– Neither Gautama nor Jesus sets out to give an explanation of the world; they do not engage in any profound philosophical speculations or learned legal casuistry. Their teachings are not secret revelations, nor are they aimed at a particular ordering of legal and state conditions.

– Both Gautama and Jesus start from the provisionality and transitoriness of the world, the instability of all things and the fact that human beings are not redeemed. This is evident in their blindness and folly, the way in which they are entangled in the world, and their lack of love towards their fellow men and women.

– Both Gautama and Jesus show a way of redemption from selfishness, fallenness in the world and blindness. This is a liberation which is not attained through theoretical speculation and philosophical reasoning but through a religious experience and an inner transformation. It is a quite practical way to salvation.

– Neither Gautama nor Jesus requires particular presuppositions of an intellectual, moral or ideological kind for the way to this salvation. Human beings are to listen, understand and draw their own conclusions. No one is required to make a confession of orthodoxy, of the true faith.

– Both Gautama's way and Jesus' way are a middle way between the extremes of sensuality and self-torment, between hedonism and asceticism.

Theirs is a way which makes possible a new unselfish concern for one's fellow human beings. In Buddha and Jesus there is agreement not only over the general moral commandments (do not kill, lie, steal, commit adultery), but also in principle over the basic demands of goodness and shared joy, loving compassion (Buddha) and compassionate love (Jesus).

But the parallels between the Buddhist and Christian ways of salvation are not limited to the founder figures. They also become evident in certain further developments, especially in monasticism.

## BUDDHIST AND CHRISTIAN MONASTICISM: SIMILARITIES

In India monasticism is an age-old institution; in Christianity it is relatively late. The question is: were the Egyptian desert fathers who introduced monasticism into Christianity for the first time in the fourth century perhaps influenced by Indian monks – who were known in cosmopolitan Alexandria? In fact for at least 600 years, since Alexander the Great's campaign in India, there had been commercial and cultural links between the great cultures of the Indus valley and the Nile valley.

Initially Buddhist monks, too, were hermits and itinerant monks. Very often they retreated during the rainy season into caves which were cool in summer and warm in winter, near to the intersections of trade routes. In time sanctuaries arose there, hewn in the rock. Only later did the monks live in established monasteries, like the present-day monastery at the foot of the Himalayas in the mountain village of Dharamsala, the Indian exile of the Dalai Lama and his Tibetan monks (Namgyal monastery).

As in Christian monasteries, the monks meet very early for morning prayer. Instead of kneeling, they prostrate themselves and touch the floor with their foreheads as a sign of the deepest veneration and self-humiliation. This is a ritual which can also be found in Christianity, when religious take vows or Roman Catholic priests are ordained. And in Buddhism too (as in a Catholic litany of All Saints) 'all saints', the whole Buddhist pantheon, are invoked: Buddhas, Bodhisattvas and great gurus, and for the Tibetans also the Dalai Lama.

Instead of prayers, which presuppose an omnipotent creator God, sutras and mantras are recited: to summon, assuage or banish the gods of nature and demons. The monks are convinced of the magical efficacy of holy words and formulae for every possible concern. There are dark rhythmic songs which do not entertain but are meant to help in meditation. Singing and reciting together makes the ego retreat, indeed get forgotten.

There are many evident similarities between Buddhist and Christian monasticism. These can be external, as in the simple uniform dress of the order and the sonorous psalmody. But there are also similarities in the basic structure:

- Both call for separation from the world (departure into 'homelessness').
- Both live strictly in accordance with a rule (*vinaya*), with commandments, prohibitions, penitential catalogues and confessions of sins.
- Both require an abandonment of possessions and sexual continence.

## MONASTICISM: CENTRAL ONLY TO BUDDHISM

However, monasticism is more peripheral to Christianity. In Buddhism it forms the centre. Jesus and his disciples were not monks, but the Buddha and his disciples were. In early Buddhism those who wanted to tread the way of redemption and retreat from the world entered the sangha, the monastic community. The Buddhist monks differed from the other Indian monks in following the Buddha as their example, accepting his teaching and his rule.

But not everyone can undertake the five special commandments for monastic novices, nor do they want to. Since Buddha's time these have been:

- Eat only once a day.
- Avoid entertainment (dance, festivities).
- Use no adornments or perfumes (unguents).
- Do not have a luxurious bed or chair.
- Have no personal money.

Far less will everyone want to adopt the more than 200 regulations (depending on the monastic community there can even be between 227 and 400) for monks. Of course, some of these rules have been adapted to modern life. At all events, Buddhist monasteries, like Christian monasteries, can have possessions. Indeed, through foundations and donations many have become rich, excessively rich. This leads to complaints among the people and power struggles, indeed wars, among the rival monasteries.

## A COMMUNITY MADE UP OF MONKS AND LAY PEOPLE

In everyday life, believing Buddhists venerate most of all the monks, the spiritual teachers (*gurus*). Conspicuous in their dark red, black, grey or saffron robes, they are quite distinct from the mass of the people. They offer the people spiritual nourishment, and in return the people give them material support.

For the monks give the people the dharma, Buddha's teaching. And they are available for domestic ceremonies: marriages, funerals, blessing

a new house or a new apartment. Then they recite from the holy scriptures whatever will bring the house and family a blessing, and drive away
the spirits with their mantras and instruments. Their resounding bass
songs are meant to assuage or banish the elemental spirits. So the monks
are allowed to accept food, money and presents from the people. Sacrificial offerings of yak butter play a great role, particularly among the
Tibetans.

At a very early stage Buddhism, which rejects an omnipotent creator
God, did associate itself everywhere with popular religion and its gods, for
example with the original Tibetan Bon religion, which was magical and
shamanistic, and Indian Tantrism. Powerful nature gods, gods of the
mountain, storm and hail, were always to be conciliated with oaths and
sacrificial gifts. Often snakes and dragons – in the East venerated as
benevolent supernatural beings – protect the Buddhist temples. These
temples are also often protected by heavenly musicians and dancers. Often
grim statues of warriors or friendly and peaceful deities guard the threshold
to the sanctuary. As in the European Middle Ages, the countless malign
spirits which are present everywhere must be driven out by a recitation of
the sutras, but also by music and noise. Prayer is constantly to be repeated
by turning prayer wheels, large or small.

In Theravada countries like Burma and Thailand, food for the monks is
sometimes still given on the streets. But as with the Christian mendicant
orders, material support today usually comes in another form. As a sign of
their renunciation of the world the monks have shaven heads and dispense
with personal property. Six items are excluded: an alms bowl, a girdle, a
razor, a needle, a toothbrush and a sieve to filter living organisms from the
water. In our day, of course, monks often also have other personal
possessions: watches are particularly popular.

## MONASTIC SCHOOLS: LEARNING AND DEBATING

As early as the age of six or seven a child can be accepted into the monastic
school – but this applies only to boys, not girls. It is a great merit and also
honour for the parents. The child is guaranteed a good monastic education. The novices learn the holy texts by heart from slim, broad-format
books which, as was customary in ancient China, are printed with wooden
matrices. But the pupils can also learn English, for instance, in the
monastery. Some contacts are made here which are useful for later life,
even if a child does not remain in the monastery after the noviciate.

So the transition between the monastic community and the lay community is very much easier than in Christianity. Monks and nuns can leave
at any time and also re-enter. In the Theravada countries, for example in

Thailand, boys have their hair cut and enter the monastery for three months to study the Buddhist teachings. Adults often enter a monastery for a short time – for 'days of reflection' or 'exercises'.

But life in the sangha comprises not only meditation and ceremonies but also the thorough study of authoritative Buddhist writings. However, the students are not only to study the dharma but also to practise it and, if they do not choose the meditative life, hand it on to others. During the debates the candidate sits. The examiner hurls questions at him and ends each one with loud clapping. This teaches dialectic and rhetoric, rapid analytical thinking and the power to convince with rhetoric.

## HELPS TOWARDS MEDITATION: MANDALAS

Meditation stands at the centre of the Buddhist monastic life. To calm the senses the Buddha himself recommended first of all observing one's own breathing while sitting still (later also when deliberately walking slowly, and eating) as an exercise in attentiveness: deliberately perceiving how the breath flows in, stays a moment, and flows out again. Breathing is a highly transitory event which could stop at any moment. Since then, this has been regarded as the basic technique for the spiritual way. The specifically Buddhist method of meditation, 'training the mind through attentiveness' (Pali, *satipatthana*) is based on the observation of breathing in and breathing out.

However, anyone who meditates will experience during this exercise that the mind very rapidly strays into all kinds of memories and fantasies. Then an image can help to focus the attention. Above all the monks of Tibet, who have learned a great deal from Indian Tantrism, can produce images for meditation, great and small, in a great variety of forms. These are called mandalas (Sanskrit for 'curve', 'ring', 'bow', 'section'). These diagrams combine concentric circles with rectangles. They set out to depict cosmic forces, the world of the gods or also the psychological personality structure of the person engaged in the exercises, often indicating the way in which these depend on one another. Here a whole mystical universe or one of its aspects is developed, symbols of both external cosmic and inner spiritual order. Buddhas, Bodhisattvas, guardian deities and guardian saints are to help to see through the emptiness of the world and its phenomena and find enlightenment.

Another form of the mandala is for a monk in his cell to pile up four bowls of stones and other objects on top of one another, to the accompaniment of invocations. The whole thing is meant to be a symbol of the cosmos: with the sun, the moon, continents, seas and the great treasures of the world. At the centre of the universe stands Meru, the world mountain, the dwelling place of the gods. The whole universe is offered to the Buddhas, deities and gurus: for the salvation of all living beings so that they may be filled with loving compassion. The person meditating concentrates his thoughts on specific aspects of the mandala, in which everything is parabolic and mysterious, and steeps himself in it: in a unity of inner world and outer world this is a way to unity with an ultimate reality. Over long years of practice, monks have learned to link colours, forms and figures in endless series and to associate every possible symbol (in modern depth psychology, too, dreams or pictorial depictions prepared by patients serve as symbols of self-discovery; the human body too is also often understood as a microcosmic mandala).

But there are other quite different forms of mandala. In the West the highly complex coloured scroll pictures (tankas), painted on rice paper, are particularly well known: these are of Buddhas, Bodhisattvas, deities, the wheel of time and of the cosmos. Often several monks work for days on a big sand mandala: the finest sand, in different colours, is scrupulously scattered with the help of needle-thin funnels to make an artistic and complex picture for meditation. To demonstrate the transitoriness of all being, this is then again scattered to the winds or tipped into a river.

With all these means it is possible to hold on to both external and internal images in meditation and finally also to develop new images which have no parallel in the external world: the art of visualization, seeing with the inner eye, say, the image of a deity, with forms and colours . . . All this is done in order to arouse religious experiences and to release spiritual energies.

## THE BASIC OBLIGATIONS OF BUDDHISTS

The Buddhist confesses the Buddha, the dharma, the sangha: the fellowship of the monks. But from the start the Buddhist community consisted of both monks *and* laity.

However, the laity is not bound by the more than 200 commandments or prohibitions of the monks but only by the beginning, the first stages of the Eightfold Path. This includes the elementary ethical obligations, five in number. We do not, though, find 'I am the Lord your God, you shall not kill . . .' in Buddhism. Rather, we find responsibilities assumed by the self: 'I promise . . . to refrain from killing.'

The fifth of these obligations is specifically Buddhist – it is not in absolutely all the texts, and is not even always rigorously observed. This is the obligation to abstain from intoxicating drinks. But the other four are the four basic ethical demands which any human being should observe, which we already find in germ in the 'indigenous religions', and which are today recognized as the four elementary

fundamental demands for a common ethic of humankind, a global
ethic, namely:
- not to kill,
- not to lie,
- not to steal,
- to abstain from sexual dissipation.
   So it is no coincidence that it was the Dalai Lama who in the
Parliament of the World's Religions in Chicago in 1993 was the first
to sign the Declaration toward a Global Ethic and afterwards to
proclaim it. It is constructed on these four constants.

There is to be no violation of bodily integrity; no violation of possessions
and property; no violation of the truth in word and deed; no violation of
faithfulness in marriage. These four or five ethical rules (*sila*) form a virtual
compendium of Buddhist morality. They are often recited in many monasteries by the monks after the 'formula of refuge' and by the lay disciples
as confirmation of their conversion. In addition, in Buddhism there is the
Golden Rule, which is directed against all selfishness: 'How can I do
something to someone that should not be done to me?'

It has to be added that Buddhist nuns – allowed by Buddha after some
resistance – clearly have an inferior status to the monks. A failure to value
women is unfortunately not peculiar to Buddhism.

## THE FIRST PARADIGM SHIFT:
## ORIGINAL COMMUNITY TO MASS RELIGION

The first monastic community, which had no needs, did not require a
temple or a monastery building. Buddha's Eightfold Path does not mention
any rites and ceremonies. The original constellation of Buddhism is the
simple religion of a monastic élite. There were Buddhist works of art only
centuries later, above all under the influence of the Hellenistic-Indian
Gandhara art school (in what is now Pakistan). This produced the first
physical depictions of Buddha – with a Greek arrangement of the folds of
his garment.

From the beginning, following the Buddha, people made memorials
only for great men who had died and above all for the Buddha himself.
Thus the massive hemispherical mound with no visible door and window,
in Sanskrit called stupa (literally 'knot of the hair') became the typical
Buddhist architecture. In the middle were the ashes of the dead person, a
reliquary or later also a text from a holy scripture. But the tremendous

changes in the stupa in subsequent centuries are only a sign of the great upheavals in Buddhist teaching, cult, discipline and art.

In the meantime a doctrine of salvation for the few radicals had become a doctrine of salvation for the many, the masses. The small original community became the great 'community of hearers' (*shravakayana*). A process also took place in Buddhism which today we call a change of overall constellation, a paradigm shift, in this case from the élite religion of the original community to the mass religion of the Buddhist state, with a developed cult, rites and ceremonies. This is, however, what the Buddha himself had described as one of the 'ten fetters' which have no value for redemption. But how could this tremendous transformation into a highly ritualized religion with countless pagodas and temples come about? That is connected with the name of Ashoka.


## THE EMPEROR ASHOKA: THE MODEL BUDDHIST RULER

The great Emperor Ashoka (268–233 BC), grandson of Chandragupta Maurya, founded the first great Indian empire after the retreat of the troops of Alexander the Great; following a bloody war it finally embraced almost the whole continent. In the rich central Indian trading city of Sanchi (near present-day Bhopal) he married the daughter of a merchant, whose son Mahendra brought Buddhism to Sri Lanka. Ashoka himself had the original stupa erected in Sanchi; it is still very close to the model of a grave mound. This is the first sign of the paradigm shift to a state and cultic religion.

The stone hedge and the four splendid doors decorated with reliefs from the second to first century BC – beautiful girls under trees support the architrave – represent the most important monuments of early Buddhist art. They served as models for Buddhist architecture throughout Asia. Sanchi has been declared part of the world's cultural heritage by UNESCO. The reliefs depict scenes from the lives of Buddha and the emperor Ashoka, especially Buddha visiting the bodhi tree, before whom even the beasts bow in reverence. But here the Buddha is not yet depicted in human form. Symbols stand for him: alongside the stupa and the bodhi tree above all the wheel of learning.

To the present day Ashoka, who as a Buddhist repented of his former bloodshed, has remained the ideal Buddhist ruler (*cakravartin*). Although his politics were controversial, his justice, humanity and tolerance towards other religions were emphasized. And in fact Ashoka now no longer wanted to change the world with the sword, but through the dharma, the law of the Buddha, which he had engraved in great stone inscriptions. All over the kingdom, including Sanchi, he had the principles of Buddhist ethics

1. Krishna: for Hindus the ideal of true humanity

2. Daoist liturgy of the dead: the lantern in the middle symbolizes the soul which is to ascend on high

3. A 'possom man' draws his own quite personal possum history in the sand

4. Khajuraho: uninhibited depictions of orgiastic groups

5. Vivekananda: (with the dark turban) at the 1893 Chicago Parliament of the World's Religions

6. The Todaji Temple in Nara: the largest wooden building in the world

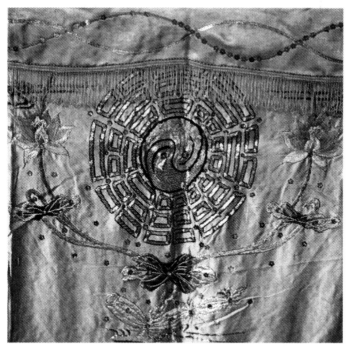

7. The Tai–ji
   diagram: the
   yin–yang
   symbol
   surrounded
   by the eight
   trigrams of
   the *Yijing*

8. The Temple
   of Heaven in
   Beijing

9. Roses mark the spots where the Jesuits of San Salvador University were brutally massacred by a death squad

10. A sand mandala: not work, but a meditative exercise

11. 'Emptiness'

12. Isaiah scroll from the Dead Sea

13. The Reform Synagogue in Berlin: a living synthesis between tradition and modernity

14. Kairouan: the oldest mosque in North Africa and the fourth holiest place in the Islamic world

15. The blessing of Easter bread in Moscow

16. Ritualized Sufi dance: an expression of being seized by God

proclaimed on pillars containing edicts, crowned with animal figures and decorated with the symbolic wheel of doctrine. Along with the rock edicts, these pillars, which still exist today, are the earliest extant monuments to bear witness to Indian art.

At the same time Ashoka founded a welfare state with hospitals for human beings and animals, whose integrity he likewise wanted to protect. He also made great donations to the Buddhist monasteries, which became the basis of their growing wealth. Only the complete abolition of hunting and the slaughter of animals proved impossible to carry through. Ashoka made it clear that the doctrine of the overcoming of suffering must not mean that Buddhists are socially passive. And with all this he founded Buddhism as a state religion.

## BUDDHISM – A RELIGION OF STATE AND CULT: THE 'LITTLE VEHICLE'

Ashoka also had the relics of the Buddha sent to those places in the kingdom where he had been particularly active. Already on Buddha's death there was a dispute among various princes in the area over the ashes and remnants of the bones of this man who eventually became very famous. Now the Buddhist cult of relics and belief in miracles spread over the whole kingdom, which surely went against the Buddha's intentions. So here already we see the Buddhist cult religion developed.

Ashoka, who was also the representative of state centralization and levelling down, was thus something like a Buddhist Emperor Constantine. Through him Buddhism in India and beyond became a state religion, a cult and a popular religion with relics and a belief in miracles. Like Constantine, Ashoka convened a council, which was in fact the third council of Buddhists. But even this council was unable to bridge the split which had slowly formed between the school of the elders, the later Theravada Buddhists, and the 'majority'.

## THE SPLIT IN THE SANGHA

For several centuries the teachings of Buddha were not even brought together in a binding canon. Rather, they were handed down and recited in very different traditions. So it is no coincidence that there were increasingly contradictory interpretations, explanations and expansions. The following parties emerged at the third council in 250 BC:
– On the one side were those who still wanted to preserve 'the teaching of the elders' (*sthaviras*). They represented the conservative monks. Their

only successors who still survive are the schools of Theravada ('Teaching of the Old'), disparagingly known as the 'Little Vehicle' (*hinayana*), because it offers a place only to a minority of monks and nuns who deny the world.

– On the other side were those monks who supported the views of the lay community and wanted to develop the dharma further. At that time they represented the 'majority' (*mahasangikas*). Only very much later, at the beginning of our era, did the 'Great Vehicle' (*mahayana*) develop out of it.

After Ashoka, the religion for monks who denied the world became a power which changed and shaped the world politically. There was no aggressive and militant conquest of the world here as there was with Christians and Muslims. A *Realpolitik* which diverges from ethical norms can no more appeal to the Buddha than it can to Jesus of Nazareth. But as in Christian Byzantium, in the Buddhism of South East Asia the secular ruler became and to the present day remains the patron of the religious community – for all the differences between sangha and church. This is a perfect unity of state, culture and religion, even in the classical Buddhist countries (of Theravada Buddhism). The state government encourages the sangha. And the sangha legitimates and supports the state government to the present day. With good reason Burma, Thailand and Sri Lanka have been called Buddhist 'church states'.


## THE 'SOUTHERN ROUTE' OF BUDDHISM: SRI LANKA AND LOWER INDIA

Already around 250 BC the doctrine of Theravada had been disseminated to Sri Lanka and mainly from there into broad areas of South East Asia. Sri Lanka developed into the main centre of the tradition. For in the eleventh century its Indian homeland was lost to Buddhism for ever as a result of Muslim invasions on the one hand and the decadence of the rich Buddhist monasteries, which had become excessively powerful, on the other. The writings of the Theravada, in Pali (a stage of linguistic development in central India), still form the most numerous and complete of the early Buddhist collections of texts. The Theravada Buddhists therefore see themselves to the present day as the guardians of true doctrine. For them this is collected in the Pali canon. And that embraces the 'Three Baskets' (*tripitaka*): the Basket of Disciplines (*vinaya*), the Basket of Teaching (*sutras*) and the Basket of Higher Teachings (*abhidharma*). Thus Buddhism initially spread from India above all along the sea route. This was a 'southern route', to Sri Lanka, Burma, Thailand, Cambodia and Laos as far as Indonesia – leaving behind grandiose examples of architecture all over South Asia.

## A BUDDHIST 'MIDDLE AGES': JUSTIFICATION BY WORKS

However, in this powerful expansion Buddhism was not spared the doubtful consequences of its 'Constantinian shift'. Something like a Buddhist 'Middle Ages' extended over the Theravada countries. For now countless stupas were built everywhere over the Buddha relics or texts, as works of merit. In this way architectural expression was given to the degree to which even for the monks Buddhist practice, instead of concentrating on gathering no karma (in order to be able to enter Nirvana), concentrated on collecting good karma: merits for a better reincarnation. But as in the Christian Middle Ages, in the long run this led to a righteousness by works, which was exhausted in the accumulation of religious merits.

So in Buddhism, too, this very first paradigm shift from the original élitist religion to a mass religion resulted in a manifest two-class society. There is no mistaking the religious and social dualism of hierarchy and people, clergy and laity. Only monks could attain enlightenment relatively easily; the laity found it difficult, and many people thought that women would do better to be reborn as men. This dualism of monks and laity in the 'Little Vehicle' sooner or later had to result in a further paradigm shift: this led to the 'Great Vehicle'.

## THE 'NORTHERN ROUTE' OF BUDDHISM: CHINA–KOREA–JAPAN

Meanwhile Buddhism had also extended by land, by a 'northern route'. At an amazingly early stage – as early as the first century AD – it travelled by the Silk Road to Central Asia and China. Then in the fourth century it travelled on to Korea and its three kingdoms. And from there finally, from the sixth century on, it travelled also to Japan. In all these instances the Buddhism took the form of Mahayana, the Great Vehicle, which was to make it possible for as many people as possible to attain salvation. Only in the seventh/eighth centuries did Buddhism also reach the 'snow land' of the wild warriors, Tibet.

## THE SECOND PARADIGM SHIFT: 'THE GREAT VEHICLE'

From the first to the fifth centuries AD there was in fact a second turn of the wheel of doctrine: the movement of the Mahayana or Great Vehicle. From the beginning this resulted in a reformulation of Buddhist doctrine.

In it, of course, the Buddhist constants – Buddha, dharma, sangha – were preserved.

However, attempts were made to discredit the Theravada Buddhism of the traditional monastic community in order to legitimate the Mahayana position by calling it a lesser, 'Little Vehicle', and representing its Pali canon as incomplete. It was said to be time to proclaim the deeper teachings of the Buddha, which led to 'perfection of knowledge' (*prajna-paramita*). Here the Mahayana relied on new sutras which without much fuss were attributed to the historical Buddha and were said to express the true nature of Buddhism.

Was this a falsification of the teachings of the Buddha? No. For the followers of Mahayana – and even more for the followers of the Tibetan Vajrayana, the 'Diamond Vehicle' – it was a development. They thought that their teachings were related to the original teaching of the Buddha as the tree is related to the grain of seed. This was an evolutionary model of thought: Christians, and Catholics in particular, know it from their own history. However, such arguments were also used to excuse even fatal deviations, which clearly contradicted the intentions of the founder figure. In Mahayana Buddhism there is a tension which is already present in original Buddhism.

## A TENSION BETWEEN MONASTIC AND LAY EXISTENCE

In the Little Vehicle the ideal was the monastic Arhat, who attains salvation only for himself: the ideal was to strive for individual redemption. Over against this, the ideal now became established of the philanthropic saint, the enlightened being, the Bodhisattva, who is likewise essentially different from the holy magician or siddha of Tantrism, endowed with miraculous powers. The Bodhisattva does not seek the shortest way to Nirvana. He strives for the redemption of others. One can call for his support in any distress, since in unbounded compassion he seeks to help all men and women to attain salvation. But those who themselves want to fulfil the Bodhisattva ideal must attain the six 'perfections' (*paramita*) in the course of their existences: generosity, ethics (*sila*), patience, energy and finally, with deep involvement (*dhyana*), the higher stages of meditation, in order in this way to attain wisdom (*prajna*), the goal of the Bodhisattva's career.

Mahayana Buddhism performed the indisputable service of resolving the basic tension between monastic and lay existence. This tension, which was already present in original Buddhism, had already influenced Theravada Buddhism on a wider front, though there it became caught up in the piety of almsgiving (*dana*). The designation 'Great Vehicle' is justified to the degree that the important thing is to move others over the wide river of suffering to the other bank (redemption). Now many people, rather than a few monks, are to be able to find a way to definitive redemption. In this way the monastic religion increasingly became a lay religion, which also promised those who are not monks, even women, the possibility of attaining enlightenment.

However, for all its openness to the laity, in Mahayana powerful hierarchies of monks formed which might even be called 'high church'. They had solemn titles (abbots, archabbots, general abbots), precious garments and great wealth in temples and monasteries. The senior monks were treated as reverently, indeed as obsequiously, as some Christian hierarchs. And when monks meet in large numbers for the autumn festival at the Todaiji temple in the old Japanese capital of Nara, the biggest wooden building in the world – from China (dressed in yellow), Korea (grey), Tibet (red) and Japan (violet) – they appear to be not only an extremely colourful but also a highly ceremonial gathering, indeed a clerical religion.

Indeed, when at this festival (*hoyo*) they recite mantras and make invocations before the statue of the great Buddha, the laity have much to wonder at but absolutely nothing to say.

### FROM THE RELIGION OF AN ÉLITE TO A TWO-CLASS RELIGION

Of course, when watching such a powerful ceremony involving Buddhists from all over East Asia, we may ask what it still has to do with original Buddhism. But as Christians we should be rather careful, since of course we can also ask what one of the great episcopal processions or events in Rome has to do with the original Jesus of Nazareth.

I believe that the decisive thing is that each of these two religions has developed: something like a change of the overall constellation has taken place – today we call it a paradigm shift. New elements are taken up everywhere: the élite religion has become a mass religion with many adherents. That has to be organized in some form or another. The result is the kind of two-class religion that we see here: the clergy are the monks who have to make all the decisions. The others, the laity, simply obey: they support the religion and also pay for it. It is the same as in Christianity.

## BUDDHISM BECOMES JAPANESE, SHINTO
## IS 'BUDDHIFIED'

In China, and particularly in Japan as we saw Buddhism had a successful history which has lasted down to our own time. If we look at some
temples in Japan we can think that we are in China: in the golden age
of the Buddhist Tang dynasty (618–907). But we are in Japan, say in
Nara, that place where the classical Chinese Tang culture established itself
in an epoch-making way. And with it came Buddhism, which as early as
594 was declared the state religion. In fact Buddhism – always with a
strongly Confucian ethos – was to shape Japan more than any other foreign
religion.

In Japan there had previously been virtually no generally disseminated
written language, no developed techniques in painting, in sculpture, in
architecture and in city building; there had been no calendar, no philosophy and no high religion. Indeed, previously there had not even been a
unitary government, a state administration and a capital. It should never
have been denied that just as Greece and Rome provided the foundations
for the cultural rise of Europe, so beyond question China and Korea,
which at that time were largely Buddhist, provided the preconditions for
the cultural rise of Japan. And just as the legacy of Greece and Rome
became mixed with a new element in the period of the Franks, namely the
culture of the Germanic barbarians, so in the Nara period the legacy of
China was mixed with the still hardly developed culture of the Japanese.

Buddhism came to Japan as a religion which had an already highly
developed organization and philosophy. But however rich its writings,
however splendid its ceremonies, and however technically refined its art,
the primal Japanese religion of Shinto with its veneration of nature and its
animism (shamanism) could not simply be suppressed.

On the contrary, Buddhism (*butsudo* = 'way of the Buddha') and Shinto
(*kami no michi* = 'way of the Kami') converged in many ways. Statues of
Buddha, and Bodhisattva, much admired, were now venerated alongside
the indigenous nature deities (*kami*), and there were 800 myriads of these.
Indeed, some Shinto deities were now understood as the manifestations
and incarnations of Buddhas and Bodhisattvas, and incorporated as guardians of Buddhism. Thus the more that Buddhism spread in Japan, the
more an amazing osmosis took place: Buddhism became Japanese and at
the same time the indigenous Shinto religion became 'Buddhified'. This
process gave rise to a specifically Japanese Buddhism.

## THE MORE-THAN-EARTHLY BUDDHA

Nara, Japan's first fixed metropolis, founded at the same time as the beginnings of the kingdom of the Franks in Europe, was built on a grid plan (drawn in 710), after the model of the then Chinese capital Chang'an or Xi'an. The Buddhist temples built in the heyday of Nara, like Todaiji (consecrated in 752), represent an extremely artistic testimony to Mahayana Buddhism. In the Tang period this international language of art dominated the whole of East Asia. The Buddhist temples were able to assert themselves as religious centres, even when at the end of the eighth century the capital was moved from Nara to Kyoto, and very much later, only in the nineteenth century, to Edo/Tokyo.

Eighteen metres high, Daibutsu, the 'Great Buddha' of Nara – designed, it should not be forgotten, by a Korean, cast from 437 tonnes of bronze and gilded with 139 kilograms of pure gold – is the largest bronze statue in the world. A 'Great Buddha' must be at least 4.8 metres (a *joroku*) high, which is said to have been the legendary size of the Buddha – almost three times that of an ordinary human being. At the back of the statue are artistically gilded wood carvings on which are depicted the sixteen incarnations of the Buddha. However, the surprising thing is that this Buddha is not, as one might assume, the earthly Buddha Gautama, but a supernatural Buddha. But how could such a transcendent figure be arrived at?

This did not happen suddenly, but only on the basis of that second 'turning of the wheel of doctrine' which I have described. As early as the third Buddhist council of 250 BC, convened by Ashoka, there was discussion of the question: is the Buddha by nature a human being or a transcendent being who transcends humanity? Is he only a human being and a teacher, as was assumed in Theravada? Or is he a superhuman, other-worldly eternal principle which is identical with the Absolute, as is now assumed in Mahayana?

Already in India the view had become established in Mahayana that it was impossible for the infinitely profound doctrine of the overcoming of suffering to have been invented by a human mind. Rather, it came from a transcendent eternal being who had taken human form in the historical Buddha Gautama. So there was a similar development with the Buddha in Buddhism to the development with Christ in Christianity: the earthly view 'from below' was increasingly replaced by a heavenly view 'from above'.

## SEVERAL ETERNAL BUDDHAS

In order to explain this 'high' Buddhology more precisely, a doctrine of three bodies (*trikaya*) was developed. There are likewise parallels to this in Christianity (the body of the earthly Jesus, the body of the glorified Christ, the body of the Christ who is identical with God's eternal Logos). Alongside the visible body of the historical Buddha (*nirmanakaya*), in the Buddha paradise there was said to be a body of rapture (*samboghakaya*) and finally the cosmic dharma body (*dharmakaya*). This is identical with the law of the universe, the Absolute.

Furthermore, if the Buddha is eternal, he can also be active at all times. According to an ancient Indian view, and already according to Theravada, the Buddha underwent countless earlier births. Mahayana went further, holding that in former ages there were further other-worldly, eternal, transcendent Buddhas. At least three are counted before the earthly Buddha. The first of them is the cosmic Buddha depicted in Todaiji: Vairochana, 'the one like the sun', who is portrayed disseminating grace with a gesture of teaching. Vairochana is the highest of the five transcendent Buddhas. He is identical to the Adi or Primal Buddha, who in turn is a personification of the Dharmakaya, the Absolute. He is so to speak 'equal to God'. Indeed, in this way this Buddhism even takes on messianic features. For after the Buddha Gautama, the fourth of the transcendent Buddhas, when the state of the world has got even worse, the fifth and last Buddha for this era of the world will appear: this is the Buddha Maitreya, 'the loving one', who will embody all-embracing love.

However, it should be remarked in passing that all these notions of the Buddha seem to have moved even further from the original Buddha Gautama than the medieval christological and trinitarian speculations moved from the original Jesus of Nazareth. So self-critical Buddhists, too, ask: can the future belong to this medieval Buddha?

## CONFRONTATION WITH MODERNITY

As early as 794 Japan's capital had been moved from Nara to Kyoto (= 'capital'). Thereupon Kyoto became the treasury of Japanese culture. This place above all, in the spiritual heart of Japan, saw the development of the tea ceremony, the art of ikebana and the culture of colourful festivals. Even today in this city, which was spared bomb damage in the Second World War, there are around 1000 Buddhist temples (and 200 Shinto shrines).

But meanwhile Kyoto has become a typically modern metropolis with

1,500,000 inhabitants. And in contrast to Kandy, Rangoon, Mandalay, Chiang Mai or Bangkok, one finds hardly any monks on the street. Today the picture presented by the city is not dominated by monastic robes, but by mobile phones, electronics, cars, mass transport and high-rise houses, which are increasingly displacing the traditional small wooden houses. Japan already entered modernity under the pressure of the West in the so-called Meiji period (1868–1912). That meant industrialization and urbanization, and also secularization and the Westernization of all spheres of life.

Buddhism did not flourish in Japan between the seventeenth and the nineteenth centuries. But in the twentieth century it developed a power of renewal which also embraced some groups in Shinto, Japan's traditional religion – from 1868 to 1945 it was the state religion. And so in our days even in the tumult and noise of the modern metropolis there are people with a religious motivation who are not afraid to go through the crowds and draw attention to their message with rattles: 'Fire, water, wind – that is the one God! Couples should honour one another! Parents should be looked after.' These are members of the Shinto sect of Tenrikyo ('teaching of the heavenly truth') founded by a Japanese peasant woman in the nineteenth century, which has its headquarters in Tenri (in the prefecture of Nara) and promises a happy life through unselfish work for the common good.

## THREE BUDDHIST OPTIONS

What is the future of religion in Japan? To which voice will the younger generation listen? This question is posed not only by representatives of the 'national religion' of Shinto, which has been heavily compromised by nationalism and militarism and which was banned as a state cult by the Allies in 1945. It is also posed by adherents of modern Buddhism, which with Shinto and other traditions of Japan for many people forms 'a shared holy way'. With the twentieth-century renewal movement, the scholarly investigation of the sources of Buddhism has once again opened up a view of the original core of the Buddha's teaching.

Now Buddhism is less rooted than Shinto in the old agricultural economy and nationalism. It must therefore also be less endangered by modern mobility, industrialization, urbanization and secularization. But it, too, is certainly threatened by that new concentration on material values which has arisen with Japan's tremendous economic boom, though today this boom seems to be in danger and people are becoming insecure. Like China, modern Japan too faces the alternatives of either a reactionary religion of the past (a renewed nationalistic Shinto) or a religionless secularism (Western materialism and consumerism). Is there a third way? It is clear that in Japan there are many people who no longer practise any religion at all. But it is also clear that many of those who do not practise religion still affirm its abiding significance.

How far Buddhism can maintain itself and which Buddhism can maintain itself are crucial questions. What does Buddhism offer to men and women today? Here in principle the Japanese have three Buddhist options. Put very schematically, they can concentrate on 'meditation', on 'recitation' or on 'action'. Since the thirteenth century, starting above all from Kyoto and in connection with the sacred mountain of Hiei, there have been three great currents, denoted by the names of great Buddhist reformers (to the present day they are eternalized in portraits on Hiei):

– the meditation Buddhism of the Zen masters Dogen (founder of the Soto-Zen sect) and Eisai (founder of the Rinzai-Zen sect);
– the faith Buddhism of Honen and his disciple Shinran, the founder of the Pure Land sect;
– the social and political Buddhism of Nichiren and many more recent religions.

I shall go on to discuss these three options, beginning with Zen meditation, which had and still has a great influence on all Japanese culture.


## CALLIGRAPHY: 'ZEN'

'Zen' is attractive to many Japanese not least because here religion and art are intrinsically combined. Many Japanese practise the art of calligraphy with pencil and brush: for them this is a way of spiritual discipline and meditation in which quite definite aesthetic and philosophical rules must be observed: 'In calligraphy you see the reality of the person,' says one of the most distinguished Japanese calligraphers. 'When you write, you cannot lie, retouch and decorate. You are naked before God.'

Ikebana ('living flowers'), the Japanese art of flower arrangement, represents a similar way. It too follows particular rules and has different schools. Thus for example a flower arrangement can represent the law of heaven (above), earth (below) and human beings (at the centre).

The sado, the tea ceremony, the tea way, in which the harmony of room, garden, floral decorations and pictures is meant to communicate simplicity and freshness, is similar. Here too there is everywhere a combination of self-discipline and aesthetics. The ceremonial preparation of the tea, which involves striving for reverence, harmony, purity and silence, is meant to lead to inner fulfilment. This is Zen culture; but what about life in a Zen monastery?

## BUDDHIST MEDITATION:
## SITTING IN CONTEMPLATION (ZEN)

It cannot be taken for granted that one will be accepted into a Zen monastery. The ritual is very strictly regulated. The postulant has to set down his request for acceptance in writing and leave it at the entrance. From the room behind the door he will then initially receive the answer, 'There is no room in this monastery. There are other monasteries in Kyoto, like Nanzen-ji.' The candidate often has to wait for hours, even days. That too is part of a well-thought-out ritual. Finally, however, the candidate is accepted.

Those people in the modern world who attach importance to religious concentration, simplification, inwardness and the immediate experience of the heart can doubtless find all this best in the meditation Buddhism of the Mahayana tradition. From the beginning, in fact, meditation is a means of intensive spiritual self-discipline on the Eightfold Path of Buddhism. But in the Theravada countries it often fades right into the background in favour of Buddhist doctrine, rites and merits.

In its heyday between the eighth and the thirteenth centuries the Chinese Ch'an reform movement of meditative Buddhism (the word is derived from the Sanskrit *dhyana* = 'recollection') took over a great deal from the nature mysticism and lifestyle of Daoism. It found a way into Japan as early as the beginning of the thirteenth century, where it was called Zen, which similarly means recollection and contemplation. 'Zazen' is practised as the royal way to illumination (*satori*): a purposeless silent 'sitting in contemplation'. Here paradoxical riddles and almost insoluble intellectual tasks (*koan*) are meant to be aids towards breaking free of the compulsions of the mind.

This way of inner recollection and emptying the spirit, in which the dualistic distinction of I/Thou, subject/object is done away with, will doubtless also be highly valued by many people in the future. A Zen teacher might speak like this:
– Do you find the traditional veneration of the Buddha excessive and his role misunderstood? In that case, in Zen you can again take the original Buddha seriously as teacher and guide. In this sense 'take refuge in the Buddha'!
– Have you had enough of the external rituals, the images, temples, sacrifices and also the philosophical abstractions and commentaries of the Buddhist schools? In that case, in Zen you can return to simple teaching, which at the same time shows a practical way of experience, the practice of meditation and the realization of the Buddhist ideal, Buddhahood. In this sense 'take refuge in the dharma'!

– Do you reject all the 'ecclesiastical' fossilizations and all the clericalism of traditional Buddhism? In that case, in Zen you will find an open community. Illumination in this life can also be attained by lay people, sometimes in unexpected things and in the ordinary events of everyday life. Everyone can dwell in the depth of the Buddha nature, which is deep in every human being, the unity and bond with the whole of reality. In this sense 'take refuge in the sangha'!

## DISCIPLINE, WORK, EVERYDAY LIFE

Thus the Buddhist constants – Buddha, dharma, sangha – continue to be preserved. But there has to be strict discipline in the monastery. The 'staff of enlightenment' (*kyosaku*) is the symbol of this. Blows with it on the back or the shoulders are not meant to be a punishment. Rather, they are meant to overcome weariness, to stop people nodding off, to relax tensions and arouse latent powers. In the Zen monastery, too, however, life does not consist only of meditation but also of work, quite ordinary housework. It consists of an alternation of silence and movement: one might be reminded of the Benedictine *Ora et labora*, 'Pray and work'. No service is to be too lowly for the Zen monk. However, begging at houses, often done urgently, for food and other gifts, is now the exception in a city like Kyoto.

But Zen meditation is possible not just in the monastery. In the modern world Zen Buddhists do not have to lead a life which is different from that of ordinary people. They can also experience illumination and the fleeting, transitory nature, the 'emptiness', of all things in the everyday world: they can be in the world and yet at a distance from it. They can clearly recognize and see through reality without being imprisoned in an ideology. This is a conscious, full life in the present moment.

The experience of meditation and specific spiritual and aesthetic rules have left a deep mark on Japanese attitudes and Japanese art.

## THE ZEN GARDEN: THE EMPTINESS OF ALL THINGS

Japanese pictures display spontaneity, asymmetry, clarity and empty space: there is a combination of the utmost simplicity and artistic perfection. The depiction of the most simple natural objects seems sketchy; many paintings set out to express the unity of form and emptiness. The Zen saying, 'The trees show the bodily form of the wind', is in full accord with this.

Even today, the meditative Zen spirit influences Japanese painting and above all the shaping of gardens. Garden layouts in the Zen spirit inconspicuously have a highly artistic form. In restrained plainness they are meant to express a natural quality, simplicity, clarity. This is also meant to be expressed by the stone garden, the gravel bed of which always has the same structure, which has been meticulously worked out with the aid of a calculator. It is meant to express freedom, openness and breadth, emptiness. The soul of the monk is to become as empty and ordered as the garden, free of greed, hatred and blindness.

But what does 'emptiness' mean? This is a difficult term for Westerners. The paradigm shift of the Great Vehicle also changed the understanding of redemption, nirvana. Nirvana is not to be attained only at the end of the samsara, the cycle of life, but in the midst of the samsara, in the here and now. Indeed, for Buddhists, in any case the things of this world have no constancy, no abiding substance, no unchangeable being. And those who are enlightened know that it is precisely this lack of substance that makes up the true nature of the universe.

This insight is meant to lead to a state of effortless being, indeed wisdom, relaxation, cheerfulness in the midst of life. Many depictions of the Buddha's smile indicate this. After his illumination he still has to suffer and die, but suffering and dying have lost their bitterness for him. Anyone who even today has seen through the reality of this world, recognizing that it is empty and without substance, can no longer be shaken by old age, sickness and death. Such people can transform their suffering into peace and joy. They know that they can participate in the Buddha nature.

The calligrapher finds it easy to write the word 'emptiness', though its meaning is difficult. It is a second important character. But the question cannot be suppressed: are those who have come to know emptiness also beyond good and evil? The Samurai warriors of the Tokugawa military dictatorship showed that meditation can be used, indeed abused, for very different purposes, as again in our century have the Japanese militarists and now many aggressive businessmen. So what moral standards should monks, managers, the military observe? As a soldier may one kill, as a politician may one lie, and as a businessman may one steal, because everything is indeed 'empty', a matter of indifference? Must not those who are on the way of enlightenment also live accordingly and follow at least the four basic obligations of the Buddha? Self-critical adherents of Zen ask precisely these questions.

## BUDDHIST FAITH: TRUSTING INVOCATION OF THE NAME OF BUDDHA (SHIN)

There is a second Buddhist school, which has what amounts to a liturgy, precisely regulated; it begins with the striking of a bell. Anyone who as a member of modern society finds the Zen Buddhist's total responsibility for his faith intolerable can be shown in faith Buddhism a way in which everything depends on trust in the Buddha, or more precisely the Buddha Amida, the Buddha of the 'Western paradise'.

It is not Zen that has the most adherents in Japan but this faith Buddhism or Amida Buddhism: above all the 'true school of the Pure Land' (in Japanese *jodo shin-so*). This was founded in a time of social and religious crisis in the Japanese Middle Ages, in the militaristic Kamakura period, on Mount Hiei, by Shinran Shonin ('the holy one') (1173–1262). He was a contemporary of the great Zen masters Eisai and Dogen, and in Europe also of Thomas Aquinas and Bonaventure. Shinran was introduced to belief in Buddha Amida by his teacher Honen Shonin (1133–1212), and from then on he saw the recitation of the name of Buddha as the only means of salvation.

The starting point of his movement had been a quite personal crisis. For like the monk Martin Luther later in Christianity, the monk Shinran had the living experience that the many works of traditional piety bring no salvation. So Shinran broke with Buddhist Orders and monastic tradition. In despair at his sense of helplessness and his uncertainty about salvation, after twenty years he left the monastery on Mount Hiei. He married, had a family and first propagated his teaching among the peasants in Eastern Japan, but later again from Kyoto. This was the message of the Pure Land. What was it about?

On a central point, with his message Shinran stands in opposition to classic Buddhist teaching. According to that teaching human beings can bring about redemption in their 'own strength' (Japanese *jiriki*) – i.e. without a gracious God and without the intercession of saints and the sacrifice of priests. However, on the basis of his own existential experience Shinran became convinced that human beings remain caught up in their passions; they are beings subject to karma. They are incapable of redeeming themselves, of overcoming their suffering by themselves. Whether monk or lay person, man or woman, educated or uneducated, human beings can attain redemption only by trust in 'another power' (Japanese *tariki*), i.e. on the basis of faith. This is what Buddha Amida promises. For tradition reports that Buddha Amida (Sanskrit *amithaba*), in earlier life a king and then a monk, is now the Buddha of 'boundless light'. In all depictions of him he sits in the middle of a lotus flower, the symbol of purity, over the swamp; he rules over the Western paradise and radiates infinite mercy and wisdom.

## BUDDHIST LITURGY

Believers are constantly strengthened in the liturgy. This already takes place through reading from a work by Shinran or a classical writer of this school. And according to Shinran it is especially important first of all to acknowledge one's own guilt or, as it is said: 'First one must acknowledge a deep sin; that is the first thing that one must do, nothing else.'

There is no doubt that here a new way of salvation is opened up which attracted many believers, even some adherents of Zen, who in the end did not want to rely only on their own strength. Moreover the promise was great: no more endless rebirths were necessary. Redemption is possible here and now. How? Simply by calling on the name of Amida Buddha in faith and trust, as it is solemnly sung in the 'Nembutsu' of the Shin liturgy. However, it is also particularly effective at the hour of death: 'Namu (veneration) of Amida Butsu (Buddha)!'

So from the prospect of awakening from death in a lotus flower in the Pure Land paradise the believer may now already derive confidence and power for everyday life. For, as one can hear from a woman preacher at the end of the ceremony: 'Now I am living at the end of the twentieth century and have many things to reflect on: the uncertainty in society and the reason why I was born.' The Amida Buddha gives an answer to this.

Of course, the result of Amida piety can be that one is concerned about faith but neglects ethics – a charge which was also made against Martin Luther and his trust in faith. Nor do people seem to need explicitly to learn the Buddha's four basic obligations. But all Shin Buddhists know very well that they are to live in such a way that they need not be ashamed before the Amida Buddha.

## SOCIAL AND POLITICAL BUDDHISM: ESTABLISHMENT OF THE BUDDHA KINGDOM (NICHIREN)

If Shinran seems to be rather like a Buddhist Luther, one could almost call another reformer the Calvin of Buddhism: this is Nichiren (1222–82). He was a contemporary of Shinran and the great Zen master Dogen. He too was in search of the Buddha's true teaching and he too looked for it on Mount Hiei. But it was the Lotus Sutra of the Buddha preaching in the eternity of his eternal dharma that fascinated Nichiren. He internalized it completely and interpreted it in a highly arbitrary way – for a time of religious decline and in the hope of a unification of Japan and a religious renewal.

When Nichiren later in his ancestral monastery in Kamakura saw salvation exclusively grounded in the recitation of the Lotus Sutra, he was expelled. But he took his message on to the streets. He vigorously attacked Zen and Shin Buddhism and even dared to admonish the government publicly. This was a crime hitherto unheard of in Japan.

Thus in the context of a religion with a mystical and inward orientation Nichiren appears as a unique prophetic figure. He was condemned to death but miraculously saved, and then banished. Finally, however, he was allowed back to Kamakura. Referring the Lotus Sutra to himself in the stories of two Bodhisattvas (first of all 'the Much Abused' and then the Bodhisattva of 'the Superior Conduct'), he now saw himself even more as the messianic saviour of the nation. He unshakeably propagated his message that there was now only one important thing, namely to recite the Lotus Sutra with full attention: 'Veneration of the Sutra of the Lotus of the Good Law' (Japanese *nam myoho renge-kyo*). In this way one could achieve Buddhahood in a moment.

However, following their founder, the Nichiren school also emphasized the social and political tasks of religion: they did not set out to console, but to establish a Buddha kingdom here on earth. In the twentieth century the million-strong Buddhist lay religions of Reiyu-Kai, Soka Gakkai and Rissho-Kosei-Kai – founded in 1925, 1930 and 1938 respectively – appealed to Nichiren. All these religions have a more or less marked ethical orientation.

Yet there is no overlooking the fact that the adherents of Nichiren are often in danger of succumbing to fanaticism; indeed, at a later stage some of them also became caught up in fanatical nationalism. But today these movements, even Soka Gakkai with its marked nationalistic orientation, are committed to peace in the world and to understanding between the religions. And as well as all its liturgy, faith Buddhism, too, sees that it has important social and political tasks.

## SOCIAL COMMITMENT LIVED OUT

Of the around a dozen universities in Kyoto, five are of Buddhist origin. Amazingly, one of these, the Ryokuku University, was founded as long ago as 1639. Today it has three campuses with around 17,000 students. The three treasures of Buddhism – the Buddha, the dharma and the sangha – are symbolized in the emblem of the university. And the university hymn begins with the words: 'Make us listen to the dharma, unchangeable down the ages.'

This university is rooted in the tradition of faith Buddhism and precisely in this way displays a modern social awareness and commitment. Other traditions, like Zen, are also taught. And at the same time the university, with its sixteen faculties, is also open to the challenges of the present time.

'Hope' is a third important calligraphic character. Japan's ambivalent economic development has shown many people that the material realm is not enough by itself and that religion is still a factor of hope. They call themselves 'engaged Buddhists', and are engaged all over the world as non-violent social critics and activists. They are opposed to war and oppression, corruption and dishonesty, fighting this evil from its roots, an excessive self-centredness. The Tibetan Dalai Lama, the Vietnamese Zen monk Thich Nhat Hanh and the Thai social activist Sulak Sivaraksa are representatives of this 'engaged Buddhism'.

### BUDDHIST ETHIC AND GLOBAL ETHIC

Meditation is and remains central to Buddhism. But in Buddhism too the problem of the relationship between meditation and action arises. And even in a Zen temple today the question is asked whether or not its ethical standards help in a catastrophic earthquake. A Shin Buddhist has things easier; he can go by the Amida Buddha, the Buddha of compassion, and to this extent Shin Buddhists are *a priori* very committed socially. And the new religions which derive from Nichiren are also dedicated to action in present-day social life: a group like Rissho-Kosei-Kai is active not only in the Third World but also in the World Conference of the Religions for Peace.

What is common to all Buddhists and all Japanese is the ethical capital that people in Japan derive from Confucianism, and here of course certain responsibilities are taken for granted. However, in Japan the emphasis has very often been only on the obligations of the inferior to the superior. Today, though, in the face of very many abuses, there is more emphasis on the responsibilities of superiors, say the politicians, towards their inferiors; here particular basic norms of morality, 'do not lie, do not steal', etc., must be taken more seriously.

To this extent it is a sign of hope that the idea of a Universal Declaration of Human Responsibilities to supplement the Universal Declaration of Human Rights should have found a footing in Japan and have been given special support here.

## TRANSITION TO A NEW GLOBAL CONSTELLATION

Like China and India, indeed basically like the whole world, Japan is in a phase of transition into a new constellation which we can only guess at in a sketchy way. Here the tremendous achievements of modernity must not be gone back on, but its inhuman limits and defects must be overcome.

Will humankind succeed in moving into a new postmodern constellation? Such 'transcending' would require:
- not only science but also wisdom to prevent the misuse of scientific research;
- not only technology but also spiritual energy to bring the unpredictable risks of a highly efficient overall technology under control;
- not only industry but also ecology, which in an age of globalization comes up against an ever-expanding economy;
- not only democracy but also an ethic which can counter the massive interests of different peoples and groups in exercising power: a global ethic, a common human ethic, in a globalized world.

## ARCHERY: A DEMAND ON THE INDIVIDUAL

But the specific contribution of Buddhism to a global ethic is that everywhere demands are made on the individual. All must tread the way themselves. Men and women make themselves what they are. They become human beings by practising humane conduct. Here it is decisive to forget the self as far as possible, to practise unselfishness. In that unselfishness the presupposition for all living beings is:
- to offer good will (*maitri*) in place of rejection and segregation;
- to offer compassion (*koruna*) in place of feelings of coldness and insensitivity;
- to offer quiet joy (*mudita*) in place of envy and jealousy; and finally,
- to offer unshakeable calm (*upekkha*) in a place where there is greed for power, success and prestige.

Indeed, in a new global constellation people could use more compassion, readiness for peace, gentleness, cheerfulness, tolerance and harmony in the spirit of the Buddha.

# V

# *Judaism*

## A JEWISH WEDDING IN NEW YORK

Picture a wedding, much like any other yet not like any other. For first, it is a Jewish wedding, and secondly it is taking place in the middle of New York. The bridegroom is Israeli, the bride American. The decisive element is the marriage agreement (*ketubba*), which is explained by the rabbi; it lays down the traditional duties of the husband towards his wife. Then it is signed by the couple: a beautifully decorated document for them to hang up in their home. This is an age-old rite in a modern setting, a joyful event. Two individuals have found each other over thousands of miles. This is a good sign that Judaism is a world religion.

But how different all the Jewish faces at the wedding are! How different Jews are, even if we merely take a representative cross-section of the 1,700,000 Jews in New York or indeed the 5,700,000 Jews in the United States. Far more Jews live here than in Israel, where only 81 per cent of the 5,700,000 inhabitants are Jews. The American Jews have no intention of 'going home' to Israel. The vast majority of them feel politically and culturally American, not Israelis living abroad. They speak English and often know no Hebrew. They may or not believe in God, and they may observe the religious law fully, only in part, or not at all.

The wedding is celebrated under the splendid baldachin, the 'chuppa'. This was originally a 'bridal chamber' (Ps. 19.6), a portable tent in which the nuptials were consummated. The rabbi first sings the ancient blessing over the cup of wine. Both the bridegroom and the bride take a sip from the shared cup.

Then follows the central part of the marriage. The couple exchange rings and make the marriage promises to each other. The bridegroom says: 'With this ring you are hallowed to me as my wife in accordance with the law of Moses and the people of Israel.' The bride says: 'I am my beloved's and my beloved is mine. This ring is a symbol that you are my husband and a sign of my love and worship.' The marriage is valid only if the bridegroom himself has bought the ring.

The rabbi repeats once again the marriage promises of both the bridegroom and the bride. The couple, he adds, have promised to work for the ongoing existence of Judaism and the Jewish people, at home, in family life and in shared enterprises. Then comes the solemn confirmation: 'So today this marriage is sealed and attested according to the law of the state of New York and according to Jewish custom.'

Finally the prayer shawl (*tallit*) is wrapped round the bridegroom and the bride; on this day it is given to the bridegroom by his parents-in-law. Then follows the concluding blessing: 'God bless you and keep you.' And may God give them the most precious gift: 'Shalom', peace, in a peaceful world.

Traditionally the ceremony ends with the breaking of a glass, wrapped in a cloth; perhaps this was originally meant to drive out the evil spirits. Nowadays it is understood as a symbol of the destruction of the temple, a sign of the remembrance of that even at this most joyful moment.

## THE RIDDLE OF JUDAISM

So according to Jewish understanding, marriage is seen essentially as an institution which ensures the ongoing existence of Judaism and the Jewish people. This very small people sees itself threatened more than others by today's multi-cultural society – by the many mixed marriages and also by a falling away from the faith. But is faith necessary for Jews?

According to the Orthodox understanding, a Jew is someone who is born of a Jewish mother or who has converted to Judaism. But this definition in no way solves the riddle of Judaism. It is a riddle for non-Jews, but it is often a riddle even for Jews themselves. Jews are not a race, so what are they?

– Jews have a state and yet the majority of them are not citizens of it.
– Jews are a people and yet not a people, a language community and yet not a language community, a religious community and yet not a religious community.

## JEWISH DRESS?

Only a minority, often called 'Hassidim', 'pious', can also be recognized outwardly as Jews. Kaftan, hat, beard and sidelocks are marks of Orthodox Jews, those who are faithful to the Law, the Torah. Their women cover their natural hair with a hat, scarf or wig. They observe not only the 'written Torah', the five books of Moses, but also the 'oral Torah', everything that is regarded as binding in the commentaries of the rabbis.

By contrast, non-Orthodox Jews at most wear a head covering (*kippa*) on religious occasions – wherever the name of God is pronounced as a sign of respect and reverence. They see no occasion in their day-to-day activities in the modern world to wear a form of dress taken over from seventeenth-century Poland, especially the black hat or cap, as the Hassidim do. Indeed, for centuries most Jews did not have any distinctive dress.

Whether or not their dress marks them out, away from New York and Israel, all over the world Jews are for the most part numerically a small minority. But in terms of intellect, religion, culture and business they are a great power which has written world history and has suffered from it: a world religion of a quite distinctive kind. This religion has its synagogues all over the world. In New York the oldest to have remained in constant use is the Central Synagogue on Park Avenue.

## A COMMUNITY OF FATE

I have taught many semesters in the United States and also in New York, and of course I have met many Jewish people of the most varied origins, cultures, languages and nationalities there. And time and again I have asked myself, 'What really unites all these people?'

If one were to question all the people coming out of synagogue and also those who never enter a synagogue, they would answer: Jews now have shared experiences behind them, shared stories and traditions. They have a shared history. Indeed, in a way they share a common Jewish destiny. And so over the centuries a community of fate has taken shape.

Of course, we want to know what the basis of this community of fate is. It is grounded in the interaction of three factors: the people of Israel, the land of Israel and the religion of Israel. That produces a definite sense of togetherness in all these people, along with an awareness of solidarity, at least in times of crisis, and a shared attitude in many things. That explains why Judaism has shown a unique and admirable power of endurance through all the centuries of peace and the centuries of persecution.

## THE HOMELAND OF THE JEWISH PEOPLE

At a very early stage, Canaan was the homeland of the Jewish people. Canaan was a narrow corridor of land lying at the intersection between the Mediterranean in the west and the deserts of Syria and Arabia in the east. To the south was the great power Egypt, and to the north its adversary,

Mesopotamia. It was and is a land of deserts, mountains and only a few fertile plains.

But the high religions of the Nile and of the Euphrates and Tigris went into decline more than 2000 years ago: we can wonder at their gigantic relics in the great museums of the world. Only the religion of the little people of the Bible was to last and have a future. This people formed not only a community of fate but also a narrative community. Its foundation consisted of stories of the patriarchs and the twelve tribes.

## A PEOPLE WHICH DID NOT ALWAYS EXIST

To begin with, these quite simple stories, centred on figures like Abraham, Isaac and Jacob, were only handed down orally. And historically they can no more and no less be verified than the epics of Homer, the Song of Roland, or the sagas of William Tell and the Nibelungs. None of them are biographies, but they are not mere fairy tales either. They are sagas.

Sagas are marked out by brevity, simplification and concentration on a few persons. As a rule they have a historical nucleus, even if this cannot be dated. And they have a historical foundation. However, particularly in the biblical stories about the patriarchs, social and cultural conditions glimmer through. We get some idea of what life must have been like in Palestine in the roughly 500 years between 1900 and 1400 BC. We already know something about this period from sources outside the Bible like Sinuhe the Egyptian, who lived there (in the twentieth century BC) among semi-nomads. These sagas, the characters in which usually have West Semitic personal names, finally came to be recorded in the first book of the Bible, the book of Genesis. This book was composed of various oral sources in a process which must have taken around five centuries.

And now comes the amazing thing: this people was very well aware that by comparison with its neighbours it was a relatively young people, and had by no means always existed. It did not link its history directly with a mythical history of the gods, as did the peoples of Egypt and Mesopotamia. Rather, it remained fully aware of how it became a people at a late stage, in an alien land. Moreover the first historical mention of the name 'Israel' does not occur until the so-called Israel stele of Pharaoh Amenophis III in the Eighteenth Dynasty (fourteenth century BC).

However, the book of Genesis first relates a long primal history which is a universal history of all humankind: the creation of the world and human beings – the fall – the flood – the covenant with Noah – the building of the tower of Babel (chapters 1–11). Only then do three cycles of sagas centred on the patriarchs or tribal ancestors Abraham, Isaac (along with Ishmael) and Jacob, who was called Israel (along with Esau), follow as a prehistory (chapters 12–36). All this is the great introduction to the story of the twelve tribes, those eleven brothers who sold Jacob's favourite son Joseph into Egypt (chapters 37–50).

## ABRAHAM: AN IMMIGRANT

Tradition says that Abraham emigrated from Mesopotamia, a land where towers were built, together with his small clan of nomads. They made a living by breeding sheep and goats; we can still find such groups all over the Middle East today. He left the rich southern Mesopotamian city of Ur, with its stepped temples (*ziggurats*), which was dedicated to the moon god Sin.

According to tradition, Abraham and his family went to the northern Mesopotamian city of Haran on the great bend in the Euphrates. From there he travelled on to Palestine, which at that time was inhabited by the Canaanites. So right from the beginning Abraham was not native-born but an immigrant, and he remained an 'alien' until his death at a great age. In his time Abraham could have lived on the periphery of the cities, as the Bedouins do today.

## ABRAHAM: THE FIRST LEADING FIGURE OF THE PROPHETIC RELIGIONS

But why does Abraham still play such a fundamental role not only in the Hebrew Bible but also in the New Testament and even in the Qur'an, where after Moses he is the most frequently mentioned biblical figure? The reason is that everyone descends from him: first of all Isaac and Jacob, the tribal ancestors of Israel and Jesus Christ, and then also Ishmael, the tribal father of the Arabs and later the Muslims.

All of them receive God's promises. Israel is to become a great people and receive a land to live in. Ishmael, too, is to become a people, and in this way Abraham is to become a blessing for all peoples.

That is why Abraham has tremendous ecumenical significance as the tribal ancestor of the three great religions which are all of Near Eastern or Semitic origin. In his time the patriarch possibly knew other gods below the one supreme God (strictly exclusive monotheism only developed over time out of henotheism). But he had no notion of a rival evil God or of a female consort deity. Therefore for all three religions Abraham is the primal representative of monotheism, the archetype of the prophetic religions.

Abraham's faith differs deeply from the religious sense which we find in the mystical unitive religions of India or the wisdom religions of China. For Abraham is the one who does not know God 'in himself', like the Indians, or simply 'above himself', like the Chinese. No, he walks and stands 'before God', and in so doing puts an unconditional, unshakeable trust, faith, in God – even where God seems to ask too much of him in requiring the sacrifice of his son. That is why the three Abrahamic religions are called religions of faith.


## STRIFE OVER ABRAHAM

The only property that Abraham acquired was a piece of land in Hebron for a family grave. But the Bible attaches importance to this: he did not take the land by force. Rather, he negotiated respectfully with the people who had been settled here for centuries, whose right to the land he recognized *a priori*.

Abraham's tomb is still pointed out to Jewish, Christian and Muslim pilgrims and tourists – in Hebron (Kiriath Arba). It is a place which nowadays has a majority of Palestinian inhabitants, with a new Jewish settlement in the centre; particularly after the massacre of 29 Muslims by a Jewish settler at Abraham's tomb, the great tomb has to be protected by a large contingent of Israeli soldiers. It is now literally a building for the three religions. For a fortress was erected over the tomb of Abraham by King Herod, and on the top of that a mosque, which was transformed into a Crusader basilica.

Today, however, in order to avoid further conflicts, Muslims and Jews may visit the tomb of Abraham and the other prophets only at different times and through different entrances. The Muslims go in at midday through the left-hand entrance, summoned by the muezzin: for them Abraham, in Arabic Ibrahim, received the original revelation which is set down without falsification only in the Qur'an. Then in the evening, the Jewish settlers enter under a strong guard by the right-hand entrance. 'Israel's people' has a claim to 'Israel's land'; there is already a basis for that in the figure of Abraham.

What Jews and Muslims have in common is easily overlooked here. After all, they are already related ethnically. Both are Semites and they have very similar languages. And Christians, too, recognize in Abraham the model of their faith. Indeed, he is the father of faith for all three prophetic religions.

## AGAINST COMMANDEERING ABRAHAM

However, over the centuries all three religions have attempted to commandeer Abraham exclusively for themselves.
- Jews have 'Judaized' Abraham: the blessing for the peoples is said to apply only to Israel's people and land; Abraham is said to be the ancestor only of the Jewish people; he already observed all 613 commandments of the Torah down to the smallest detail without having learned them.
- Christians have 'Christianized' Abraham: all the promises given to him are said to have been fulfilled in Jesus Christ and in him alone.
- Muslims have 'Islamicized' Abraham: he is regarded as the model Muslim, whose practice distinguishes him from Jews and Christians; Islam is said to be fundamentally the earliest religion.

But despite all the different interpretations and emphases, Abraham remains the primal witness to belief in that one and the same God who is the God of Jews, Christians and Muslims. Thus Abraham is the first great leading figure of those three religions which with good reason have been called Abrahamic religions. For as I have indicated, even apart from their common descent, Jews, Christians and Muslims continue to have a similar basic understanding not only of God but also of the world and human nature. They also have a similar understanding of history, both individual histories and the history of humankind. History does not run in cosmic cycles but progresses purposefully down the ages. It is a history in which the mysteriously invisible God is constantly at work.

So Judaism, Christianity and Islam are said to be the three great monotheistic religions. They are also said to be ethical religions. That is because for all three, human beings are dependent on God, who is merciful (*ha-rahman*, Arabic *ar-rahmani*) and just. But at the same time human beings are responsible for their own actions – as God's image or God's representatives.


## THE HOUR OF THE BIRTH OF THE PEOPLE OF ISRAEL:
## THE EXODUS

Of course, the Jewish ethos is bound up with a second great leading figure: with Moses and the exodus from Egypt. Traditionally the Jewish family celebrates this fundamental event of Israelite history, 'the liberation from Egypt', every year. Israel's primal confession is prayed at every Jewish morning and evening prayer: the confession of the one God who has freed Israel from Egypt. But this fundamental event of Jewish faith is also commemorated especially at the feast of Pesach or Passover: the saga tells how as a last plague inflicted on the Pharaoh the angel of the Lord had all the firstborn of Egypt killed, but spared the Israelites. Moreover the word 'Passover' means 'God's passing over', 'being spared' by God.

Some biblical scholars conjecture that behind the Pesach sacrifice lies a sacrificial rite involving blood to ward off the demons, the kind of rite which was performed at the old nomadic spring festival to protect the new life of the flocks in these regions. At any rate the nomadic festival and the agricultural Mazzoth festival, the Feast of Unleavened Bread, seem to have been fused into one and associated with the recollection of the exodus from Egypt.

What happens when an Orthodox Jewish family celebrates the Passover meal? The head of the family, dressed in the white garment of the high priest, speaks the blessing (kiddush = sanctification), the invocation of God who has 'created the fruit of the vine and hallowed Israel and the seasons'.

In the book of Exodus, in the narrative of the exodus from Egypt, we read: 'And on that day you will explain to your son, "This is because of what the Lord did for me when I came up out of Egypt"' (13.8). Then the youngest male in the family puts the traditional question, 'Why is this night not like any other night?' The answer is: 'On all other nights we eat leavened (bread) and unleavened, on this night only unleavened, on this night only bitter herbs.'

A reading from the Haggada, the 'story of the exodus', is appointed for this night. In the book from which it is read there will be many pictures (those in the Sarajevo Haggada are famous), especially of the forced labour in Egypt, the obdurate Pharaoh and the ten plagues inflicted on his people, together with their escape from the Egyptians through the Red Sea.

The skilfully constructed exodus cycle in the Bible is in some respects obscure, and many historical details are disputed. Only a few of the tribes may have been involved in the exodus, the so-called Yahweh or Moses group. But regardless of the historical details, the recollection of the liberation of the people from servitude in Egypt which once took place is, and still remains, fundamental to the self-understanding of the whole people of Israel. That is why the narrative of the exodus, read out by the father of the household, stands at the centre of the Pesach festival. This is the hour of birth of the people of Israel.

The Passover meal is now produced: a lamb shank, an egg, spring produce and mazzoth, bread which was baked unleavened because of the great haste of the exodus. The breaking of this bread and the distribution of wine remind Christians of Jesus' last supper, which some assume to have been a Passover feast.

Another characteristic of the Jewish Pesach is that not only is unleavened bread eaten, but bitter herbs are also handed round. These are to recall the bitterness of the slavery in Egypt. This is a bitterness which is tasted with abhorrence by everyone after the meal.

Four cups of wine are drunk. A fifth cup is filled but not emptied. This is 'Elijah's cup'. It points to the hoped-for final redemption of the people of Israel. So the door is opened: time and again, at every Passover, the return of Elijah, the herald of the Messiah who is at the door, is expected.

## MOSES: A SECOND LEADING FIGURE OF THE PROPHETIC RELIGIONS

However, the great symbolic figure of the people of Israel is not Elijah, but Moses. He, God's messenger, leader of the people, giver of the Law, indeed God's representative, is a highly complex charismatic figure. He is an inspired leader, but does not himself fight. He is a vehicle of revelation, but at the same time a man with many weaknesses. He is the founder of a cult, but does not personally offer any sacrifices.

Certainly the individual religions have also attempted to commandeer Moses solely for themselves: they have 'Judaized' him (as 'rabbi' Moses), Christianized him (as a 'model of Christ') and Islamicized him (as the 'forerunner of Muhammad'). Nevertheless, for all three religions he is and remains the great leader of the liberation and wilderness wanderings. And alongside Abraham he is the primal image and model of all the prophets: he is the second great leading figure of all three Abrahamic religions.

Moreover, Moses is the typical prophet in the spirit of a Near Eastern-Semitic religion of faith and hope. This religion experiences God as a 'Thou', as a reality which addresses human beings and expects a response, responsibility, from them. The call of Moses to be liberator of his people takes place in front of a thorn bush which burns but is not consumed. When he asked who was calling him, Moses was given by the God Yahweh the mysterious answer *ehyeh asher ehyeh*, 'I am there as I there shall be' (Ex. 3.14). That means: I shall be with you, leading, helping, strengthening and liberating. Faith in this God remains the constant foundation of the people of Israel: a God who is experienced not as a despot and slave owner but as a liberator and redeemer.

## THE COVENANT ON SINAI: THE CENTRE OF JEWISH RELIGION

The Sinai cycle was probably originally handed down independently. And again it is not easy to discover the history behind the narratives about the appearance of Yahweh – was he a mountain God? But where is the mountain of God? – the 'Ten Commandments' and the making of the covenant. Be this as it may, present-day Mount Sinai is an age-old cultural area. Here words have been found which were scratched by Semitic forced labourers of the Egyptian Pharaoh in the copper and malachite mines of Sinai. These inscriptions are the earliest evidence for the Canaanite-Phoenician 22-letter alphabet (which was also adopted by the Greeks).

The Sinai tradition indicates that there was a quite special relationship between Yahweh and the Yahweh group. This was the basis of that special relationship between God and Israel which would later be called 'covenant' (*berit*): 'You shall be to me a kingdom of priests and a holy people' (Ex. 19.6). Here we really are at the centre and foundation of the Jewish religion. There can be no Israelite faith, no Hebrew Bible, no Jewish religion, without a confession which is formulated increasingly clearly, the 'covenant formula': 'Yahweh is the God of Israel and Israel is his people!'

## THE SOLUTION TO THE RIDDLE

It is only in the light of this basic notion that we can understand the abiding riddle of the Jewish people. That is the only explanation of:
- its originality from an early date;
- its continuity in the long history down the centuries to the present day;
- its identity under the various epoch-making constellations or paradigms, despite all the difference of languages and races, cultures and regions.

The people's obligation under the covenant corresponds to God's covenant promise. The legislation corresponds to the making of the covenant. Covenant (*berit*) and covenant law (*torah*) belong together. But at the beginning the Torah was unquestionably not yet an all-embracing corpus of law. It was less a matter of 'law' in the strict sense than of 'instructions', 'commandments'. Many biblical rules about behaviour in fact derive from the non-Yahwistic nomadic environment and have now been subordinated to the will of Yahweh; many were codified only after the settlement in Palestine.

## THE SINAI COVENANT PRESUPPOSES A
## COVENANT WITH HUMANKIND

The Sinai covenant is rightly seen as an exclusive, indissoluble agreement between God and this one people which is binding on both sides. By it Israel clearly dissociates itself from the nature myths of the polytheistic religions of its environment. But the Sinai covenant must not lead us to forget the covenants which preceded it: the wider covenant with Abraham, which also included the children of Ishmael, and even more the earlier covenant with Noah, which was utterly universal.

For the covenant concluded with Noah, as the survivor of the great flood, was a covenant with the whole of creation. It applies to human beings and animals, to circumcised and uncircumcised, and knows no distinction of race, class or caste, indeed no distinction even of religion. Its sign is not circumcision, as with the covenant with Abraham, but the rainbow which forms an arch over the whole earth, all men and women and all peoples.

According to the Bible, this universal covenant already brought clear obligations for humankind as a whole, so that it might be preserved and not destroyed. The covenant with humankind is matched by an ethic for humankind. We could call this preservation of order a minimal fundamental ethic of reverence for life: do not murder and do not eat the flesh of living animals. The reason for not murdering is 'for God has created the human being – every human being – in his image' (Gen. 9.6). Indeed, according to the first pages of the Bible, every human being is 'God's image and likeness' (Gen. 1.26). So Adam is not, say, the first Jew, just as he is not the first Christian or the first Muslim either. 'Adam' is simply 'the human being': 'Adam' is the model for all human beings.

## THE DECALOGUE – THE BASIS FOR A SHARED FUNDAMENTAL ETHIC

On the basis of the Bible the Jews are called 'God's chosen people'. However, for believing Jews that is not an expression of superiority and arrogance, but the expression of a special obligation: an obligation towards God's covenant, God's instruction, in Hebrew the Torah.

That certainly does not mean that all the countless commandments of the Jewish sacral law were given from the very beginning. And of course outside Israel, among the other peoples, there were also elementary commandments requiring humane behaviour. But the new thing was that these commandments were now put under the authority of one and the same God. People were no longer told in general terms, 'You shall not kill, lie, steal, commit adultery.' Now they were told, 'I am the Lord your God. You shall not kill, lie, steal, commit adultery.'

At a very early stage these commandments were brought together, the most important of them in the 'Ten Words', the Decalogue. They were also taken over by the Christians. There are parallels in the Qur'an. They form the basis for a shared fundamental ethic of the three prophetic religions. Grounded in faith in the one God, these Ten Words form the Jews' great legacy to humankind.

## ISRAEL: FIRST OF ALL A TRIBAL SOCIETY

We do not know precisely how the land gradually came into the possession of the Israelites. But in due course a community of fate developed among the tribes of Israel. In the twelfth century BC the great families, clans and tribes were still living in a pre-monarchic, pre-state constellation. This was a tribal paradigm, in which there was a loose federation of tribes with a patriarchal order, with elders, several Yahweh sanctuaries and a Yahweh priesthood.

In times of a common threat charismatic judge figures (*shopetim* = 'judges') appeared. But there was neither an administrative apparatus nor a professional army. In the early centuries the primal constellation for Israel was not a state but a tribal society.

But in the face of the external threat posed by the Philistines and internal political problems, the tribes of Israel finally adopted an institution which had long since been established in the small states around: kingship. The first king, Saul (1012–1004), initiated this paradigm shift from a pre-state to a state constellation. His primitive little fortress in Gibeah has been excavated quite recently – it is the first significant Israelite building known to us. But Saul failed, both as a person and as a warrior.

## ISRAEL BECOMES A STATE

It was the Judahite David from Bethlehem (1004–955), at first Saul's ally and then pursued by him, who formed the tribal society into a state. He definitively established the kingdom paradigm of the monarchical period (Paradigm II). With him Israel also began to write its own history.

David, a man of charisma, vision and bravura, was a great politician, a supreme commander and organizer. With extraordinary political acumen and efficiency he permanently combined the kingdoms of the north and the south, Israel and Judah. He captured the Jebusite city of Jerusalem and made it the capital, and established his residence on the hill of Zion: the 'City of David'. However, the Zion Gate which is pointed out to tourists today does not come from his time, any more than does the tower of David.

But the new capital would hardly have attained the sacral character which it still has to this day had not David wisely introduced into it, in a solemn procession with music and cultic dance, the portable holy 'ark of God', the symbol of the tribal alliance and the presence of Yahweh. In Jerusalem the tent sanctuary was erected. And alongside the military and civil administration, the Canaanite cultic priestly administration was also organized and

'Yahwized'. Indeed, it was through King David that in Jerusalem Yahweh became a kind of state deity. It was through David that Jerusalem became the cultic centre for all Israel and Judah, a unique 'holy city'.

## DAVID: A THIRD LEADING FIGURE OF THE PROPHETIC RELIGIONS

Like Abraham and Moses before him, David too has been perceived selectively and commandeered by the three prophetic religions. David has been:

- 'Judaized': he has been stylized as the one who was faithful to the Law and taught the Law and in this way advanced to become the type of the coming Messiah.
- 'Christianized': he appears as only the forebear of Jesus, as the type of the coming Messiah.
- 'Islamicized': he is regarded as a prophet who is the model for the Prophet Muhammad.

Nevertheless, David is and remains the third prophetic leading figure of the three Abrahamic religions: as the most important king in Israelite history he is regarded as the ideal blend of a good ruler, a brilliant poet (the Psalter was attributed to him), an exemplary man of prayer and a great penitent. And whether individual psalms come from David or from others, at all events they are the richest and deepest expression of prophetic piety 'before God'. The great king of Judah and Israel was to have misfortunes only with his successors.

Down all the centuries to the time of David Ben-Gurion, Israel's first prime minister after the Second World War, the kingdom of David, which had been occupied 3000 years earlier, remained the paradigmatic ideal of the Jews. This comprised:

- A strictly organized state of Israel, united under 'Davidic' leadership.
- Jerusalem as the religious and political centre of the kingdom (Mount 'Zion' later became a designation for the whole city).
- A strong army, an administration which functioned well, and a clergy which was integrated into the state.
- National identity within the secure frontiers of a great empire.

Prayers are still offered at David's legendary tomb in Jerusalem; they often involve the traditional movement of the whole body. To the present day David's kingdom, with Jerusalem as the capital, remains the political ideal. For some, even the frontiers of his empire are the goal to be aimed at, although these frontiers had been disputed since the time of David, and the kingdom fell apart again after the death of his son Solomon.

David is not glorified in the Hebrew Bible. Rather, his adultery with the beautiful Bathsheba is severely censured by the prophet Nathan. Indeed, most of the great prophets of Israel were opposed to the kings and priests, as is attested in the writings attributed to them, preserved not least in the age-old manuscripts discovered at Qumran, which are on display in the Hebrew Museum in Jerusalem.

## THE PROPHETS IN OPPOSITION TO PRIESTS AND KING

About 70 years after David's accession, around 927, there was a fatal division of the kingdom. The image which had been presented by the rule of his son Solomon, the builder of the first temple, who was very fond of pomp, was all too divisive. 'Solomon in all his glory' lived like an oriental potentate with a great court (harem); he engaged in great building projects and enlarged his army. Harsh forced labour and mass impoverishment were the consequences.

After Solomon's death the northern kingdom (with its new capital, Samaria), split off from the southern kingdom (with its old capital, Jerusalem). Subsequently the two kingdoms lived side by side, sometimes related by marriage, sometimes in fratricidal war, until first the northern kingdom and then also the southern kingdom perished.

All in all, the monarchy of the first united and then divided kingdom lasted only 400 years. This was also the period of classical prophecy, which uniquely set the Israelite religion apart from all other religions. In what other religion had prophets stood out so boldly against kings and priests?

Here I am referring to the great individual prophets like Isaiah, Jeremiah or Ezekiel, who already understood themselves to be specially called as heralds of God. They received the instructions of God directly and handed them on to the people: 'Thus says the Lord'. These heralds did not foretell a distant future but were watchmen who issued warnings, criticisms and admonitions about their own day.

The prophetic critique, which is always formulated powerfully, attacks the unbelief and self-righteousness of the people, the ritualistic worship of the priests, and the unjust legal practices of the rulers. But these prophets also proclaimed salvation for the individual and for the people. At any rate, there were no invitations to 'holy wars'; on the contrary, there were many speeches against war and in favour of peace among the nations. But throughout, the prophets always fought for belief in the one God who tolerates no other powers and figures alongside himself.

What is particularly impressive is the prophets' dedication to a fundamental ethic: their humane demands for justice, truthfulness, loyalty, peace and love were presented as demands of God himself. There could be no service of God without the service of human beings: Israel owed this basic insight above all to its prophets. Indeed, the powerful voices of the prophets have rung out down to the present day, even if in all three Abrahamic religions time and again attempts have been made to domesticate them by interpretation and to subordinate them to teachers of the Law and hierarchs, so that prophecy seems to be quenched in these religions.

## THE DOWNFALL OF BOTH KINGDOMS: THE END OF THE MONARCHY

Some prophets – who are therefore called 'prophets of doom' – threatened the downfall of both kingdoms. And indeed as early as 722 the Assyrians conquered the northern kingdom of Israel, deported the inhabitants to Mesopotamia and settled their own people in Samaria and the surrounding area. From then on the area was inhabited only by a mixed population, despised by the Jews of the southern kingdom. This population was known as the 'Samaritans'.

Barely 150 years later, in 587/86, the southern kingdom of Judah was conquered by the Neo-Babylonians; Jerusalem was stormed and plundered. The temple of Solomon and the ark of the covenant went up in flames.

The prophet Jeremiah had warned that rebellion against the Babylonians was useless, but his warnings went unheeded. He was persecuted, indeed during the siege of Jerusalem even imprisoned for high treason. The Babylonians freed him, but he was forced by rebels to emigrate to Egypt, where he died.

The Israelite upper class as a whole, along with the king, were deported to Babylon, where the king died. The end of the Davidic kingdom had come, the end of an era. For around 2500 years (apart from the interlude of the Maccabean period) the Jewish people was to lose its political and state independence. First of all followed the almost 50 years of the 'Golah' in Babylon, the Babylonian exile (586–538).

## ISRAEL BECOMES A THEOCRACY

Since the Babylonian exile Israel has lived in a tension between homeland and Diaspora ('dispersion'). This has time and again produced new stimuli. For from the exile on, the majority of Jews have usually lived outside their homeland. From the start they have not wanted to return there, since things were better for them in the Diaspora.

However, already in Babylon the new post-exilic paradigm which replaced the kingdom paradigm of the monarchical period was being prepared for:

– Only now did circumcision, the sabbath and the laws relating to cleanness and diet develop as the marks which distinguished the Jews from other peoples; circumcision, for example, was widespread in the ancient world, as in Egypt, but not among the Babylonians. It is still widespread even in secular Jewish circles.

– Only now were the different traditions systematically collected: the 'narratives' (haggada) and also the 'laws' ('halakha' – 'way of life').

And what about the political power? For 200 years this had been in the hands of the Persians, then of Alexander the Great and his successors, and finally of the Romans. Israel no longer had a monarchy. Instead, after the exile, it received a new, second temple and, along with it, a whole temple hierarchy in Jerusalem, which was now regarded as the sole centre of the cult. Granted, this second temple no longer contained the ark of the covenant. But it possessed a great seven-branched lampstand (*menorah*), which was to become an important motif in Jewish religious art and in 1948 was adopted as the emblem of the new state of Israel.

At the same time the state now had a quite specific body of holy scriptures which became binding law. Only now did Judaism become a religion of the book with a precisely defined canon of scriptures. This consisted of Law/Instruction (*torah*), Prophets (*nebi'im*) and Writings (*kethubim*), which together form the Hebrew Bible (called Tanak, after the initial consonants of the three parts).

The form of rule under the Persians, Alexander the Great and the Romans was theocracy: a 'rule of God', but one in which God no longer also ruled over the state, as in the time of the monarchy, since the state was now pagan. God ruled only over the community of those who believed in Yahweh. Thus the paradigm of post-exilic Judaism was theocracy instead of monarchy. In practice it was exercised on the one hand by the priesthood (the hierocracy of a supreme council and high priests) and on the other through the divine law (nomocracy). The conflict between Jesus of Nazareth and the Jewish establishment was about this historical constellation. The independent religious jurisdiction which still exists in the present state of Israel goes back to this paradigm. For many Jews, in Jerusalem in particular, theocracy remains the ideal form of government.

## THE DESTRUCTION OF JERUSALEM AND THE TEMPLE

However, subsequently Zealot groups again wanted to fight against the power of Rome for the state independence of Israel which had been regained for a few decades under the Maccabees in the second century BC by a revolution of the whole people. The Zealot revolutionaries were inspired by a widespread apocalyptic expectation of the messianic kingdom. But the apocalypse did not turn out as they expected. The terrible events can be described quite briefly:

- The Jews lost the first Jewish–Roman War between 66 and 70. This resulted in around 600,000 Jewish dead. Jerusalem was devastated, the temple was burnt down, and the menorah was taken through Rome in Titus' triumphal procession. It can still be seen depicted on his triumphal arch, but it was destroyed in the Vandal attack on Rome.
- The Jews also lost the second Jewish–Roman War between 132 and 135. Here too the results were devastating. Around 850,000 Jews were killed, Jerusalem was razed to the ground, and all Jews were banned from it on pain of death. Indeed, a new Hellenistic city was constructed, dedicated to the Roman Jupiter Capitolinus: 'Aelia Capitolina' instead of 'Jerusalem'. The theocracy definitively came to an end.

## WHY JUDAISM SURVIVED

This was a national catastrophe worse than the exile. To the present day it is publicly lamented by Jews at the so-called West or Wailing Wall of the destroyed temple.

But amazingly enough, even without a monarchy, without a temple, without a priesthood, without a supreme council and high priest, the Jewish people survived. Indeed, the Jews survived without the whole theocratic system that had been built up since the Babylonian exile. They survived, though they were now scattered all over the world.

This survival is certainly not just a biological fact. Nor is it merely a continuum with a psychological foundation; far less is it a historical miracle. Beyond any doubt this survival of the Jewish people had to do with the survival of the Jewish religion. For it was their religion which gave the homeless people a new spiritual home. This has remained important for Orthodox Jews to the present day:

- The Torah scrolls took the place of the destroyed altar, and prayer, good works and the study of the Torah took the place of the temple cult.
- The scribes, the rabbis, took the place of the hereditary priesthood, and the status of rabbi attained by learning and study took the place of the inherited dignity of priest and levite.

Women had played a great role as tribal mothers and prophetesses, but now they were in many ways subordinated to men and separated from them in prayer and worship, as was also customary at that time for Christians and Muslims. However, for God, men and women are equal.

And both men and women may put petitions to God, written on scraps of paper, in the cracks in the Western Wall of the temple.

Now everywhere synagogues appeared in place of the one temple of Jerusalem. The synagogue was a novel type of house for assembly, prayer and community; it probably originated in the Babylonian exile, where in any case people did not have a Jewish temple. This was a revolutionary development in the history of the world religions, which became a model for both Christian churches and Muslim mosques. Synagogues became widespread in Palestine, Babylonia, North Africa and Europe.

## THE JEWISH MIDDLE AGES

Torah – rabbis – synagogue: these were now the pillars of the long Jewish Middle Ages, which began as early as the first/second century and were to last until the eighteenth century. By around 600, Judaism as it had taken form before and after the destruction of the Second Temple in 70 had been completely transformed. The messianic hope was now bound up with strict obedience to the Law with its 613 commandments (*mitzvoth*) and thus also blunted. A national religion with a messianic orientation now became completely a Torah religion.

Being part of a nation now faded right into the background, to be replaced by a ritual and moral purity which set Jews apart from all other nations, and more than ever Jews led a segregated existence. This was already ensured by the requirement of ritually pure (*kosher* = 'usable') food. In addition, eating the flesh of pigs was banned, nor could milk and meat products be consumed together during the same meal. Initially the Jews themselves wanted a separate district (later 'ghetto') to live in. They learned and discussed together in the school. Learning became an aim in life, and reading the scriptures and commentaries a favourite occupation.

So all in all, after the downfall of the Second Temple and the theocratic system a new paradigm of the rabbis and the synagogue emerged for those Jewish Middle Ages, which were not to be interrupted by a Reformation and were to end only with the modern Enlightenment. In the first centuries the centre of Judaism was again Babylon, until the caliphate of Baghdad perished in the Mongol attack of 1258. From the eighth to the eleventh century Judaism enjoyed a heyday in Spain under the caliphate of Cordoba. And finally it enjoyed a further heyday in the tenth/eleventh centuries in Central Europe and especially in Germany.

## THE FORMATION OF ORTHODOX JUDAISM

Now the Jews lived in a ghetto which had been forced upon them. Two things in particular were important for their life there:
– The rabbis, the scribes, were now the dominant force in Judaism. And they exclusively came from the 'pious' = 'Pharisaic' trend, the only one of the parties within Judaism to survive the catastrophes of 70 and 135. The separatist Pharisaic form of life became the rabbinic form of life. And the rabbi became the norm and model for his community.
– The rabbis were the ones who incessantly commented on the Torah (the five books of Moses). Now the Torah was revered in worship like a queen, clothed in velvet and silk, adorned with silver and crowned. A fifty-fourth portion was read every sabbath, so that the whole Torah was heard in one year.

Thus already in the first post-Christian centuries an oral Torah appeared alongside the original written, biblical Torah: first of all the Mishnah, which comprised the whole religious law of the oral tradition, and later the Gemara, which in turn commentated on the Mishnah. Both together formed the Talmud. With its bewildering abundance of expositions, narratives and discussions this still forms the normative foundation for religious teaching and religious law for Orthodox Judaism. The Bible (the extent of which was now laid down canonically) gave way to the oral tradition, which had equal rights. Allegedly it had likewise already been revealed on Sinai.

This medieval rabbinic paradigm also still remains alive in the state of Israel, in so far as the chief rabbinate there has a dominant influence on religious, private and family law. The result of this is a fundamental conflict between the Orthodox and secular Jews. But by comparison with the significance of the oral tradition in Catholicism, where it is also important, rabbinic Judaism is less interested in right faith ('orthodoxy') than in right action in conformity with the Law ('orthopraxy'). All the numerous commandments and prohibitions of both the written and the oral Torah are unconditionally to be regarded as God's revelation: the regulations about the sabbath, purity or food and about prayer and worship.

The numerous commandments covered the whole day (from early to late), the whole course of the year (work days, sabbaths and festival days) and the whole course of life: from birth and circumcision through sexual maturity, marriage and family, to death and burial. But what stamped rabbinic piety and lifestyle in this medieval paradigm was not complaint about the burden of the Law but rather gratitude for the Law, God's great gift to humankind, and joy in the fulfilment of the Law. However, the shadow side was a now almost complete religious and social self-segregation from all that was not Jewish, the foundations of which had already been laid in the Babylonian exile.

## ANTI-JUDAISM IN THE CHRISTIAN CHURCH

The non-Jewish world often reacted to the survival of Jews, not with respect but with aggression and repression. Even in pre-Christian times there was a 'pagan' anti-Judaism: the first pogrom of Jews in world history took place in Alexandria in AD 38. And finally a Christian ecclesiastical anti-Judaism developed out of the pagan anti-Judaism. From around the time of the Emperor Constantine this no longer expressed itself sporadically, to a limited degree and in an unofficial way, like the pagan anti-Judaism, but permanently and universally. Judaism was officially cast off and undermined by the Christian church – because of the Jewish rejection of the Messiah Jesus and their guilt for his crucifixion. However, Constantine did not enact special church and state laws against the Jews, accompanied by repressive measures; these were decreed only by the Christian Emperor Theodosius II in the fifth century and by Justinian in the sixth. Both these decrees governed the medieval legislation enacted about the Jews by both state and church.

However, Jewish history in Christian times must not be depicted just as a history of suffering. As more recent Jewish historians in particular have established, over large areas it was an amazing history of success: up to the beginning of the Crusades largely good relations prevailed between the Christians and the Jewish minorities, who were able to assert themselves far better in the Christian empire than any other minority or small people.

## THE JEWS IN MEDIEVAL GERMANY: WORMS

The city of Worms was the location of the oldest Jewish communities in Germany, which are attested historically as early as the tenth century. However, Jews had already come to the Rhine with the Roman legions. The Jews in Worms had a synagogue from the eleventh century on, and even earlier their own cemetery, the oldest in Europe, which still exists today.

From the middle of the eleventh century to the end of the Middle Ages Worms was a spiritual centre of European Jewry. Henry IV gave the Jews of Worms some privileges in 1084; they were directly under the jurisdiction of the king. Great Jewish scholars, 'the wise men of Worms', worked in the talmudic school in Worms. It was here that Rabbi Solomon ben Isaac, called Rashi (1040–1105), was active. For a long time he was regarded as the standard commentator on Bible and Talmud; his authority was comparable to that of the last head of the school of Babylonia (*gaon*).

But what a contrast there was between the modest synagogue and the all-powerful Christian church! At first here, too, synagogue and church lived peacefully side by side. But at the end of the eleventh century the first atrocities were perpetrated. In its historic fight against Islam the church thought it had to class the Jews with the Muslims. With the First Crusade of 1095, 'Crusaders', peasants and other people from places around attacked the Jews of Worms, settling old scores. There were 800 martyrs, some of whom in their despair first killed their children and then killed or burned themselves.

The community reconstituted itself, but there were also persecutions in the thirteenth and fourteenth centuries, and many Jewish communities by the Rhine and the Moselle were exterminated. The year 1349 was another nadir, when the plague was everywhere attributed to the Jews and relatively few even in Worms could escape massacre. As we know, even the Reformation – with Luther's decisive appearance at the Diet of Worms – brought no relief for the Jews.

However, the rabbinate at Worms with the Chief Rabbi continued to provide the norms for German Jews. And the mikveh, the bath of cleansing at the synagogue, remained in use. Those who had made themselves ritually unclean through touching a dead body or through menstruation could cleanse themselves by immersing themselves in 'living', flowing water, in this case rain water that had been collected.

The homeless Jews were expelled in hundreds of thousands from France and England and later also from Spain and Portugal. The consequence was a great migration of the Jews ('Ashkenasy') settled in Germany ('Ashkenasia'). In the sixteenth and seventeenth centuries the economic and cultural centre of Judaism shifted to Poland, a land which offered a refuge and gave scope for development.

## JEWISH SECRET TEACHING: KABBALA

The tremendous pressure of suffering was also essentially responsible for the fact that above all after their expulsion from Spain in 1492, at the time of the Reformation, masses of Jews explored the secret teaching or Kabbala (= mystical 'tradition'). This was a Jewish form of 'gnosis', already developed from an earlier period, which aimed at 'knowledge' of the mysteries of the Godhead. This was said to be the real content of the Torah. Indeed, some kabbalists even attempted to lead people to a state of being filled with God in ecstasy and joy.

The kabbalistic movement reached its high point between the fourteenth and the seventeenth centuries and increasingly took on messianic features. But this very connection with Jewish messianism was an essential factor in its decline during the seventeenth and eighteenth centuries. For two successive pseudo-Messiahs, who had a tremendous following, were both ultimately converted to Islam. So the Kabbala was unable to develop a special new paradigm for Judaism, which remained with the rabbinic paradigm.

The kabbalistic piety that still remained ultimately came to be concentrated in the East European Hassidim, 'the pious'. They were frustrated by dry rabbinism. They thought that prayer and union with God in everyday life were more important than all the tedious study of the Torah. So they cultivated a piety of ardour and joy with an emphasis on the feelings. This was often accompanied with ecstasy, miracles and visions. Joyful loud ceremonies in their own house of prayer and enthusiastic or meditative prayer which was often also focused on the letters of the Bible are still popular among the Hassidim even today. Figures of suffering and salvation, the righteous or the holy, play a great role here. All in all this was a special religious world which prolonged the Jewish Middle Ages into modernity.


## JEWISH ENLIGHTENMENT: MOSES MENDELSSOHN

However, this medieval 'pious' Judaism was now challenged by modernity in Europe, which in the seventeenth century made a powerful beginning with new philosophy, science and state constitutions. However, it was more marked in Western and Central Europe than in Eastern Europe, which was retrograde both politically and socially. Jews were involved everywhere from the beginning: in the foundation of the modern colonial economy, in the development of a modern European system of business and finance, in realizing the modern state and also in laying the foundations for a modern rational philosophy. But the expulsion from the synagogue in Amsterdam in 1656 of the young philosopher Baruch de Spinoza, the ancestor of modern biblical criticism and the representative of a new all-embracing understanding of God, is symptomatic of the crisis of Jewish Orthodoxy.

Only in the eighteenth century did a man now emerge in Berlin who could claim to be both Jewish and modern at the same time. He was the philosopher, writer and critic Moses Mendelssohn. He became the initiator, symbol and idol of the specific Jewish form of Enlightenment (haskala). From Berlin he exercised an influence all over Central and North-Eastern Europe. He was the first really modern Jew. He defended

Judaism both wisely and passionately as a religion of reason, which he tried to combine with a faithful observance of the traditional Jewish duties and rites.

Thus by his enlightened Jewish philosophy of religion and the use of the German language, Moses Mendelssohn prepared for the integration of Jews into German society; indeed, he embodied this in his person. He encouraged the adoption of Western culture by Judaism and at the same time a general education for Jewish boys and girls in the schools. Mendelssohn was a friend of Gotthold Ephraim Lessing (1729–81). Lessing used this most significant figure of the German Enlightenment, who argued firmly for tolerance, freedom and humanity, as a model for his Nathan the Wise. For Lessing, Mendelssohn composed a posthumous apologia, which he completed a few days before his death in 1786. Three years afterwards the political turning point indeed came – not, however, in Berlin but in Paris.

## EXIT FROM THE GHETTO

The French Revolution brought the Jews unrestricted citizenship – as a model for all Europe. Like the earlier American Declaration of the Rights of Man in 1776, so too the French Declaration of 1789 included the Jews. However, the unrestricted citizenship granted by the parliamentary decree was not for the Jews as a religious community but for Jews as individual citizens.

This was then also endorsed by Napoleon, who appointed a 'Grand Sanhédrin' and with his armies initially also imposed the Code Napoléon on Germany. There it was to lead to the third fruitful interaction in world history between Jewish culture and an alien culture – after the interaction between Jews and Hellenistic civilization in Alexandria and between the Jews and the Moors in Spain. Finally the walls of the ghetto fell even in the papal states – in 1870, immediately after the definition of papal infallibility – with the invasion of Rome by the Italian army of liberation.

Only in Eastern Europe did the Jewish masses, almost untouched by the Enlightenment, remain under the influence of Hassidism. Sparked off by pogroms (Russian for massacre) and compulsory measures in Russia, Romania and Poland, this was to lead to renewed wanderings of the Jews: this time back to the West, to Western Europe and finally to the United States.

So from the nineteenth century on the Jews were fully exposed to the spirit of modernity, earlier and in a more radical way than the Muslims. Now there was also an exodus from the cultural ghetto. In Germany in particular there was a great discussion about the reform of Judaism. With its rigorous asceticism the early Jewish 'back to the Bible' movement of the 'Karaites' (from *kara'im* = 'readers') which was very widespread from the ninth to the twelfth centuries had not yet been able to consolidate itself in the face of the rabbinic establishment; and there had been no Jewish Reformation, which could have been the presupposition for a Jewish Enlightenment. But now, conversely, the rational Enlightenment formed the presupposition for a religious reformation of Judaism. A historical-critical science of Judaism developed, and Jewish students thronged into the professions that were now open to them. They became attorneys or doctors; however, posts in the civil service were still closed to them.

## MODERN REFORM JUDAISM

Throughout Western Europe (though not in Eastern Europe) a change now took place, from the medieval-rabbinic paradigm of the dispersed people of God to the modern assimilation paradigm of enlightened Reform Judaism. Under German-Jewish influence this new overall constellation of a national and cultural assimilation of the Jews became established to an even greater degree in the United States. Here, after the early immigration of Sephardic Jews in the seventeenth and eighteenth centuries (the Touro synagogue in Newport, Rhode Island, is visible evidence of this), there was a mass immigration of often highly educated German-speaking Jews and rabbis.

What were the goals of the Jewish reform? In brief:

- Instead of medieval segregation, Jews aimed at the legal, political and social integration of both individuals and the 'cultic community' into the modern nation state.
- Instead of the traditional rabbinic-talmudic education, Jews wanted to have a modern general education.
- Instead of rabbis who were legal experts and judges, now rabbis held office who had an academic education and were active as preachers, pastors, liturgists and teachers.
- Instead of a ghetto life there was now a modernization of the whole Jewish lifestyle from dress to diet.
- Instead of a largely incomprehensible liturgy a Reformed Jewish liturgy was now celebrated in the vernacular, with preaching and music and with no segregation of the sexes.

All in all, this was an amazing religious and cultural reformation. Even in synagogue architecture and art, as for example in the Reform Synagogue in Berlin, an effort was made to achieve a living synthesis between modernity and tradition. New ways were also taken in music. The Berlin composer Louis Lewandowski was the most influential figure here in the

Jewish world of the West. His recitatives, performed by the cantor, were traditionally Jewish. But his choral works were in the style of Felix Mendelssohn-Bartholdy, grandson of the great Moses Mendelssohn.


## THE DISPUTE OVER TRENDS

But now in the United States in particular, as previously in Germany, powerful counter-forces made themselves felt: there was an Orthodox Judaism, a secularized Judaism and, in the middle, a conservative Judaism. The consequence is that even today the different Jewish groupings in the United States, Europe and Israel live in different currents (denominations), in divergent paradigms which came into being at different times. In Judaism the divisions are not over dogmas but over how to put the Law into practice, and especially over the regulations relating to the sabbath, cleanness and the food laws.

At this stage four main currents can be distinguished:
– The Orthodox, the preservers of tradition, who regard all religious commandments as having been revealed by God and therefore argue that religious practice should remain unchanged. Many of these Orthodox (above all from Eastern Europe) still live spiritually in the Middle Ages and go about on the streets of New York, London and Berlin wearing the dress of the country population of seventeenth-century Poland.
– The Reformed or Liberals, who feel completely at home in modernity. Reform Judaism seeks reconciliation with modernity. It regards the message of the prophets as central. Therefore it rejects some archaic traditions and makes deep changes in worship and practices. Not only have the sermon, the pulpit, the gown, the organ and the choir been taken over from Christians. Men are no longer required to have their heads covered. Women can be ordained to the rabbinate.
– The Conservatives, who attempt to combine Orthodoxy and Enlightenment. This Conservative Judaism is open to modernity but at the same time wants to preserve the traditional religious practice and especially Hebrew in worship. The spiritual and material challenges of modernity are to be accepted as a positive factor; the tradition is not to be given up but to be developed further.
– And perhaps the largest group is that of the non-religious: in Germany and Eastern Europe, and in America initially, they even form the majority. These do not want to belong to any synagogue, do not want to have anything to do with religious practice, and at most celebrate the festivals out of tradition. They include Jewish socialists, agnostics, atheists and later Zionists. They are repelled by the rigidly legalistic Orthodoxy, have internalized the European criticism of religion (Marx and Freud are of Jewish

origin) and therefore reject any religion. Their Judaism is no longer governed by belief in God but increasingly by a 'Zionist' faith in a state of Israel.

But the experiment of the modern assimilation of Judaism was abruptly broken off, especially in Germany, where it had begun and where it had gone furthest. There are now hardly any Jewish families whose roots go back to the time of the building of the beautiful Berlin Synagogue in Pestalozzistrasse.

## EVERY INDIVIDUAL HAS A NAME

Even now it is horrific that in the land of Mendelssohn and Lessing, after initial discrimination and persecution a monstrous mass murder of around 6,000,000 Jews was set in motion. This was a unique event in contemporary history, not only because of the monstrous number of victims, but because a state had prepared for all this ideologically, planned it systematically and carried it out in an organized way.

'The aim: a so-called final solution of the question of European Jewry involves around 11,000,000 Jews.' It was with this aim that the Wannsee Conference was held at the Wannsee Villa on 20 January 1942 in the utmost secrecy. The 'annihilation of the Jewish race in Europe' which had already been threatened by Hitler in his Reichstag speech of 30 January 1939 and ordered orally on 12/18 December 1941 was to be implemented. Reinhard Heydrich, the chief of the secret police, presented the overall plan for the 'practical implementation of the final solution of the Jewish question' and the secretary, Adolf Eichmann, along with Heinrich Müller, head of the Gestapo, was responsible for organizing it. It was carried out ruthlessly and with technical and bureaucratic perfection by the whole apparatus of the state and an enormous host of helpers. Almost every professional group and institution, even at community level, was involved in discriminating against and segregating the Jews.

So this was no more and no less than the mad attempt to exterminate a whole people. Jews today call it the 'Shoah', the 'catastrophe'. Others speak of the 'Holocaust', the 'whole sacrifice', of the Jewish people. Indeed it was the will of Hitler and his minions that not only the Orthodox, who had not assimilated, but also the Reformed Jews, who were fully assimilated, indeed all Jews, including the old, children and infants, were to be exterminated.

'Every human being has a name.' It took around 28 hours on Holocaust Memorial Day (Yom ha-Shoah) to read out the 55,696 family names and first names of the deported and murdered Berlin Jews on the monument in the rebuilt New Synagogue in Berlin which stands as a warning: from Aal, Jutta to Zyzman, Leo.

The Holocaust was the result of an anti-semitism which was based on biology and race and was widespread in Europe at that time. But this would have been impossible without the almost 2000 years of theological anti-Judaism in (almost all) the Christian churches. Here the baneful silence of Pius XII and the German, Austrian and Polish bishops (not to mention the German Protestants) was a crucial factor.


## A FUTURE FOR JEWS IN GERMANY

At the end of the Second World War no one would have thought that Jewish children could again have a future in Germany in particular, far less in the old imperial capital of Berlin. For a long time a majority of Jews in Israel, Europe and America completely rejected a life in Germany after the Holocaust. But now in Berlin there is the Heinz Galinski School: a new Jewish school.

Already at the beginning of the twentieth century the Viennese lawyer and journalist Theodor Herzl had propagated the view that the Jewish people, rejected and homeless in Europe despite all the Enlightenment, again needed their own Jewish home; the people without a land needed a land without people. The first Zionist congress took place in Basel in 1897 under Herzl's leadership. It called for 'a national home for the Jewish people in Palestine'. In the course of the twentieth century, following five great waves of immigration (*aliyah*) into Palestine, resolutely carried forward, this state for the Jewish people was finally founded in 1948.

And what is offered to the children in the new Jewish school in Berlin with a great deal of effort, is quite naturally taught to the children in the state of Israel from an early age: there as a matter of course New Hebrew is the everyday language.

But however welcome these developments in Germany and in Israel are for the Jewish people, Christians must not forget **their** guilt: it is not repression but critical memory that will be of help **here**.


**THE COMPLICITY OF CHRISTIANS**

People still ask today how this monstrous catastrophe, the Shoah, could come about. It is clear that Hitler and his minions alone do not explain the whole catastrophic development. It would have been impossible without the disregard, tolerance, complicity of the leading élites in the civil service, in the army, in business, and unfortunately also in the churches.

For what would have happened if in 1933, immediately after Hitler's declaration of government, the German bishops had not capitulated, to the dismay of many Catholics, but protested?

What would have happened had the Vatican not as early as 1933 given respectability to this regime with a concordat, but had warned against this man, whose programme and book *Mein Kampf* made his aims completely clear?

What would have happened if the 14,000 Protestant pastors in Germany had clearly not only announced their reservations within the church, but also offered political resistance?

None of this happened, and it should not be said that it would have been impossible. Konrad Adenauer, a witness whose testimony is beyond suspicion, wrote in a letter of 23 February 1946: 'I believe that if on a particular day the bishops had unanimously made a public statement from the pulpits they could have prevented much. That did not happen, and there is no excuse for it.'

The Holocaust is a warning sign to the whole of humankind of what happens when we replace belief in the one God and his commandments with belief in one Führer, one Nation, one Race.

Fortunately we have moved on. In the Jewish school in Berlin it is evident that Jewish life is again possible here in the old and new capitals, indeed in the world and above all in the state of Israel.


## THE REBIRTH OF THE STATE OF ISRAEL

The Holocaust was the nadir and the conclusion of modernity. The revival of Judaism and especially the state of Israel is the starting point for a new, postmodern era. The foundation of the state of Israel is the most important event in Jewish history since the destruction of Jerusalem in AD 70.

The state of Israel which was founded in 1948 has developed enormously over the decades: economically, politically and culturally. Modern Tel Aviv is a symbol of this. There have been imposing achievements in the spheres of agriculture, technology, health, education, sport and defence. For Jews all over the world, after 2000 years the state of Israel has again provided a spiritual centre and a real homeland. However, by far the majority of the almost 6,000,000 American Jews have not wanted to go back to Israel, nor do they want to go back now – not least because of the tensions there. Reformed rabbis cannot function legally in Israel, nor can

Conservative rabbis. No Jew is circumcised, married or buried in Israel without the blessing of an Orthodox rabbi.

But to the horror of the Orthodox 'up' in Jerusalem, where many men exclusively study Torah and Talmud at the state's expense instead of earning their own living, 'down' by the sea, in modern Tel Aviv, only founded in 1901, with its 1,000,000 inhabitants, the atmosphere is not very religious; indeed it is highly secular. And today Western secularism is the basic attitude of many Israelis. However, for the Orthodox such a life void of religion amounts to giving up Judaism. What is the use of a purely worldly life without orientation on the tradition? Without the study of Torah and Talmud?

Only a few turn to the modern sects, for example those from India. By contrast, there are countless secularists who have prescribed for themselves a political substitute religion: 'Israel over all'. This is an Israelism fixated on the Holocaust as the centre of Jewish history.

The state with the emblem of the menorah, the seven-branched lampstand, is a parliamentary democracy with a modern administration, army and police, and modern science, business and trade unions. However, today Israelis hardly ever speak of a moral Jewish 'model state'. Some of them hope for a change in the fundamentalist-religious legislation and an end to the authoritarian politics of occupation.

In the 1930s and 1940s Jewish freedom fighters, at that time called 'terrorists', also attempted to implement their legitimate claim to self-determination with violent means. In the 1970s and 1980s Palestinian freedom fighters did the same, and again were called 'terrorists'. But neither side achieved peace through armed struggle. The Palestinians feel that their treatment by the Israelis is humiliating. The Israelis have a legitimate need for security. To most Israelis, however, it is clear that being the strongest military power in the Middle East will not be enough legitimation for Israel in the long term.

**THE PALESTINE QUESTION**

Israel could become a mediating peaceful bridge country in the Middle East. Theodor Herzl's dream is only half fulfilled. Israel has a land but no peace.

Israel was not a land without people, which the people without a land could simply enter. A Muslim Arab population has been settled here for around a millennium, and it is to them that we owe the great walls and gates: the Damascus Gate, for example, the entrance to Arab Jerusalem.

The Palestinian problem is so to speak the shadow side of the state of Israel. There have been five wars in five decades. But today many Israelis, too, see that a people of barely 6,000,000 Jews can flourish only if it has peace with the 140,000,000 Arabs around and also gives the Palestinians the right to a state.

However, there will be peace in the Middle East only if the ethnic and religious resentments and aggressions are broken down on both sides. More than anywhere else it is true here that there can be no peace among the nations without peace between the religions.

## TWO OLIVE BRANCHES

In the Israeli coat of arms, the menorah, the seven-branched lampstand, is the symbol of Jewish identity and history. But the menorah is framed by two olive branches. They are meant to express the longing of the Jewish people for peace. At a time when the European states, the former 'arch-enemies' Germany and France, Germany and Poland, and also the United States and Russia have sought and found peace and collaboration, it must be possible also to create a peaceful future for Israelis and Palestinians, between Jews and Arabs, in the crisis area of the Middle East. Indeed, especially in the Middle East, after living side by side for centuries and finally lining up against one another, Jews, Christians and Muslims need to achieve

- responsibility for one another;
- trust in and ways to one another;
- conversations and encounters with one another, with no intention of conversion, but aimed rather at furthering justice, freedom and solidarity.

But no Israeli government can ignore the fundamentalist Orthodox, even if they are only a minority. And these want a Judaism dominated by religion. They still live in a medieval counter-world: 'the Law over all'. Everyone is to observe the halakhah, the religious law: from a rigorous observance of the sabbath through the commandments about food and cleanness to the segregation of the sexes.

## JUDAISM BETWEEN SECULARISM
## AND FUNDAMENTALISM

Every religion today is involved in a basic conflict between tradition and innovation. And in Judaism in particular, all the religious problems of the beginning of the third millennium are concentrated as in a burning glass. As the oldest of the three prophetic religions, Judaism can certainly see itself as independent of the other two and so it apparently does not need to engage in dialogue. But most Jews even now live as a minority among a Christian or Muslim majority population; they are dependent on this population and its government, and so despite everything are dependent on others. Indeed, time and again cultural and spiritual changes have taken place.

But more and more Jews are aware of the period of time that separates them from the Holocaust; they see how problematical it is to derive Jewish identity only from the trauma of annihilation. As for example in the Beit Daniel synagogue in Tel Aviv, there is a concern for a Judaism which has a religious foundation and at the same time is contemporary, rooted in faith in the one God and expressed in the Shema Israel, 'Hear, Israel': 'Hear, Israel, the Lord our God, the Lord is one' (Deut. 6.4).

Thus the central element of Jewish faith has been preserved and what was never lost over more than 3000 years, through all the eras of history, has been revived: belief in God and his covenant with his people.

A renewed Jewish religion is founded on the Torah, which is not to be followed slavishly. Such a religion can also give Jews today a spiritual home.

– It reminds them of the great religious tradition of the people.
– It shapes the cycle of life from birth to death, structures the cycle of the year with the great festivals, stamps the cycle of the week in the alternation of weekday and sabbath, and supports the cycle of the day with prayer and commandments.

At the end of worship the Torah scrolls are rolled up again, wrapped up and shut away. The young people are cheered on with songs and sweets. For the members of the synagogue, worship gives joy and strength for everyday living. Theirs is an everyday life in which a middle way has to be taken: one must not isolate and encapsulate oneself, but one must not become totally assimilated and fuse completely with secular society either.

## THE DECALOGUE AS AN ABC OF HUMAN BEHAVIOUR

How far modern Judaism still is from this middle way between a religionless secularism and a fanatical fundamentalism became evident in the middle of Tel Aviv, where the Israeli Prime Minister Itzhak Rabin was murdered.

Here Judaism should have contributed its whole tremendous religious and ethical legacy to this new world era. For there is hardly any other people which has something as substantial and striking to offer as Judaism with its Ten Commandments.

As the German writer Thomas Mann explained after the terrors of National Socialism, these are the 'basic instruction and rock of respectable humanity', indeed the 'ABC of human behaviour'.

And this 'ABC of human behaviour' must also be applied to global politics and global economics in a time of globalization.

– Of course, global politics must recognize national interests, the real divisions of power. But that does not mean that the political end hallows all means, that the political end also hallows political murder, treachery, even war.

– And of course the global economy, too, has to recognize particular economic laws and consider the practicability of implementing all that it has to offer. But again that does not mean that profit, however justified it may be, hallows all means, including breaches of trust, including boundless avarice and social exploitation.

Without a global ethic, global politics and global economics threaten to end in global chaos. At all events, without a global ethic there can be no better world order, an order which brings more justice.

## WHAT WILL THE FUTURE BE?

At present no one knows how the cultural battle between the secular and the religious will turn out.

It is certain that the people in Israel also yearn for peace, for friendship, for love and for a successful life. Judaism, this religion of admirable continuity, vitality and dynamics, will certainly find a way here and elsewhere to a future in which it becomes possible to experience what one of its primal words says every day: Shalom, God's peace for the people and the peoples.

# VI

# *Christianity*

## IS CHRISTIANITY TO BE DESPAIRED OF?

Shall we find the essence of Christianity in the slums of Latin America? Many people have written off Christianity; they despair of it. They have turned their backs on the churches. They identify Christianity with bureaucracy and pomp, with doctrinal dictates, hostility to sex and misogyny. They see an authoritarian institutional church which is lacking in insight.

Of course, all this can also be found in San Salvador, the capital of the smallest and at the same time the most densely populated republic of Central America (it has 6,000,000 inhabitants, 93 per cent of whom are Catholics). But there is more than that. Among the flood of poor people living below the fenced and fortified villas of the white upper class in the wretched district of La Chacra, where around 20,000 people are living in miserable hovels, for many Christianity is a great hope.

The people here identify Christianity simply with their pastor, the Jesuit father Daniel Sanchez. For almost fifteen years now he has looked after all the physical and spiritual concerns of these people. In a time when there is an utter lack of priests, from the grass roots he has built up a living community life with a whole series of small teams for worship, singing, catechesis, helping neighbours. Here the church is not a 'holy rule', a 'hierarchy', but a fellowship of believers, *Iglesia popular*, as it is alive in countless slums and villages of Latin America.

## A LIVING CHRISTIAN COMMUNITY

Here the priest is not the lordly figure in a two-class church made up of clergy and laity but rather the servant of the faith community. Of course, this community is delighted that it still has a pastor. Without his inspiration, co-ordination, leadership and sometimes even mediation, much would be impossible.

El Salvador is the country with the highest crime rate on the whole continent; several people are murdered every day. But Daniel Sanchez need not fear, since he is constant contact with all the people here, who value him and love him. He and his fellow-workers, men and women, attempt to bring about at least on a small scale a culture of non-violence, social justice and peace in the face of a culture of violence. Here Christianity is being lived out.

For example, there is a celebration of Mothering Sunday, and so the mothers are particularly welcomed and valued. The preacher sees a mother's love in the light of the love of God himself, who is both Father and Mother to us – and that notion causes no offence here.

There is much that is reminiscent of the earliest Christianity. As in Paul's church in Corinth, in this worship everyone has something to say. Women, too, tell of their experiences and read the Bible as if this were personally written for them. They recognize themselves again in the earliest Christian communities. Here the women are not silent in the assembled community, as they are told to be in an authentic passage in Paul, but take it for granted that they can speak. All pray and sing together and celebrate the eucharist. This is a church which understands itself to be the people of God.


## LITURGY AND SOCIAL COMMITMENT

But at the same time it is clear to everyone here that the Christian faith must have practical consequences. It cannot in any way justify oppression and exploitation, but must try to overcome them. The service of God and the service of fellow men and women, liturgy and social commitment, belong together. However, in the time of the military dictatorship, those who pressed for social reforms and human rights were in danger and feared for their lives, even at the altar.

One name stands for many of these people: Oscar Romero, the Archbishop of El Salvador. He had grown up in the church establishment. But the tremendous need of his people and the murder of a priest who was his friend changed his life. He became a committed defender of the rights of his oppressed people, and in 1980 he had to pay for that at the altar with his life.

**WHAT IS THE ESSENCE OF CHRISTIANITY?**

If one stands at the place from which Monseñor Romero was shot at the altar, directly from a car, one quickly becomes aware what Christianity is all about. Of course, one could also cite the Protestant theologian and resistance fighter Dietrich Bonhoeffer, or the American

civil rights activist and pastor Martin Luther King, or the Polish priest Jerzy Popieluszko, and countless others. Common to them all is that:
- They were committed Christians.
- They stood up for their people in a non-violent way.
- And they were all eliminated with brute force.

In this way, however, they have all become like the one who was their model in living, suffering and fighting: Jesus of Nazareth.

That brings us to the centre of things. What really is the essence of Christianity? The essence of Christianity is not, as some people think, a great theory, a world-view, or even a church system. It is simply and solely this Jesus Christ.

And all those who attempt to orientate their whole personal agendas – and every man or woman has his or her own agenda – on this Jesus Christ are Christians. Basically no organization, no institution and no church can honestly call itself 'Christian' unless it can truly appeal to him in word and deed.

## WITNESSES OF FAITH

I could never have imagined it: in 1989, nine years after the murder of Romero, here in San Salvador my friends, six Jesuit professors in the Universidad Centroamericana, run by the Order, where I had been their guest in 1987, were brutally murdered by a death squad. The victims were six fathers, including the Rector of the University, Ignacio Ellacuria, and two servants. Jon Sobrino, one of the best-known liberation theologians, who happened to be travelling abroad at the time, is the only one of my friends left in San Salvador. I could hardly recognize them on the fearful photographs of the shooting.

They were teachers at the university, and at the same time for decades had devoted themselves to the poorest of the poor, who according to the Bible are given God's special care. None of them wanted to become a martyr. None of them was an ascetic: they were all quite normal people, but committed Christians. They simply wanted to live their lives in accordance with the will of God. That meant devoting themselves to the good of their fellow human beings, as disciples of the crucified Jesus. So they did not preach intolerance, hatred and violence, but openness to all, goodness, the practice of forgiveness and solidarity, love of God and love of neighbour: loving the other as one loves oneself.

The spirit of this Jesus was alive in all these figures, as it has been in countless others who in their own way are credible and committed representatives of Christianity, honest witnesses to a faith which is orientated on Jesus himself. There are many who are united by an orientation on the concrete human figure of Jesus, who from the beginning has been called 'Christ', 'Anointed', 'Messiah': among them are Albert Schweitzer, the doctor in the primal forest; Dag Hammaskjøld, the UN Secretary-General; Pope John XXIII; Patriarch Athenagoras; Archbishop Helder Camara; Archbishop Desmond Tutu; Mother Teresa; Abbé Pierre.

All these people believed in the Christian cause because it is embodied in this one person, unique, unrepeatable and indispensable.

– Only through his spirit has Christianity remained present as a spiritual power. The Christ is its basic inspiration.

– Only through his name are the writings of the New Testament which are so diverse, and the Christian churches, which again are so diverse, held together. The Christ is their founder figure.

– Only on the basis of his history does something like a shining 'golden thread' run through the fabric of church history, which is often torn and dark, but is constantly woven afresh. In all of Christian tradition, liturgy, theology and piety, Christ forms the basic motif which for all the decadence has never been completely lost.

But precisely for that reason, time and again we need to reflect on the origins: on the Bible, the foundation document; and on Jesus Christ, the founder figure. He, and not Christianity as it really exists at any particular time; he, and not some authority from state or church, is the criterion for what is Christian. The decisive thing must be to live as closely as possible to this origin, this foundation, this centre.


## A JOYFUL MESSAGE

Yet we know this Jesus only over a vast span of time. And every people and every generation has the right to bring out its own dimension of this unique figure. However, here the criterion must not be a dreamed-up Christ but a real Christ: the quite concrete human figure who is quite irreplaceable in history.

Indeed, all the prominent Christians of our century make it clear in their own way that the decisive features of the leading figure to whom they relate are quite unique. Certainly, we can argue over many of the details in the New Testament sources, all of which were composed by human beings, but this New Testament is far and away the most closely studied book in world literature. And there have been virtually countless investigations of each of its sentences in every possible language. There are lengthy dissertations on almost every word used in it. Many of the details are unclear or can be interpreted in different ways.

However, for the Christian witnesses of our century the decisive feature of the message of Jesus was completely clear. He brought the good news of a new freedom: a refusal to allow oneself to be dominated by avarice and a desire for prestige, the will to power, sexual drives and the quest for enjoyment and pleasure, and a desire to become free for God and for one's fellow human beings. Men and women are not to become ascetics; we know very well that Jesus took part in banquets. But people should not selfishly look after their own interests and satisfy their own needs.

Rather, the important thing is to live in accordance with God's will, with an eye for the kingdom of God, and to keep the well-being of one's neighbours in view: the important thing is not to want to dominate them but to try to serve them. The important thing is to show a new solidarity with the weak, the insignificant and the poor, to practise goodness and forgiveness. It is important not just to observe commandments, not to kill, lie, steal, commit adultery, but to be unpretentiously committed to one's fellow men and women, in a love which also respects opponents and does not liquidate the enemy. This is a message of non-violence, mercy and peace.

## A DRAMATIC FATE

Had Jesus died a normal death at a great age in Galilee, that remote corner of the Roman empire, his sayings, his parables, and the so-called Sermon on the Mount would hardly have been handed down to posterity. For the force of his message has to do with his dramatic fate, which came to a climax in the holy city of Jerusalem.

The Jew Jesus did not proclaim a Jewish divine state or the establishment of a church. Rather, he preached the coming kingdom of God with its promises and its standards. But what he said and what he did led to a confrontation with the religious and political establishment: a life-and-death conflict. The way in which he dealt with the religious law, with the regulations about sabbath, cleanness and food, was too liberal for them. His solidarity with the poor, the wretched, the 'poor devils', was too scandalous: he took pity on the people. He paid too much attention to those who broke the law, the 'sinners', thus offending the pious. In the case of the individual, endless forgiveness, renunciation without getting anything in return, service without hierarchy – those were the focal points of his parables and his actions.

This was a historical conflict involving a historical figure: whenever Jesus wanted to go to the temple he had to go along a street built under King Herod (it has been rediscovered only in recent excavations). Today we can also see the entrance to the temple where Jesus' conflict with the religious establishment of his time escalated. And the protest action against the temple trade, its hierarchy and those who benefited from it, was probably Jesus' decisive provocation, which finally led to his arrest and condemnation. Today, likewise, all we can still see is the old entrance arch (which has long since been walled in). The temple court where Jesus taught and disputed has been preserved. Finally, on the other side of the city, the Roman praetorium can be identified. Here Jesus of Nazareth was condemned as a political revolutionary by the Roman governor Pontius Pilate, though he was nothing of the sort.

His fearful end is known, and the church of the Holy Sepulchre recalls it all: he died as a young man of around 30, after an amazingly short activity of at most three years, perhaps only a few months. He was betrayed and denied by his disciples and followers; he was mocked and scorned by his opponents. He was abandoned by God and his fellow men and women. He died in the most cruel way, with a form of death which according to Roman legislation could not be inflicted on criminals who were Roman citizens. Only escaped slaves and political rebels died in this way, on the cross. The last sign of life from the tormented man was a cry. Since then the cross has been the distinguishing mark of Christians. And it is the cross that makes it possible for them also to cope with the negative elements in human life and society: suffering, guilt, meaninglessness and death.

## APPOINTED SON OF GOD

It is still a real question even today: how could the shameful cross of Jesus become the sign of salvation for the first believers? It is a fact that they soon saw the cross in a quite different light. Why? On the basis of particular spiritual experiences, visions, 'appearances' and at the same time patterns of interpretation from the Hebrew Bible, they had come to the conclusion that this Jesus had not remained dead but had been raised by God to eternal life, had been received up into God's glory.

How was that to be imagined? We cannot either conceptualize or find an apt image of the reality of God; even art comes up against its limits here. But since then Christians have been convinced that this Jesus Christ did not die into nothing, but into the most real reality, into God himself.

Already during his lifetime this enthusiastic and prophetic figure, without office or title, but only with words and acts of healing, claimed an authority which transcended that of a rabbi or prophet. Some saw him as the Messiah. To justify himself in the great dispute he always appealed to God himself, whom he dared to address with scandalous familiarity as 'Abba' ('Dear Father'). On the basis of their resurrection experiences he was invoked by the earliest community as 'Son of God' – a title which had previously been reserved for the kings of Israel.

But whatever the many titles given him may be, Jesus is and has himself remained the living embodiment of his cause. With him the kingdom of God has dawned for Christians. They follow him and his way. The crucified Christ is the great sign of hope for eternal life, as the beginning of Paul's letter to the Romans says: he has been 'designated Son of God in power by resurrection from the dead' (Rom.1. 4). But it is also a historical fact that the divine sonship of Jesus became a sign of division: first between Christians and Jews and then also between Christians and Muslims. This was a tragedy of religious history.

### THE COMMON ROOTS OF JUDAISM, CHRISTIANITY AND ISLAM

Probably in no other place in the world are the oppositions between Judaism, Christianity and Islam more intensively experienced than in Jerusalem.

Nevertheless, it would be foolish to want a priori to set these three prophetic religions against one another. For the first Christians remained integrated into Judaism. They read the same Hebrew Bible, prayed the same Psalms, even observed the Jewish Law and the sabbath. They performed the baptism of John and broke the bread at supper – but now in the name of Jesus.

As soon as we compare the three religions of Near Eastern origin with the religions of the two other great religious river systems of India and China, it immediately becomes clear that they have far more in common than everything that separates them.

1. All three, Judaism, Christianity and Islam, are religions of faith. They believe in the one God; and Arab Christians also address God with the name Allah.

2. All three have a historical stamp: they do not think in cosmic cycles, but in the light of God's creation look towards a consummation of the world and human life.

3. All three have been shaped by great prophetic figures: they are not mystical religions but prophetic religions in the historical sense.

4. All three have set down their message in holy scriptures: they are something like religions of the book.

5. All three have a common basic ethic: great commandments for humankind which they feel to be the will of God himself.

## THE GREAT DISPUTE IN THE EARLIEST CHURCH

There is still a dispute among Jews as to how far they need to observe the religious law beyond a fundamental ethic. This was a question which was also disputed among the first Christians.

The first members of the earliest community in Jerusalem were all Jews, regardless of whether they spoke Aramaic or Greek. But when the first non-Jews wanted to join the young Christian community, the conflict came to a head: the first Christians took it for granted that they should observe the Torah and its ethical demands. But a dispute increasingly arose over whether those who believed in Christ, even if they were of non-Jewish origin, should observe all the 613 cultic and ritual commandments of the Jewish law, the halakah. Did the Gentile Christians in fact have to adopt the Jewish way of life: circumcision, festivals, the countless regulations relating to the sabbath, cleanness and food?

So the first great controversy in the earliest Christian community was not over dogmas like the divine sonship of Christ or the Trinity, but over the Jewish religious law. How far had the Jewish religious law still to be observed? Was it also to be compulsory for those who believed in Christ, who were not born Jews but Gentiles?

No, said the apostle Paul, a Jewish Christian who had grown up in a Hellenistic milieu, in the city of Tarsus (today in southern Turkey), and who was responsible for the Gentile mission. On the basis of the experience he had at his call (his 'Damascus experience') he felt authorized to proclaim Jesus, the Messiah of Israel, as Messiah of the whole world: not just of the Jews but also of the Gentiles.

The test case came very soon. It was sparked off by what is still one of the most important questions of the Jewish religious law: what may one eat? What is 'kosher' ('clean') and what is not? Associated with this was the question: who eats with whom? In 48, an 'apostolic council' in Jerusalem seemed to have found a compromise which Gentile Christians could accept: freedom from the religious law – but only for believers of Gentile origin.

But there was nevertheless a further conflict, in the Syrian capital, Antioch, which after Rome and Alexandria was the most important city in the empire. It was there that the first Gentile-Christian community was formed. Peter, called Cephas, 'the rock', who was responsible for the mission to the Jews, had gone there. At first he ate with the Gentile Christians, as Paul did. But he stopped doing so as soon as over-zealous adherents of James the brother of the Lord (with Peter and John one of the three pillars of the earliest community), who was a strict observer of the law, arrived from Jerusalem. These called for strictly kosher eating and segregated themselves.

Paul, who saw his whole work, the mission to the Gentiles, endangered, now passionately and publicly defended the freedom of Christians, in particular in the matter of eating together. In the second chapter of his letter to the community in the Roman province of Galatia he personally reports: 'However, when Cephas came to Antioch, then I did oppose him to his face since he was manifestly in the wrong. Before certain people from James came, he used to eat with Gentiles; but as soon as these came, he backed out and kept apart from them, for fear of the circumcised . . . and the rest of the Jews put on the same act as he did.' And Paul goes on: 'When I saw that their behaviour was not true to the gospel, I said to Cephas in front of all of them, "Since you, though you are a Jew, live like the Gentiles and not like the Jews, how can you compel the Gentiles to live like the Jews?" '

Then follow his words about the justification of the sinner by faith which were to make history: 'We (Peter and Paul) who were born Jews and not Gentiles have nevertheless learnt that someone is reckoned as upright not by practising the Law but by faith in Jesus Christ; and we too came to believe in Christ Jesus so as to be reckoned as upright by faith in Christ and not by practising the Law: since no human being can be found upright by keeping the Law.'

Thus whether Jew or Gentile, man or woman, human beings are justified by God not through the works of the Jewish ritual law but through faith and trust in God who has manifested himself in Jesus Christ. From now on Gentile Christians were free from the strict Jewish religious law.


## THE LOSS OF JEWISH ROOTS

This was certainly a local dispute, but it had historic consequences and victims. For Jewish Christianity came off worse in this controversy. Not only did it remain numerically small; with the catastrophes of the Jewish–Roman War it lost its centre, the city of Jerusalem, which is holy to all Jews. In 70 the temple was destroyed and in 135 the whole city.

The Jewish Christians went eastwards into Transjordan and spread to Babylonia and Arabia, indeed to Ethiopia and southern India. But everywhere they led a quite isolated existence. Over the decades they were denounced as heretical sects by Gentile-Christian bishops and theologians, now quite arrogant, because they wanted to combine their beliefs in Christ with the observance of the Jewish religious law (which after all was legitimate for Jewish Christians). Even more important, the Jewish Christians did not share in the development towards a 'high' Christology, expressed in Greek categories, which increasingly deified Jesus.

Very much later, Jewish Christianity in its dispersion often turned into Manichaeism and Islam. This loss of its Jewish roots did inestimable damage to Christianity. It resulted in a one-sided Hellenization of its beliefs and the way in which it ordered its life. With Jewish Christianity the bond between synagogue and church fell away.

## CHRISTIANITY BECOMES GREEK

Hellenistic Gentile Christianity had long since embarked on its tremendous triumphal course, with the bold missionary journeys of the apostle Paul which he undertook from Antioch from the 40s on. Here believers had for the first time been given the name 'Christians' (*christianoi*). Paul founded communities in Asia Minor and on the Greek coast.

Like Jesus and the earliest community, the apostle thought that he was living in the 'end time' (his view was 'apocalyptic'). That means that he expected that the end of the world would come very soon. Moreover, as his authentic letters attest, he did not appoint any permanent church hierarchy: there was no episcopate (bishops) and no presbyterate (elders). Nor did he practise the laying-on of hands or ordination. Rather, he left behind communities with authorities and functions which were charismatic and 'democratic'. All the members had different gifts, tasks and charisms: they formed a fellowship of brothers and sisters in freedom and equality. For here women, too, took on important functions of leadership. All in all this was an ideal of the earliest Christian community which many churches today still remember.

Paul's letters were written in Greek, at that time the international language for communication between urban populations. The four Gospels, the Acts of the Apostles, indeed all the New Testament writings have been handed down to posterity only in Greek, with the exception of a few Aramaic words like *maranatha* ('Lord, come'). With Paul the transition from Jewish Christianity (partly Hebrew- and Aramaic-speaking and partly Greek-speaking) to an exclusively Greek (and only later Latin) Christianity was ushered in. The loss of Jewish Christianity was not, it seems, to be lamented. For a Christianity reconciled with the Greek world could now become a universal religion for humankind which embraced and united all peoples, cultures and continents.

## THE HIERARCHY IS ESTABLISHED

In Antioch in Syria, one or two generations after Paul, as is attested by Luke's Acts of the Apostles, the Pastoral Letters and the letters of Ignatius of Antioch, for practical reasons a 'hierarchy', a 'holy rule', became established: this was a monarchical episcopate, indeed a three-tiered hierarchy of offices made up of bishops, presbyters (priests) and deacons. Soon it was also predominant in the Pauline communities, and from the Eastern churches also found its way to the West and to Rome. However, according to the New Testament evidence there can be no question of an 'institution' of this hierarchy of offices by Christ or the apostles: nor – despite all the church ideology – can it be declared to be immutable. Rather, like the exclusive 'apostolic succession of the bishops' (isolated from the pastors and laity) it is the result of a historical development which presumably could hardly have been avoided. Churches *can* be ordered in this way, but they need not be.

All along the line, a Graeco-Hellenistic theology became established in place of the Jewish-Christian theology (which has been handed down only in a few documents). Of course, the first creeds and the first Roman eucharistic prayer were formulated in Greek. In the briefest space of time, in this way a Christianity with a Hellenistic colouring spread throughout the then inhabited world, the ecumene: all over the Roman empire from the Caspian Sea and the Black Sea to Spain and Britain. In contrast to the vanishing Jewish Christianity, there was a doubtless imposing world-wide 'ecumenical' Hellenistic paradigm of Christianity.

## A SILENT REVOLUTION 'FROM BELOW'

For almost three centuries the Christians had been an oppressed and sometimes also persecuted minority. But in a silent revolution 'from below' this unpolitical, peace-loving little Jewish 'sect' of Christians developed the power to change the world. Slowly it became the world religion through which East and West were to be bound more closely together than even through Alexander the Great.

Beyond doubt the new religion in its first decades was a moral power which changed society in the spirit of Jesus by a new ethical ideal:
– Its action was not simply in good Roman style, in accordance with law, custom or class morality, contributing as spectacularly as possible to one's own praise and glory.
– Rather, it was action from a spiritual centre, from an undivided and simple heart, which recognized fellow men and women as brothers and

sisters. This led to an constant everyday solidarity with the marginalized, the suffering and the poor, and an organized concern for the needy, the sick, the orphans, widows, travellers, prisoners and the old. There is no question that down all the centuries which followed, the spirit of Jesus of Nazareth kept establishing itself, despite all the failures of individuals, institutions and constitutions, wherever not only words were spoken but quite practical discipleship in his name took place.

The inculturation of Christianity proved successful to a breadth and depth hitherto unprecedented: instead of being confined to its rural, Palestinian, Near Eastern homeland, Christianity was now inculturated in the Hellenistic-Roman world culture. In the third century, great theologians like the Alexandrians Clement and Origen created a combination of faith and science, theology and philosophy, church and culture. And this formed the presupposition for a link between Christianity and empire. It was only a matter of time before that came about. It happened in the fourth century.


## CONSTANTINOPLE: THE SECOND ROME

It was the Emperor Constantine (306–37) who, after times of the most severe repression and persecution by the state, at the beginning of the fourth century finally ushered in the unavoidable political shift. With the shift of political paradigm, Christianity also received another centre: instead of Jerusalem, this was first of all Rome and soon Constantinople, erected by the Emperor Constantine in place of the ancient Greek Byzantion. 'Byzantium' became the centre and leading church of Christianity, the second Rome. The small communities of Christians now became great organizations. The minority became the majority, the persecuted religion the only legitimate religion, the underground church family the state church.

Hagia Sophia was to be the symbol of this Christian state church; it was built by the Emperor Justinian (527–65) in the sixth century. A gigantic mosaic on the balcony – happily preserved from deliberate destruction – clearly illustrates the new Christian ideology of the state. In this paradigm Jesus Christ is understood as the ruler of all (pantocrator), who stands in the place of God. And in God's name the emperor rules the state and the church as autocrator (self-ruler). The emperor, and the emperor alone, convenes, guides and approves those ecumenical councils which lay down the norms for right belief, 'orthodoxy'. At that time there was no mention of a 'pope', even in ancient Rome.

## FROM CHRISTIAN FAITH TO ORTHODOX DOGMA

Now church dogma, too, developed in that new imperial constellation of state and church. When every possible theological option clashed, it became imperative to interpret the relationship of Jesus to his God and Father ever more precisely in intellectual and conceptual terms, with categories from Greek physics and metaphysics (the Greek terms were *physis*, *ousia* and *hypostasis*, the Latin *natura*, *substantia* and *persona*). This entangled the theology of the Greek church fathers in intellectual problems which were almost insoluble, and at a very early stage first of all split the theologians and then the church.

Paul and all the Christian theologians of the first three centuries had unmistakably maintained the Jewish belief in one God by always clearly subordinating Christ to the one God and Father. But at the first ecumenical council in 325 – convened by Constantine (without asking the Bishop of Rome) at his residence in Nicaea – Christ was put on the same level as God: he was said to be *homo-ousios* = of the same substance with God, the Father. This was a formula with which the emperor wanted to resolve the seemingly endless disputes, above all with the followers of a certain Arius. However, it created more problems than it solved. In the end it proved to be baneful. Jewish Christians, who doubtless rejected it at the council, even if they were unable to prevent it, in this way saw themselves finally excommunicated. The formula remained incomprehensible to Jews and later to Muslims. And Christians today also have insuperable problems with it, as they do with the trinitarian dogma of the one God in three persons, which developed from it later.

But it was this dogma of the Trinity, established in the fourth and fifth centuries, that became the crowning glory of the Christian state religion, which under the Emperor Theodosius (379–95) was already fully institutionalized at the end of the fourth century: the Catholic Church was now the state church and heresy was a crime against the state. The consequence was that the persecuted church often became a persecuting church: in the name of Jesus Christ, the preacher of non-violence and peacemaking (or even in the name of the Trinity), those who believed otherwise, first of all the Jews, were persecuted, and soon even executed, and priceless cultural items (books!) and art treasures were destroyed.

Faith was now no longer primarily understood as believing trust in God and his Christ, as in the New Testament. Faith was now above all right belief, orthodoxy, the conviction of the 'correctness' of particular teachings of the church about God, Christ and the Holy Spirit, as these had been formulated by the seven ecumenical councils and sanctioned by the state. It was this claim to 'orthodoxy' that distinguished the Byzantine church from earliest Christianity and finally also from other churches, and at the same time became its proper name.

Meanwhile the Western, now Latin, church had gone its own way under the Roman bishops and had attempted to establish the primacy of the Bishop of Rome in the East as well. In the eleventh century, after a long process of alienation, there was a final split between the pope, who had become very grand, and the Byzantine church: in 1054 the Roman bull of excommunication was laid on the altar of Hagia Sophia by the cardinal legate. However, the then emperor Constantine IX Monomachos, depicted on a mosaic in Hagia Sophia, was to hand on the insignia of the empire to the Grand Prince Vladimir of Kiev. After the fall of Byzantium this became the legendary basis for the theory of Moscow as the third Rome, which arose very much later.


## THE SLAVONIC WORLD:
## RELIGIOUS AND CULTURAL SPLIT

Already around the end of the first millennium, the process of Europeanizing and Christianizing the southern and eastern Slavonic peoples, which was essentially directed from Byzantium, was complete. The three most important developments can be sketched out briefly.

Together with his brother Methodius, the distinguished Byzantine scholar and missionary Constantine is rightly called 'apostle and teacher of the Slavs'. Constantine, whose later monastic name was Cyril, devised the first Slavonic script. This Old Slavonic (Glagolitic) alphabet, later simplified as 'Cyrillic' script, is still in use today. Because in their worship in Moravia and Pannonia the brothers Methodius and Cyril did not use Latin like the Franks or Greek like the other Byzantines, they made a Slavonic Christianity possible. First of all they laid the foundations for a Byzantine-Slavonic ecumene among the southern Slavs (the Bulgarians and later the Serbs).

The fate of Hungary, the West Slavs (Bohemia and Poland) and the western South Slavs (the Croats and the Slovenes) was different: on the basis of the old division of the empire into East and West Rome these did not orientate themselves on Byzantium but on Rome. So the Slavonic world was divided between the Byzantine and the Roman churches. At a very early stage two completely different paradigms emerged here: on the one hand the Hellenistic paradigm of the early church and on the other the medieval Roman Catholic paradigm. As early as the ninth century the fate of what was later South Slavia (Yugo-slavia) was decided by this division. Very different developments followed: different alphabets, different liturgies and liturgical languages, different cultures, and often different regimes. The most recent fragmentation of Yugoslavia into the old religious and cultural units could probably have been avoided only had there been ecumenical collaboration between the churches in time and had the politicians been firmly committed to a federal solution (for example on the model of the Swiss Confederation).

But the tribes of the East Slavs were to be more significant for world history. They similarly adopted Byzantine Christianity and built up the Russian empire: in a first phase, in Kiev, the kingdom of Rus, from which Russians, Ukrainians and Byelorussians come. The founding date of Russian Christianity is taken to be the conversion of Grand Prince Vladimir and the mass baptism in the Dnieper by Greek priests in the year 988. After two centuries of Tatar rule the kingdom of Kiev was to be followed in the second phase by the kingdom of Moscow, and in the third phase by the kingdom of St Petersburg.

## MOSCOW: THE THIRD ROME

Almost at the same time, Byzantium was conquered by the Turkish Muslims, in 1453, and Russia was freed from Tatar rule, in 1448. After Kiev, Moscow and in it the Kremlin became the spiritual and secular centre of the Russian kingdom, the seat of the czar and a metropolitan, later the patriarch.

The Cathedral of the Dormition of Mary is the main church of czarist Russia. It is modelled on the church of the same name in Vladimir (which between the Kiev kingdom and later the Moscow kingdom was for a short time a power centre in Rus). Ivan III (1472–1505), who also built the Kremlin wall, had it erected. He entrusted the new building to the Italian architect Fioravanti, since all the Russian architects feared the czar's wrath. Fioravanti combined the traditional Byzantine architecture with elements of the Italian Renaissance. But tradition has it that after completing the building this architect, too, fell out of favour with the czar and died in prison in Moscow in 1486. However, in an unparalleled way his church became the model for all the later cathedral buildings of Eastern Europe.

This was the place where from then on the czars were crowned, the metropolitans and then the patriarchs were elected and buried, and important state decrees (*ukáz*) and excommunications were proclaimed. The most famous case was precisely a century ago: in 1901 it was here that Leo Tolstoy was expelled from the church. The Monomach throne, from which the czars pray, is a particularly splendid feature. It is no coincidence that the transfer of the Byzantine imperial insignia by Emperor Constantine IX surnamed Monomachos to the Grand Prince of Kiev, Vladimir Monomach, is engraved here. This legend gives its credentials to the third Rome, which replaced Byzantium (called by the Russians Zargrad, 'Emperor City').

The church of Russia already existed a thousand years ago. The splendour with which this church is still developing even today is utterly Byzantine: precious brocade garments, richly decorated episcopal crowns, fragrant thuribles and candles decked with flowers in abundance. The requirement that priests and monks should be bearded is also Byzantine. The East Slavonic tribes took over the language of the Slavonic liturgy and literature from the South Slavs, the Bulgars, but everything else from Byzantium, the Emperor Constantine's second Rome. When the Russians under the Grand Prince came to Byzantium before their baptism and there experienced the worship of the court, they did not know whether they 'were in heaven or on earth, for on earth there is no sight of such beauty'. That is what we read in Russia's oldest chronicle, written by the monk Nestor in the Monastery of the Caves in Kiev at the beginning of the twelfth century.

For almost 500 years (988–1448) Russia was a church province of the patriarchate of Constantinople. Not only the early church norms embodied in the rule of faith, the canon of scripture and the office of bishop but also the whole of Russian church organization has a Byzantine stamp, along with its dogma, liturgy, theology, discipline and piety, even if many forms and norms have been adapted to the Russian character. In other words, the Russian church is part of the Byzantine form of Christianity and conditioned by the historic role of Russia. Here it makes the fate of this paradigm of Christianity quite clear.

## SUBJECTION OF THE CHURCH TO THE STATE

Following the conquest of Constantinople by the Turkish Muslims – after 1100 years Constantine's work had come to a sorry end – the Russian church had become autocephalous: it made the claim to choose its 'own head'. On the other hand, over the course of time the subjection of the church to the state, which was already latent in the Byzantine model of the harmonious 'symphony' of church and state, intensified. In this model, the state authority protects and dominates the church, and the church justifies and supports the state authority ('Caesaropapism'). So no rivalry could arise in the East like that in the Latin West between emperor and pope.

To this degree the thrones standing at the same level in the Church of the Dormition of Mary, which suggest the equal status of czar and patriarch, are deceptive. In reality the church increasingly became part of the state. This was a dependent relationship which was to become complete and definitive under the Enlightenment and modernization which took place in the modern period under Peter the Great; he replaced the patriarch by an initially progressive state authority (the 'Holy Synod'). But Ivan III already had himself addressed as 'autocrator' ('self-ruler') of Russia and in dealing with foreign powers took the title 'Czar (emperor) of Moscow and all Russia'. In fact he was married to the niece of the last Byzantine emperor, who had fallen, sword in hand, at the conquest of Constantinople by the Turks on 29 May 1453. This provided powerful support to his self-confidence and claims.

So Moscow entered into the heritage of Constantinople. Moreover after 1589 Czar Boris Godunov finally made the metropolitan see a patriarchate, albeit the last in the series of five Eastern patriarchates. Only now did the ideology of a third Rome appear: since the first Rome had become heretical and the second Rome had fallen, Moscow understood itself to be the new centre of Orthodoxy, and saw Orthodoxy as the last bastion of true Christianity: the Russians were an elect people and their czar was the only Orthodox ruler. All that was Russian was now regarded as Orthodox, and all that was foreign was suspected of heresy.

## A DISPUTED CHURCH

In the Kremlin the grandiose worship of the time of the czars has been restored in all its Byzantine splendour after the collapse of Communism. In radiant light the interior of the Kremlin cathedral now shines out more brightly than ever before, at a very early stage decorated throughout with dozens of splendid frescoes depicting the lives of Mary and Jesus. On the pillars, 135 martyrs of Orthodox Christianity are depicted – the great pride of Orthodoxy.

But many Russians have by no means forgotten that the Orthodox church, along with the aristocracy, the army and the police, guaranteed and backed the czarist regime, so that the 1917 Revolution was directed against both state and church. The church had been given back its patriarchate, but in the person of the patriarch Tikhon it turned against the Revolution. According to Lenin's altered version of Marx's saying, religion was in fact not only the 'opium of the people' but also opium deliberately offered to the people, which the Bolsheviks were to fight against with every possible means.

However, the church rightly retorts that under Stalin, Lenin's revolution became a brutal and murderous regime of terror: thousands of clergy were arrested and deported, thousands of houses of God were devastated or closed. Millions of people, both believers and unbelievers, were sent to the 'Gulag archipelago'.

But after almost 70 years of oppression, in 1989 the turning point also came for the church, and it became evident that despite vigorous persecution, contrary to the prophecies of Feuerbach and Marx, religion had not died out but had remained alive. That can be experienced not only in the Kremlin cathedral but also in every Russian parish church.

## THE ORTHODOX EASTER FEAST

It is above all the liturgical feasts which from olden times have meant much to the Russian people. They still mean much today. First of all comes the feast of Easter, *the* most exalted feast of Christianity. On the basis of the Julian calendar, once introduced by Julius Caesar and still used in the Russian church, it is usually celebrated on a different Sunday from that in the Western church, which uses the Gregorian calendar, improved by Pope Gregory XIII in 1582.

Even in the time of the Communist oppression, thousands upon thousands silently entered or stood before the few churches that were open. Today, however, Easter can be celebrated loudly and joyfully everywhere. Countless Muscovites do celebrate Easter and have Easter bread broken, for example, in front of the Nicolai church. They then take it home for the family festival. They also like to be sprinkled with holy water.

The feast of the resurrection of the Lord is very much a feast of candles, light and joy. In early times, on this night one could hear the many thousand bells of Moscow's forty times forty churches ringing. They were silenced in and after the Revolution. But 'risen' from their decades of silence, today many of them ring out again.

In the East it is not so much the crucified Christ as the risen Christ who stands right at the centre of the liturgy. He is the great centre of hope for eternal life. This hope is expressed in the cry of the priest to each individual, 'Christ is risen', to which the faithful joyfully respond, 'Yes, he is risen indeed'. The liturgy ends with the priest's kiss of peace and the receiving of the eucharistic gifts. The bread, dipped in the wine, is offered with a spoon.

## THE CULT OF IMAGES AND MONASTICISM

The veneration of icons is utterly characteristic of Orthodoxy. Whereas the 'Constantinian' basilicas and mosaic art were still common to both Western and Eastern churches, the religious images or icons (the Greek *eikon* means 'image') are a specifically Eastern development. First of all they were only pictures of pious memory, which were meant to strengthen prayer. But as early as the sixth and seventh centuries they became pictures for cultic veneration. Some believe that these pictures would communicate the help of the biblical figures or ancient saints depicted on them.

This was a pious movement among the people, unpopular with the hierarchy and the emperor but supported by the monks. The monks, too, were a special development characteristic of Eastern Orthodoxy. For in the East the monks saw themselves as the guardians of right teaching, as spiritual guides to the people, indeed as the inner core of the church, largely removed from the authority of the patriarchs and the bishops. In fact, in the church they took the place of the intellectuals, and even today they occupy both the bishops' thrones and the patriarchate, along with the professorial chairs. Students must therefore decide before they are ordained priest whether they want to remain unmarried and aim at a higher career, or become married worldly priests with no prospect of episcopal consecration.

Under the influence of the monks a practice that was strictly taboo among Christians in the first centuries as idolatry became established: lighted candles or lamps were put in front of pictures, and incense was offered. Indeed, the pictures were kissed, washed, clothed and venerated with genuflections. The Orthodox explanation was that this did not involve any superstition whatever. But many people believed in the spiritual power of the icons themselves, which were made, distributed and looked after by monks. With good reason 'miracles' were attributed to particular pictures.

The consequence was a vigorous dispute over images in the Byzantine church which lasted for more than a century. Could pictures made by men really communicate God's grace? The picture-breaking (iconoclastic) movement, though long favoured by the emperors and their armies, finally succumbed to the power of the monks and the longing of the people for something to look at and to give help, for grace and miracles. With great effort, theology justified the depiction of the divine in the face of the biblical prohibition against images by a reference to the 'incarnation' of God in Christ. At a synod in Constantinople in 843 a decision was finally made in favour of the images. And every year, down to the present, this event is celebrated on the first Sunday in Lent with the 'Feast of Orthodoxy'.

In all this we must not forget that under the 200-year rule of the Tatars, the descendants of the Mongol Genghis Khan, it was above all the Orthodox Church which maintained a sense of national unity at a time when the kingdom was divided into principalities, in a state of economic decline and cultural decay. Since then an Orthodox church has been the symbol of the one Russia in the face of the Tatars, the non-Christians, the non-Russians. Since then 'being Russian' has also meant 'being Orthodox'.

And whatever criticism we may have of the monks, someone like Sergei of Radonezh, the most revered monastic saint of Russia, founder of the Monastery of the Trinity at Sergiev Posad (known under the Communists as Zagorsk), which was the model for around 180 further monasteries, embodies the ideals of Russian piety as these live on down to Dostoevsky's *The Brothers Karamazov*, with the sympathetic figure of the 'starets', the charismatic 'elder', as the spiritual leader. These ideals are simplicity, humility, compassion, social and national commitment. The world of images, monks and monasteries forms a counter-reality of sacred values to the second culture, a subculture which even in the view of present-day Russian theologians has remained alive under the Byzantine-Christian culture: a 'night culture' made up of old pagan Slavonic or Tatar elements.

Thus consciously or unconsciously there are still many believers in Eastern Europe, clergy even more than laity, whose spiritual and religious lives are lived completely within the Hellenistic-Slavonic paradigm of the early church. The liturgy has hardly changed, and their theology even less. This gives the Orthodox churches a strongly traditionalistic and monastic character; on the other hand it is very religious and festive. Be this as it may, when in 1971 I visited the central cathedral of Russia as a museum, I would never have dreamed that one day I would be privileged to take part in the Easter worship of the Patriarch of Moscow and all Russia here.

## THE DANGERS AND THE HOPES OF ORTHODOXY

I cannot conceal my sympathy for the Orthodox Church. In many respects it is closest to earliest Christianity. It does not have the same centralistic government as my own church, and it allows at least its priests (but not its bishops) to marry. It also allows the eucharist to the faithful in both kinds, bread and wine. And it has survived under all kinds of political systems, even the last persecution for 70 years under the Communist regime, with thousands of martyrs. That is above all because of its grandiose liturgy, its hymns. All this is very gripping for someone from the West.

However, we cannot overlook the fact that the distance from primitive Christianity is enormous. The average believer has difficulties in recognizing Jesus' supper in the ceremonial liturgy. And the link with the state, too, is not at all characteristic of earliest Christianity.

But all that is a challenge for the Orthodox Church today to use the power of its liturgy to increase the element of proclamation: the message itself, preaching, and also the education of children in the schools. All that is a great challenge for the Orthodox Church. And I also think of the bond, indeed the reconciliation, with the Latin church of the West, with which after all it was associated for 1000 years. A great task of the twenty-first century is to do away with this schism, which has lasted more than 900 years. However, here it is above all and primarily Rome that has to make a move.

## ROME'S PRIMACY OF HONOUR IN THE EARLY CHURCH

Even Catholic historians concede today that we read nothing about Peter in Rome anywhere in the New Testament, and there is nowhere even the hint of a specific 'successor' to Peter. Neither the New Testament nor the earliest New Testament sources know a Bishop of Rome. Neither the letter of the apostle Paul to Rome nor the earliest writing of the Roman community to Corinth mention such a bishop. That is inconceivable if in fact there was one. A monarchical episcopate can be demonstrated in Rome only at a late stage, around the middle of the second century.

However, today even Protestant scholars no longer dispute that the church of the imperial capital, which was both large and prosperous, without doubt always claimed for itself the tombs of the two chief apostles Peter and Paul, who were always venerated together in the beginning. The Roman church had attained high moral authority as guardian of the apostolic tradition both through its charitable activity and also through its fight against Gnosticism. Since the downfall of Jerusalem, the church of the old imperial capital itself had beyond dispute enjoyed the primacy of honour rather than powerful Byzantium. But the church of Rome with its many house churches and grandiose old basilicas like Santa Sabina was not yet an authoritarian centralist institution. Still, the emphasis on law and order, a talent for organization and a realistic political sense were already typical of Rome.

In Rome people remained aware that the church derived from Judaism. In Santa Sabina, on one of the oldest Roman mosaics, there is a symbolic portrayal of the church of the Jews. In time this was suppressed by the church of the Gentiles, primarily with a Hellenistic stamp. However, in Rome in due course the East Roman Greek paradigm was replaced by a Latin theology, church order and liturgy: the specific Roman Catholic paradigm. Instead of Greek, which had long prevailed even in Rome – in education, trade, travel, church and culture – between 360 and 382 the language of the people, Latin, was generally and definitively introduced into worship. After the shift under Constantine new basilicas were built, still without domes, and completely orientated on the altar and the bishop's chair: these were no longer secular rooms for meetings and assemblies, but places of worship. Here the earliest Christian thanksgiving festival developed into the sacrifice of the mass, which now increasingly became more a solemn ceremony. What had once been the simple table at which a meal was eaten now became the sacrificial altar.

The rise of a new paradigm in the Western empire, which since the end of the fourth century had been separated from the Roman Eastern empire, had been long heralded:

– Theologically. In spiritual terms, at the end of the fourth century Western Latin Christianity still appeared as an appendix to the dominant East Roman Greek Christianity: the ecumenical councils, convened solely by the emperor in Constantinople, all took place in the East with scant participation from the West. But at the same time the brilliant North African Augustine already initiated that Western-Latin paradigm of theology which was to prove fundamental to the whole of the Latin Middle Ages. His monumental theology of history, which saw history as a clash between the City of God and the City of the World, was particularly influential.

– Politically. In the middle of the migration of the peoples, in 476 the empire of West Rome perished with the deposition of the last emperor. But only two decades later the barbarian ruler Clovis, king of the Franks, was baptized. This ushered in a development which in the year 800 led to the coronation of Charlemagne as emperor by the grace of God and the pope. He claimed a similar position of power in the church of the West to that claimed by the Byzantine emperor in the East. Thus to the indignation of Byzantium a West Roman empire was founded to rival East Rome; the Muslim armies had in any case robbed Byzantium of the areas in which Christianity originated, the eastern and southern Mediterranean.


## THE PAPACY BECOMES ESTABLISHED

However, the decisive development was that after the transfer of imperial government to Constantinople, the bishops of Rome exploited the power vacuum in the West. They attributed more and more power (*potestas*) to themselves, first in the church and later, as a result of the confusion caused by the migration of the peoples, also in the state. Now talk of serving the church and state was a mere formality.

First of all Rome had made hardly any legal claims with reference to Peter. The passage in the Gospel of Matthew, 'You are Peter and on this rock I will build my church' (16.18f.), which is so important for bishops of Rome today and which now adorns the dome of St Peter's in black letters two metres high against a gilt background, is not quoted in full at all in any of the Christian literature of the first centuries. Only in the middle of the third century does a Roman bishop (Stephen) refer to it for the first time in a dispute with other churches about the pre-eminence of Peter. And only long after the shift under Constantine was the quotation about the rock used to support a Roman claim to primacy. Even then, none of the Christian East went along with this interpretation, any more than Augustine did. For here in general the 'rock' was still thought to refer to Peter's faith in Christ, which is the foundation of the church. Even in Rome itself, people would have nothing of a legally assured authority of Peter over the whole church, far less of the legal primacy of a successor of his in Rome; and understandably in the East people will have nothing of this even today.

Only in the time after Constantine, from the second half of the fourth century onwards, did the bishops of Rome energetically make increasing attempts also to establish a monarchical church structure in practice. But even at the first ecumenical council at Nicaea in 325, whereas Rome enjoyed the same privileges as the great old sees of Alexandria, Antioch and Jerusalem, it did not exercise any primacy over the whole church. Even the most important bishops and theologians of the Western church, Ambrose and Augustine, do not know such primacy.

At the second most important ecumenical council, held at Chalcedon in 451, the Roman bishop Leo the Great achieved a great success with his Christological formula, presented by legates, that Christ is one person in two natures. But even here no one thought of according Rome a position of pre-eminence over the other churches. On the contrary, Leo, who was already dreaming of a *plenitudo potestatis* ('fullness of power') allegedly given to the bishop of Rome by Christ and who therefore gave himself the title of the pagan Roman high priest, 'Pontifex maximus', was forced to recognize that in its famous canon 28 the same council had accorded the see of New Rome (Constantinople) the same primacy of honour as the old imperial capital. Leo's subsequent sharp protest against this promotion of the second Rome was completely useless. Still, he was the first of the bishops of Rome to be buried in Constantine's church of St Peter. And in future Rome would be fond of referring to him for its own claims: because of his theory of primacy and praxis the title 'Pope' in the strict sense was bestowed on him.

However, Eastern Orthodox Christians felt and still feel it arrogant that an individual bishop in the church should attempt to attribute to himself the quite personal responsibility and authority of the apostle Peter. Above all, it seemed unacceptable that every possible legal consequence of an absolute claim to rule should be derived from the apostolic authority of Peter – by a skilful combination of theological and legal arguments. Moreover, the insatiable Roman quest for power did not shrink subsequently from adopting the crudest forgeries. One might think of the

Donation of Constantine (the claim that before travelling to the East, Constantine had bestowed an imperial status on the Bishop of Rome and primacy over all the churches). One might think of the forgeries of Symmachus ('The first see is judged by no one') and above all of Pseudo-Isidore, to the effect that the early church was already ruled by papal decrees down to the smallest detail. These manipulations, which are unique in world history, are by no means a curiosity of the time, but a power factor even today. In the Catholic Codex of Canon Law which was revised in 1982 they may be veiled, but they are still effective in the papal absolutism which is once again cemented there.

## THE SPLIT BETWEEN THE EASTERN AND WESTERN CHURCHES

Even now the Roman primacy of jurisdiction (not just the primacy of honour as the first patriarchate in rank) still clearly poses the great unresolved question between the Eastern and Western churches. It has never been discussed at an ecumenical council between East and West, far less decided. Here beyond any doubt the novel Roman theory and practice of primacy is most to blame for the split between the Eastern and Western churches. Even in the West, there were many setbacks and much stagnation before the Roman Catholic paradigm, initiated theologically, politically and legally by the popes, could also be implemented in practice. At an earlier stage, numerous popes were deposed (by the Byzantine or the German emperor), and there were papal trials and condemnations. Down to the eleventh century Rome was not regarded as a real teaching authority in the legal sense, far less were papal decisions regarded as infallible. Just as there were heretical emperors (in the iconoclastic dispute), so too there were heretical popes (the most famous case is Honorius I in the seventh century, who was condemned as a heretic by several councils).

However, the papacy, which in the tenth century (known as the *saeculum obscurum*, the dark century) was in complete decline, was reformed by the German emperors through a series of popes whom they nominated, most of them from Germany. Strengthened in this way, in the eleventh century it turned against its imperial protectors and at the same time thought that it could engage in a new trial of strength with Byzantium. In old Rome, in line with the forgeries, the whole church was now increasingly derived from the authority of the pope.

And it was no coincidence that the Cardinal Humbert of Silva Candida who for the first time laid the foundation for the absolute rule of the pope in the church and his superiority to any worldly authority was the papal legate who in 1054 fatefully excommunicated the Orthodox patriarch and the whole of the Eastern church in Hagia Sophia in Constantinople. This is regarded as the definitive break between the Eastern and Western churches. It was sealed by the baneful Fourth Crusade (1204), which resulted in the conquest and plunder of Constantinople by the Latins and the appointment of a 'Latin' emperor and patriarchate. Humbert had come to describe the relationship of the church and the pope as simply that of door and hinge, family and mother, building and foundation, river and spring. At that time this was still pure theory, but it soon also became Roman practice.

## A REVOLUTIONARY NEW CHURCH CONSTITUTION

In the meantime the apostle Paul, who had once resisted Peter face to face, had decisively lost significance by comparison with Peter: Peter alone had to support all the papal claims to power. Triple papal crowns, the 'fisherman's ring', pontifical garb – these were now the papal insignia, and the statue of St Peter in St Peter's, Rome, is still adorned with them on the feast of St Peter. In the course of the centuries the successor of the Galilean fisherman has become the Lord of the church who loves to command *urbi et orbi*, the city and the earth.

When a pope like John Paul II stands at Bernini's Confessio over the tomb of St Peter he is the embodiment of an absolutist monarchical conception of the church which was unknown in the first millennium. Only in the eleventh century, under the regime of the iron Gregory VII (1073–85; previously he was the colleague of Cardinal Humbert) did this conception become established in the West with a revolutionary new church constitution, the 'Gregorian Reform': the whole church, orientated on the pope, had the authority to interpret the gospel in doctrine and practice in a binding way for everyone. The pope wanted to be not only the successor of Peter, but the representative of Christ, indeed of God himself.

Thus the paradigm shift was complete – away from the collegial ecumenical paradigm of the early church to the explicit Roman Catholic paradigm of the Middle Ages. With the help of all the forgeries, an image of the church and church law was suggested and propagated which was wholly centred on papal authority: the holding of councils was bound up with the authority of the pope; all important matters in the church were subject to the pope's judgement; state laws which went against it were of no significance; the bishops were completely dependent on the pope – all this was in the forged decretals and their later official confirmations.

## THE ROMAN SYSTEM

The Catholic Church was a new Roman empire. One expression of this which still exists today is the bestowal of the pallium on the newly appointed archbishops from all over the world on the feast of St Peter. The pallium is a sign of archepiscopal authority. The pope has reserved to himself the right to bestow it in person. Thus he controls and rules even here. For only with the pallium may an archbishop exercise his rights as a metropolitan. He receives it only when (like all the bishops in the world) he has previously sworn a personal oath of obedience to the pope in the liturgy – although Jesus himself prohibited swearing. The oath has the following wording: 'I . . . archbishop of . . . will always be true and obedient to the Blessed Apostle Peter, the Holy, Apostolic Church of Rome and to you, Summus Pontifex, and your legitimate successors. So help me, almighty God.' No wonder that after a such a solemn oath to the pope even previously critical professors of theology show the same kind of uncritical obedience to the pope as the German generals under oath once showed to the 'Führer'.

However, we should certainly not throw the baby out with the bath water, and reject the Catholic Church along with the Roman system. There is no doubt that for the Catholic Church all down the centuries Rome has also been a factor of continuity: the continuity of Christian faith, rites and ethics. Nor should we dispute that in principle the substance of Christian faith has also been preserved in Rome: the same gospel, the same rite of initiation (baptism), the same community rite (eucharist), the same ethos (love of neighbour).

But criticism of the Roman system must be formulated just as clearly: the differences between the old and the new paradigms are blatant. Whereas the ecumenical paradigm of the early church was fundamentally sacramental, collegial and conciliar, the new medieval Roman Catholic paradigm is primarily legalistic, monarchical and absolutist:
– We no longer have the scheme of the early church and the Orthodox church today: God – Christ – apostles – bishops – church.
– What we have is the new constitution of the medieval church : God – Christ – Peter – pope – bishops – church.

Only since the high Middle Ages has the Catholic Church had the appearance that it presents to us today:
– The pope claims the primacy of honour over the whole church, over all patriarchs, bishops, priests and every believer: this is still rejected by the Eastern churches.
– The authority of the clergy is in principle superior to that of the laity: this led to the great dispute between the pope and the emperor and then

between the pope and the modern state, a dispute which the papacy has
lost all along the line.
  – The prohibition of marriage is now a law which applies to all the clergy:
this goes against the millennia-old tradition of priestly marriage even in the
Western church and causes countless unnecessary problems, at present
above all a catastrophic lack of priests.
  Down to the Second Vatican Council (1962–5), the Western church
essentially retained the form that it had taken in the high Middle Ages.
Indeed, some Catholics fixated on Rome still remain imprisoned in this
medieval paradigm. But this Roman system clearly contradicts the gospel.
For the church of the New Testament is:
  – not centralized: but the Ecclesia Romana claims to be the 'mother',
with the pope as 'father';
  – not legalistic: but the pope wants to be executive, legislative and
judiciary at the same time, supported by a canon law which he himself
has fabricated, the interpretation of which requires a science of canon
law;
  – not politicized: but the Roman Church sets itself up alongside the state
power as an independent institution of government with an international
status, a diplomatic service and special rights;
  – not clericalized: but a patriarchal hierarchy and a clergy of celibate
males set above the people clearly dominates the laity;
  – not militarized: but over the centuries a militant church has manifested
itself in 'holy' wars of conversion, wars against heretics, crusades (even
against fellow Christians) and wars of religion, and also in persecutions of
Jews, burnings of heretics and witches. Even today it has an Inquisition
and mercilessly persecutes 'deviants' (today there is psychological rather
than physical burning), waging campaigns world-wide in its fight for a
medieval sexual morality.
  John XXIII and the Second Vatican Council, which was held in St
Peter's between 1962 and 1965 (I myself took part in it as a theologian),
attempted to reorientate the Catholic Church on the gospel, to restore the
collegiality of pope and bishops which existed in the early church, and to
restore the unity of the church of Christ which had been broken by papal
absolutism. It did so with only modest success, for the overdue reform of
the papacy and the Roman Curia could not even be discussed, and
consequently the changes made were only cosmetic. It is true that since
then representatives of Eastern Orthodoxy have even taken part in the
papal liturgy, but they have done so without receiving communion. For
the fact remains that the tremendous Roman claim to power is still the
great block on the way to unity between the Eastern and Western churches.
Even Pope Paul VI conceded this three decades ago. Will we perhaps yet
experience the voluntary renunciation of power by a pope in the spirit of

the Sermon on the Mount? Or do we have to wait for a Third Vatican Council or a second council in Jerusalem for that?

### CAN THE PAPACY BE REFORMED?

I studied in Rome for seven years and know it so to speak from within. For all my criticism of the papacy, I remain convinced that a pastoral ministry to the whole church on the model of the apostle Peter is meaningful, if it is practised in the spirit of the gospel. Nor can it be disputed that the papacy has done great service in holding together at least the Western churches, preserving their unity and freedom. And the Roman system has often proved more efficient than the somewhat loose church alliance of the Eastern churches. To the present day, wherever the pope is credible, he can address the conscience of the whole world as a moral authority.

Many Catholics, too, criticize the Roman claim to power: they feel that the Roman system has developed further and further away from the original Christian message and church order. Since the high Middle Ages the negative aspects have been obvious. Since this time there have been complaints about:
- the authoritarian-infallible gestures in dogma and morality;
- the regimentation of the laity, the clergy and local churches down to the smallest detail;
- in general, the completely fossilized absolutist system of power, which is orientated more on the Roman emperors than on Peter, the modest fisherman from Galilee.

These complaints are more than 500 years old. At that time they led to a historic conflict between the pope and a young German monk. In 1519 this monk had stayed in the monastery of the Augustinian Hermits in Santa Maria del Popolo on an official journey to Rome. His name was Martin Luther.

## MARTIN LUTHER: THE REFORMER

The crisis of the Roman Catholic paradigm had already long been in the making. By its destruction of the universal power of the emperor, the universal papacy had weakened itself and encouraged the rise of the nation states, above all that of France. And the reversal of papal world power into papal impotence took place amazingly quickly: the exile of the popes in

Avignon in the south of France lasted through almost the whole of the fourteenth century: first there were two and then three popes at the same time. Finally, the reform Council of Constance was held at the beginning of the fifteenth century. Although this one ecumenical council to be held north of the Alps failed the Bohemian Jan Hus by treacherously executing him as a heretic although he had been promised safe passage, it did take up the tradition of the early church in so far as it defined the supremacy of the council over the pope and in addition called for regular councils. But even at that time, Rome learned nothing from this reform council: its decisions were undermined, with the result that under the immoral Renaissance papacy there was an unprecedented decadence in the church, the clergy, theology and pastoral care. Only art thrived.

It was the rebuilding of St Peter's which finally provoked the historic conflict: how was its building to be financed without indulgences, without money for the remission of sins? The Roman Curia collaborated with German bishops and bankers in exploiting the faithful. In this profound crisis of medieval Christianity – precisely a century after the successful reform Council of Constance – in Germany in 1517 that insignificant, unknown monk became an epoch-making prophetic figure. With tremendous eloquence and effectiveness, within a few years he developed a new Reformation paradigm of Christianity in keeping with the gospel. This was a programme which he himself embodied powerfully. His name was Martin Luther (1483–1546), and he was a German professor of biblical studies.

The replacement of the old paradigm took place with unprecedented rapidity and drama. Martin Luther published his Ninety-Five Theses against indulgences in Wittenberg. There is an argument as to whether they were really nailed up to the north door of the castle church; in any case, the original wooden door was destroyed in a fire). A heresy trial opened in Rome. Luther refused to recant. Rome threatened him with excommunication and called for his writings to be burned. Luther appealed to a general council. The papal nuncio had Luther's writings burned in Louvain in Flanders. Luther responded in Wittenberg by burning the bull of excommunication and the papal canon law. Emperor Charles V ordered the monk and professor to appear before the Reichstag in Worms. On 18 April 1521 he made his defence, concluding with the following sentences: 'Unless I am convinced by the testimony of the Scriptures – for I do not trust either in the Pope or in Councils alone, since it is well known that they have often erred and contradicted themselves – I am bound by the Scriptures I have quoted, and as my conscience is captive to the word of God, I cannot and will not retract anything, since it is neither safe nor right to go against the conscience. God help me. Amen.'

## RETURN TO THE GOSPEL

What was Luther's concern? It was quite simply that the church should return to the gospel of Jesus Christ, of which he had had living experience in holy scripture and especially in Paul. He therefore translated the Bible into German, so that the one Lord of the church, his message and his fate should again be comprehensible to people. Specifically that meant:

– At that time there were numerous church traditions, laws and authorities: for Luther the fundamental and abiding criterion of being a Christian is 'scripture alone'.

– There were numerous saints and official mediators between human beings and God: for Luther the mediator and centre of scripture is 'Christ alone', the crucified.

– For believers, numerous demands had to be fulfilled and numerous efforts had to be made ('works'), all of them laid down by the church, to attain the salvation of their souls. For Luther, according to Paul grace and faith come first and last. Men and women are justified not by works but 'by grace alone'. We do not earn this grace but have it 'through faith alone', through an unconditional trust in God and his Christ.

Thus a new form of Christianity rapidly became established, in the face of vigorous resistance from Rome. Indeed, a 'new' form of the church developed, as Protestant worship showed. No longer as in the Middle Ages was everything fixated on the hierarchy and its pomp; rather, the pastors and the worshippers together formed the fellowship of the faithful. Here was a community which prayed together, especially the Psalms: 'The Lord is my light and my salvation, whom then shall I fear? The Lord is my refuge, of whom shall I be afraid?' (Ps. 27). And this was a community which sang together: the hymn rapidly made the Reformation popular in Germany.

All in all Christians had a new freedom: this message was to give people, and especially the young, steadfastness in life. 'For freedom Christ has set us free. So stand firm and do not allow others to impose the yoke of slavery on you again' (Gal. 5.1). This saying of Paul has been a key feature of the rite which since Luther has been characteristic of the church of the Reformation: the rite of confirmation, strengthening in the faith. In it young Christian men and women are formally accepted into the community. After they have made the confession of faith with prayer and the laying on of hands they become adult members of the community, with all the rights and duties which go with that. Only now are they also admitted to the eucharist.

Of course, nowadays all Protestant pastors ask themselves how many of those who have been declared adult Christians will also continue to play an active part in congregational worship and at the eucharist. This has been a weak point in the Protestant churches from the very beginning. Already in Luther's time there was the first great split in the Reformation, specifically over the eucharist.

## THE WESTERN CHURCH IS SPLIT

It is historically certain that Rome (and not Luther) is chiefly to blame for the theological dispute over the right way of salvation and rapid escalation of practical reflection on the gospel into a fundamental dispute about authority in the church and the infallibility of pope and councils. A pastoral primacy of the pope or a papal primacy of ministry orientated on the gospel which led to mediation and inspiration would have been initially acceptable even to Luther in the interest of the unity of the church; some of his one-sidedness and exaggerations could have been corrected in an understanding dialogue.

But in Rome – and in the German episcopate – at that time people could not and would not hear this call for repentance and conversion, reflection and reform. Think of all that would have had to be changed. The whole of theology would have had to be reorientated, and the whole church restructured. A paradigm shift *par excellence* would have been due, a change in the overall constellation: a new understanding of God and human beings, of church and sacraments, the abolition of indulgences, the introduction of the vernacular in the liturgy, the abolition of the law of celibacy and much more.

But Rome and the German episcopate were neither willing to take this course, nor capable of doing so. Rome could excommunicate Luther, but the radical reshaping of church life in accordance with the gospel and the progress of the Reformation movement were unstoppable. So the new Reformation paradigm of theology and church was soon solidly established. However, the price to be paid was that to the great schism between East and West was added the no lesser split in the West between North and South. This was a historic development of prime importance with incalculable effects on state and society, business, science and art, which was soon also to make its mark on the world stage: Latin America became Catholic and North America became Protestant.

Finally, what seemed to have begun so well with Luther soon began to show signs of fragmentation. The Reformation programme had been illuminating, but its implementation was dubious. For:

1. Luther had summoned up spirits which could only be got rid of by force. There was an outburst of enthusiasm, especially in the Anabaptist movement, which quickly caused Luther to establish a second front. His

left-wing opponents made him seem conservative, and the side that he took in the peasant wars – against the exploited peasants, and for the rulers and nobility – made him seem reactionary.

2. Unity in the Reformation camp itself could not be preserved. Differences over the understanding of the eucharist finally alienated Luther from his more radical Swiss colleague Ulrich Zwingli, who came from Zurich. The victor on the world scene proved to be John Calvin (of Geneva), who adopted a middle position and as the great inspiration and organizer of an international network made Protestantism a world power. 'Reformed' Christianity as the consistent Reformation also became politically active: through the Huguenots in France, the Calvinists in the Netherlands and the Puritans in England. Calvin's presbyteral-synodical church constitution then became indirectly significant for the development of modern democracy.

3. The Reformation did not just come up against growing political resistance; the original enthusiasm for reform soon ran out of steam. The many people who were not ready for the 'freedom of a Christian' also lost the support of the church when the Roman system collapsed.

4. The ideal of the free Christian church which Luther had enthusiastically painted for his contemporaries in his programmatic writings of 1520 was not realized in the German empire. The Lutheran churches which had been freed from the 'Babylonian captivity', i.e. that of Rome, quickly came under no less oppressive dependence on the secular rulers and city magistrates. In Germany the Reformation did not prepare the way for modernity and freedom of religion, but initially favoured the state authorities and princely absolutism.

In England, where for a while the moderately Reformed Anglican state church seemed to have been replaced by a Puritan Presbyterian church (under Oliver Cromwell), on the whole people kept to the 'third way' on which they had set out. This *via media* attempted to integrate the medieval Catholic paradigm and the Reformation-Protestant paradigm.

But in England in particular, finally new Protestant alternatives developed: those free churches based on voluntary membership which rejected any form of state church and any financing by the state (hence the 'Independents') and which with freedom of religion established the autonomy of the 'congregation'. In the United States the future was to belong to the 'Congregationalists', together with the Baptists and later the Methodists. There, too, a great variety of non-conformists from the European continent found a new home – under the banner of religious freedom.

But whether Lutheran, Reformed, Anglican or Free Church, all the churches of the Reformation granted the laity what right down to the Second Vatican Council was constantly refused them by Rome: communion from the chalice.

## AMBIGUOUS RESULTS OF THE REFORMATION

Martin Luther was fundamentally right: sinful human beings are justified before God only through God's grace on the basis of trusting faith and not on the basis of their own pious achievements. Forty years ago, as a Catholic theologian I wrote a doctoral thesis in Rome on this question, which in Luther's time was the occasion and core of the schism in the church. My thesis established a fundamental consensus between the two doctrines and at the time won the approval of perhaps the most important Protestant theologian of the twentieth century, Karl Barth, along with many others (*Justification*, 1957).

Only now is there a Joint Declaration on the Doctrine of Justification, published by Rome and the Lutheran World Alliance in 1997, which states that the reciprocal doctrinal condemnations of the time have been superseded. Of course, it would be consistent for that to be followed by a recognition of the church as the church of Jesus Christ, a recognition of the validity of its ministries and a restoration of eucharistic communion. I hope to live to see this.

For the time of confessionalism is over:
– Since Vatican II the Catholic Church has realized a whole series of Martin Luther's concerns: it attaches great importance to the Bible; it has a liturgy in the vernacular; there is participation of the laity and decentralization. However, it needs even more concentration on the gospel to resolve the law of celibacy: orientation on the original Christian message.
– Conversely, however, the Protestant churches need more Catholic broadness: there is all too much provincialism, there is an increasing fragmentation into sects and there are many little popes instead of the one pope.

But even today we must see that the great challenge to both churches is posed by the Enlightenment and modernity, which came only two centuries later. The foundation for this challenge was not laid in Wittenberg, nor even in Rome, but in France, England and Holland. And above all in the United States of America.

## CHRISTIANITY CONFRONTED WITH THE REVOLUTION OF MODERNITY

Those who see the monumental copper Statue of Liberty on Liberty Island at the entrance to New York Harbour should know that this work by

F.-A. Bartholdi, who came from Alsace, which was erected in 1886, was given to the United States by France – in grateful remembrance of the alliance with France during the American War of Independence. Moreover the tablet in the statue's left hand also bears the date of the Declaration of Independence, 4 July 1776. An imposing sign of freedom for millions of people and a sign of gratitude for what the French Revolution of 1789 owed to the American Revolution of 1776 stands off the shore of Manhattan: Liberty enlightening the world.

For us today, the most important result of the French Revolution is the Declaration of the Rights of Man. Among those who drafted it in Paris, on the American model, were the American champion General Lafayette and the American ambassador Thomas Jefferson. On 26 August 1789 it was passed by the revolutionary parliament. In it freedom is the central concept, the most influential of the three revolutionary watchwords: freedom, equality and brotherhood. The individual rights of freedom (of conscience and expression of opinion) are to be matched by political rights (the sovereignty of the people, free elections and a separation of the powers) and economic rights (the inviolability of property). But this document is no 'bourgeois' declaration to mask a selfish preoccupation with possessions. Rather, it is the Magna Carta of modern democracy. Here was a development which overwhelmed the church. Moreover the popes condemned 'the abominable philosophy of human rights' (Pope Pius VI). This was an unmistakable signal that the march of the official Catholic Church into the cultural ghetto had begun. Following the natural scientists and intellectuals, now more and more of the middle class and the workers turned their backs on the Catholic Church.

However, modern times, modernity in the strict sense had already begun 150 years before the French Revolution: with a new belief in human reason. This now became the arbiter in all questions of truth. All the traditional authorities – whether Aristotle or scholasticism, the pope or the Bible – therefore found themselves in a crisis, a crisis of legitimation. This rational modernity had already been heralded in the seventeenth century. Great names here stand for great programmes:

– René Descartes: he was the father of the new rationalist philosophy and introduced a 'Copernican shift' of thought. The whole of reality was now constructed in terms of the human subject.

– Galileo Galilei: he was the pioneer of new empirical mathematical science. This was the presupposition for the technology and industrialization which soon began and reached their first climax in the nineteenth century.

– Cardinal Richelieu: he was the patron and virtuoso practitioner of a new secular understanding of the state and politics. The state and politics were no longer governed on confessional or even religious and moral principles, but were to be understood in terms of practical interests. The state was the natural product of a treaty between people and government and therefore autonomous over against the church.

The revolution in modern philosophy, the natural sciences, technology and industry was completed in the democratic revolution of state and society. What does this modern development mean for Christianity?

## CHRISTIANITY ON THE DEFENSIVE

At a very early stage, Christianity, both Roman Catholic and Reformation, was put on the defensive. For the paradigm of modernity, this meant:

- There was now an emphasis on original natural religion rather than on the Christian revelation in history.
- Now tolerance of all confessions and religions was propagated instead of religion as a confession.
- There was now a call for Enlightenment instead of a call for reformation.
- There was an emphasis on human freedom generally (freedom of religion and conscience, and at the same time on freedom of assembly, speech and the press) instead of on the freedom of Christians.

But the churches often persevered in their medieval or Reformation Gothic. All too often fixated on their great past, they rejected the new momentous paradigm shift. The slogan of the Roman Catholic paradigm was 'Pope and Curia' and that of the Reformation paradigm 'The word of God'. But the slogans of modernity were 'reason', 'progress', 'nation'.

In reactionary Catholic France, where religion had been totally discredited by the absolutist *ancien régime*, with the 1789 Revolution the Enlightenment had taken a turn which was sharply hostile to the monarchy and the church: 'Priests to the lantern!' In the free United States of America the Enlightenment remained in principle well-disposed to religion. Certainly there was a separation of church and state, but this was in the context of the religious freedom of the individual and society. A national state church was rejected *a priori*; too many immigrants and their descendants were religious dissenters. In general the conviction prevailed that the peaceful co-existence of faith communities in mutual tolerance was to be guaranteed. The government was to be favourable to any religion and not hinder the free practice of religion. There was not a total break with the past as in France, but the establishment of a modern liberal democracy of a kind which then also gradually became established in nineteenth-century Western Europe.

Now global perspectives increasingly came into the foreground: at first imperceptibly, the Eurocentric constellation was replaced by a polycentric constellation of different world religions. And the further the world horizon extended geographically, culturally and spiritually, the more the relativity of Christianity with a European stamp became evident.

But the further modernity progressed, the more its own relativity also became evident: too much that was negative may have happened in the name of God, but too much that was negative also happened in the name of reason, progress and nation.

## MODERNITY IN CRISIS

There is no mistaking the fact that today for many people the modern belief in progress, reason and nation seems to have faded into the twilight. The two faces of modernity are perhaps clearer on Wall Street, New York, than anywhere else:

– More and more people today are enjoying modern freedom and prosperity. But more and more people are failing to make like progress in matters of morality and ethics.

– More and more people are finding that they are caught up in a financial and economic situation which operates globally.

– More and more people are calling for fairer distribution and welfare for those who are disadvantaged by globalization.

– More and more people are sharing in the fruits of a highly efficient mass technology. But more and more people want an equal degree of control: they want humanization instead of rationalization.

– More and more people are affirming the democracy that is slowly also becoming established outside Europe and North America. But even more people still see no peace and no new world order. Truly, the towers are reaching higher and higher to heaven, and there is less and less heaven on earth.

## IN THE TRANSITION TO THE NEW GLOBAL ERA

What was already in the making as early as 1918 and broke through in 1945 became evident to all in 1989: our world is in transition into a new era, a postmodern paradigm. This as yet has no name, but it can be described negatively as:

– post-colonial and post-imperialistic: the model of truly united nations;
– post-capitalist and post-socialist: the model of an eco-social market economy;
– post-ideological and post-confessional: the model of a multi-cultural and multi-religous economic world community. Is that an illusion? That depends on us.

What is Christianity to contribute to this new global constellation? Three imperatives are urgent:

- Instead of condemning modernity there is a need to affirm its humane content: no traditionalism or fundamentalism, no subculture in the cultures, whether of Catholic, Orthodox or Protestant provenance.
- But at the same time there is a need to combat the inhuman constraints and destructive effects of modernity: no ultramodernism or postmodernism (random pluralism), no modernist concessions and no sell-out of the substance of religion.
- And thus there is a need to transcend modernity and anti-modernity by showing new dimensions of hope which are:
  - cosmic: partnerships with nature instead of domination of nature;
  - anthropological: men and women with equal status instead of a patriarchate;
  - social: fair distribution between poor and rich instead of antagonism;
  - religious: instead of a pre-modern religiosity and the modern absence of a religious sense a new openness to that very first and last spiritual reality which in the Jewish-Christian-Muslim tradition with a much misused name we call God.

The new global constellation requires a new world order, and this cannot be introduced without the support of the religions by the nations. In the new millennium the global organization of the United Nations – often criticized and even more often ignored and left in the lurch – faces immense tasks in this respect:

- The headlong globalization of the economy, technology and the media calls for global guidance by a global politics.
- But a global politics needs to be founded on a global ethic which can be supported and lived out by people of all cultures and religions, believers and non-believers alike.

**THE VISION OF HOPE**

There are people who believe that a clash of civilizations, say between Muslim and Western culture, is inevitable. Such a view is superficial and overlooks what the civilizations have in common. However, humankind must make a great effort if it is to avoid such a clash. Since the 1980s I have been campaigning for the programme 'No world peace without peace between the religions!' And in 1992 (and again in 1994 and in 1999) I was allowed to speak on this topic at United Nations Headquarters. Here I had a very positive response.

For precisely here there is an awareness that the religions have an immense potential for conflict which is exploited by some who are religious and some who are not. But the religions also have a by no means small potential for peace which has similarly developed. For it was men and women with religious motivations who without violence and bloodshed committed themselves to change, radical change in their countries: in Poland, in East Germany, in South Africa, in Central and South America and in the Philippines.

The conclusion to be drawn is that a clash of civilizations and religions must be avoided. And it can be avoided if sufficient people, men and women, and above all politicians and religious leaders, devote themselves to it. That is my realistic vision of hope.

No survival of humankind without peace among the nations! But no peace between the nations without peace among the religions! And no peace among the religions without dialogue between the religions!

## FOR THE SAKE OF THE CHILDREN

No, we have not given up hope. The peoples of the earth must not give up hope, if only for the sake of the children, the coming generations. And the children who one day will themselves be shaping the future could use what Jesus of Nazareth proclaimed and lived out 2000 years ago: tolerance, understanding, goodness, a readiness to help, sharing, forgiveness, love. Even after 2000 years these ideals are certainly not out of date.

The globe is threatened from within. It could fall apart. But the globe can also be made whole, more peaceful and more humane. That happens wherever people talk to one another, tolerate one another and respect one another instead of threatening and fighting one another.

For nations, groups and individuals the Golden Rule is more topical than ever. Jesus formulated it not only negatively but also positively: 'What you want to be done to you, do to others.' This is a fundamental orientation for the whole of a long life.

Violence is a problem in any society. But the saying of the great prophet Isaiah about 'beating swords into ploughshares' (2.4) is understood today in all nations and religions.

Young people should already learn that violence is not a means of controversy. Only in this way will we see the slow rise of
- a culture of non-violence and reverence for all life;
- a culture of the partnership of men and women;

– a culture of solidarity and justice;
– a culture of tolerance and truthfulness.

But wars above all are inhuman. They must be prevented by every possible means. After all, did not Jesus of Nazareth say, 'Blessed are the peacemakers, for they shall be called the children of God' (Matt. 5.9)?

# VII

# *Islam*

## MUSLIMS IN MARSEILLES

Notre Dame de la Garde is the landmark of the most famous French port, which has given its name to the French national anthem. Countless sailors have made a pilgrimage here to the Madonna, to give thanks for rescue from shipwreck.

Marseilles was founded by the Greeks as long ago as 600 BC and since Roman times has been the greatest trading port in the Western Mediterranean. For more than 1600 years it has been an episcopal see. Medieval Marseilles flourished at the time of the Crusades.

Many people from all over the city and all over the world have begged for help at this pilgrimage place, praying for support in all the manifold storms of life. There are countless pictures, countless anxieties. But there are some situations in which people can no longer help themselves. Nothing has changed here.

However, we should not be deceived: neither here in Marseilles nor anywhere else in France is the church the great spiritual landmark for society. Much is a relic of the past. In recent times the Catholic Church has lost its monopoly in the market of doctrines of salvation. France is more secularized than most other European countries. The number of practising Catholics has declined to a few per cent, often no greater than that of the Muslims who are settled there: at around 4.5 per cent they form the highest proportion of the population in any European country. There are more than 3,000,000 Muslims in France, and soon there will also be 3,000,000 Muslims in Great Britain and in Germany. By now in Europe the Muslims form the largest religious community after the Christians. And this trend is continuing.

## CALL TO PRAYER: MUEZZIN, MINARET, MOSQUE

Prayer plays a central role in all three Abrahamic religions (Judaism, Christianity and Islam). But it is the Muslim's duty (*fard*) to perform ritual prayer (*salat*) five times a day at particular times. He is publicly summoned to prayer by the muezzin, from high up the tower of the mosque, the minaret. The call is given in the morning, at noon, in the afternoon, at sunset and in the evening. Today, though, the announcements are very often made by tape and loudspeaker, sometimes in noisy competition. Here the instruction contained in the Qur'an itself is forgotten: ' "It is the same whether you call on God or on the Merciful: His are the most gracious names." Pray neither with too loud a voice nor in silence, but seek between these two extremes a middle course' (surah 17.110).

The mosque (*masjid* = 'place where one prostrates oneself', place of worship') is a place not only for worship and personal prayer but also for meetings, negotiations and judgment; it is also a place for theological instruction and study. Its furnishings include the prayer niche (*mihrab*) in the direction (*qibla*) of Mecca, the pulpit (*minbar*) for the leader of Friday worship, a Qur'an stand, lights and lamps, mats and carpets. The Muslim house of God has no images, statues or devotional objects. Words of the Qur'an, artistically formed in large Arabic letters, are enough, together with non-representative ornaments. There is no solemn music, whether instrumental or choral. The solemn recitation of the Qur'an is music enough.

### THE MUSLIMS – OUR NEIGHBOURS

I went to the office of the sheikh of the Islah mosque. I had come straight from Notre Dame de la Garde. Sometimes Muslims, too, take flowers, candles and incense there. For Mary and above all her son Jesus play a significant role in the Qur'an. That means that the Christian and Muslim faiths are not totally opposed, as they are so often made out to be.

However, here in Marseilles, as in other cities of Europe, there are great tensions between Muslims and non-Muslims and fears on both sides:

– Non-Muslims feel threatened by the revolutions in Iran, Sudan and Afghanistan and the terrorists in Algeria and Egypt.

– But Muslims also feel threatened: by social restrictions, unemployment, possible deportation; by the military intervention of the West in Iraq, and by the one-sided policy in Bosnia and above all in Palestine.

If a 'clash of civilizations' is to be avoided in a city, a land, the world, then this can be done only through dialogue and understanding. There are fanatics in Islam, but there are also fanatics in Judaism and Christianity, everywhere.

Of course, violence must be resisted everywhere. But in principle understanding, tolerance, a democratic disposition should be shown to people with a religious commitment. And here it is a great help if one reflects on religious roots, and in particular on the common roots of Judaism, Christianity and Islam in belief in the one God of Abraham.

## DAILY RITUAL PRAYER – THE ESSENTIAL SYMBOL OF ISLAM

The equality of all Muslims before God is particularly evident in worship: no dress separates clergy from laity, no liturgical drama separates the sacred from the profane, no mystery play separates the initiated from the innocent. In principle any Muslim can lead the prayer as an imam. There is no priesthood and no ordination of priests, no holy of holies, no sacrificial altar, no special dress for religious dignitaries and no separate space in the mosque for a clerical caste.

The daily ritual prayer is disciplined, its course precisely laid down and completely focused on the one God. All are incorporated into the well-ordered ranks of the praying community: every individual is caught up in the great rhythm of this tremendous simple and direct rite of personal and communal worship of God. The most important of the five prescribed movements is the double 'prostration' of worshippers before their Creator and Judge, in which the forehead touches the ground. In this way those who pray indicate that human beings owe their existence utterly to God, that their fate constantly depends upon a higher power. This is the deepest expression of 'Islam', 'submission' to God.

In the view of many Muslims the opening surah of the Qur'an (*al-fatiha*) contains the foundation, the sum and the quintessence of the whole Qur'an: 'In the name of God, the Compassionate, the Merciful. Praise be to God, Lord of the Creation, the Compassionate, the Merciful, King of the Last Judgment. You alone we worship, and to You alone we pray for help. Guide us to the straight path, the path of those whom You have favoured, not of those who have incurred Your wrath, nor of those who have gone astray.' The only petition that is expressed in the obligatory prayer is the petition for 'right guidance'. Could not such a prayer also be prayed by Christians? We shall have to work out the distinguishing features of Islam, but do so in an objective and not a derogatory way.

## ISLAM AS A THREAT

For some people in the West, after the collapse of Communism Islam has had to take on the role of the enemy. To have an enemy is good in many ways. It serves various functions, not only social and political, but also in the sphere of individual psychology:

– Having an enemy unburdens us: neither we nor our friends are to blame, but the enemy. Our suppressed feelings of guilt and inferiority, our aggressions and frustrations, can innocuously be diverted outwards and projected on the enemy. In the enemy we have a scapegoat.

– To have an enemy brings people together: though we may be at odds in many respects, we are sworn to resist the enemy. A common enemy strengthens cohesion. It leads us to close ranks and exclude deviants. To have an enemy encourages thinking in terms of blocs.

– To have an enemy polarizes. By reducing possibilities to an either-or, people can effectively categorize others in the political dispute as friend or enemy and exploit them accordingly. If we do not know what we are for, at least we know what we are against. The fronts have been drawn. We all know where we stand. To have an enemy forces everyone into a friend-foe syndrome.

– To have an enemy promotes action: we do not need our own information and orientation. We may and should defend ourselves against the others, aliens, enemies, both outside and within. So not only mistrust but also hostility, and if need be even violence, is appropriate against things and persons: this can be physical, psychological, political and indeed military force. If we have an enemy, our inhibitions about killing are overcome. Having an enemy easily leads to war, cold or hot.

## SELF-CRITICAL QUESTIONS FOR CHRISTIANS

Where Islam is concerned, our media love to show fanatical bearded mullahs, uninhibited violent terrorists, super-rich oil sheikhs or veiled women. The countless peace-loving, tolerant and open Muslims in Europe in particular suffer under such stereotypes, which emphasize Islam as a religion above all of internal intolerance, external militancy, and rigidity and regression in every respect.

Self-critical questions for Christians come thronging in. Isn't all too often a negative picture of Islam compared with an ideal picture of Christianity? Aren't there also intolerance, militancy and regression in the West, indeed in Christianity itself, and conversely, aren't there also tolerance, a love of peace and progress in Islam? Doesn't such a scheme of friend and foe denigrate and exclude what is alien in us? Is this a picture of Islam as it really exists? Christians should understand Islam as it understands itself. Critical questioning can then be allowed; competition for a deeper understanding of God is thoroughly desirable.

## ISLAM: AT THE SAME TIME THE NEWEST AND THE OLDEST RELIGION

A mere look at the map of the world provokes the question: why will soon a billion people in the belt around the equator confess Islam, from the Atlantic coast of Africa to the Indonesian islands, from the steppes of central Asia to Mozambique in Africa? Why has this religion been able to bring together in a great religious family such different people as the nomadic Berbers, the black East Africans, the Arabs in the Middle East, but also Turks, Persians, Pakistanis, Indians, Chinese and Malays?

For Muslims themselves, Islam is the newest and therefore also the best religion. Granted, previously Jews and Christians had already received God's revelation, but unfortunately they had falsified it. Islam first presented it again in an unfalsified form. So for Muslims Islam is also the oldest and most universal religion. For Adam, the first human being, was already a 'Muslim'. Why? Because Adam already practised *islam*, which literally means submission to God's will in living and dying.

## CALLIGRAPHY INSTEAD OF DESCRIPTIVE ARTS

Unlike the Jews in later times, even now Muslims do not have the slightest inhibitions about speaking the name of God. But when it comes to the prohibition of images, if anything they are even more radical than the Jews. For them, scripture takes the place of the prohibited images and calligraphy the place of the descriptive arts: in earlier times, too, calligraphy was cultivated in the highest circles.

The script of classical Arabic developed out of a form of Aramaic. The Aramaic alphabet of the Nabataean Arabs (whose capital was Petra in present-day Jordan) is its forerunner. Trilingual Christian inscriptions in Syriac, Greek and Arabic from the year 512/513 are the earliest evidence of Arabic script discovered so far. This is a consonantal script, written from right to left; over time its vowels were provided with little 'diacritical' (distinguishing) signs to avoid ambiguity and misinterpretation.

Even today the calligrapher still uses the traditional writing instruments, a quill or a reed pen made of bamboo. But above all he needs intellectual and aesthetic capabilities. Usually he is the master of several kinds of script. A calligrapher loves to show his ability with the two decisive names in the Islamic confession of faith; this is the basis of all Muslim practice.

## THE FOUNDATION OF ISLAM: THE CONFESSION OF FAITH

The confession of faith (*shahada*) is indisputably and beyond question the central message of Islam. It is of the greatest conceivable simplicity and in fact can be rendered with two words.

The first word is Allah. Muslims believe in the one God who does not tolerate the 'association' of any kind of goddess, a son or a daughter. Belief in Allah, the one God, is the first obligation for Muslims and the foundation of the Islamic community, the sole content of their prayer liturgy. It is the spiritual bond of unity for all Islamic tribes and peoples.

The second word is Muhammad, in other words the confession of the last, definitive Prophet, the 'seal' of the prophets. Just as according to Islamic understanding Moses brought the Jews a book, the Torah, and Jesus brought Christians the Gospel, so too Muhammad brought the Arabs a holy book, the Qur'an. Thus Muhammad, too, is not just an ordinary prophet (*nabi*); because he has brought a holy book like Moses, David (the Psalms) and Jesus, he is a special emissary of the one God. Nevertheless, in no way is he more than a man. The Qur'an says: 'I am no more than a mortal like yourselves. It is revealed to me that your God is one God' (surah 41.6). Here we can see what is common to the three religions of Semitic Near Eastern origin and what distinguishes them.

## THE DISTINCTIVE FEATURE OF THE THREE MONOTHEISTIC RELIGIONS

There is no mistaking what Judaism, Christianity and Islam have in common: belief in the one and only God of Abraham, the gracious and merciful Creator, Preserver and Judge of all human beings, in Arabic called 'Allah' by both Muslims and Christians.

But what distinguishes the three religions is clear. What is most important is:

- for Judaism, God's people and land;
- for Christianity, Jesus Christ as God's Messiah and Son;
- for Islam, the Qur'an as God's word and book.

## THE QUR'AN: A BOOK

For Muslims the Qur'an is a living, holy book in Arabic. Every word in this description is important.

It is a book. As such it has the advantage that all believers know where they are. The book contains everything that has been directly revealed by God. It unequivocally states the will of God. Therefore here too nothing is to be changed. On the contrary, it is not a matter of change but of internalization. Even as schoolchildren, Muslims are to memorize as many texts as possible.

It is one book. The Qur'an is not, like the Hebrew Bible, a collection of very contrasting writings which at first sight seem to have no common denominator. Nor does it consist, as the New Testament does, of very different proclamatory texts which are even contradictory in many details, and themselves indicate that they do not contain all the source material about Jesus. No, for Muslims the book is a single book of revelations which came to one and the same Prophet; these revelations are therefore consecutive and despite all the differences of time and style form a unity. Only after Muhammad's death were they collected into a book, divided into 114 sections (more or less according to length). The sections are called surahs (*sura*, plural *suwar*), and these in turn are made up of verses ('signs', *aya*; plural *ayat*). There is already mention of a book (*kitab*) in the Qur'an itself.

It is an Arabic book. The Qur'an is the earliest Arabic literature in prose (it was preceded by collections of verse). More than almost anything else it furthered the dissemination of Arabic in word and script, and even now is normative for syntax and morphology. But more importantly, at the same time the Qur'an is a book of revelation given to the Arabs, so that now finally they too possess a scripture like the Jews and Christians. They are a 'people of the book'. They now possess a holy book which through the beauty, the impressive melody and the often passionate rhythm of its language can even bewitch and charm the non-Arabs among the Muslims. For them, too, Arabic is the language of worship and for them, too, Arabic script is their own. Even Muslims who favour reform think that only those who understand pure Arabic can understand the Qur'an and that therefore every Muslim must make the effort to learn Arabic. Through the Qur'an Arabic has become the sacred language of the whole of the Muslim West.

## THE QUR'AN: MADE PRESENT BY READING

The Qur'an is a living book. It is neither a venerable book from the past nor a private book of devotion and contemplation. It is a book which time and again is recited aloud in public: 'Qur'an' comes from the verb qaraa = 'read aloud', and means 'reading' in both senses of the word: both the act of presenting and reciting, and what is recited, the lectionary. What the Prophet heard he handed on to his fellow men and women. The Qur'an is a book of surahs and verses written in resonant rhymed prose which can and should be recited or sung. Its words and sentences accompany the Muslim from the hour of his birth, when the Qur'an confession of faith is sung in his ear, to his last hour, when words of the Qur'an accompany him to eternity. By hearing, memorizing and reciting the Qur'an, the Muslim confesses God's revelation and at the same time appropriates it.

The Qur'an is a holy book. It is not a book like any other, to be touched with grubby hands and to be read in an impure spirit. Before reading this book one must cleanse one's hands with water or sand and open one's heart in humble prayer. It is not a profane book, but is sacral through and through, and in this respect it is omnipresent. Its verses, artistically engraved in stone or painted on pottery, adorn sacred buildings, and also decorate works of metal and wood, porcelain and miniatures. Strikingly beautiful, written in different scripts, the copies of the Qur'an themselves transcend everything else. They often have precious bindings and usually are adorned with coloured decorations.

## FOR MUSLIMS THE WAY, THE TRUTH AND THE LIFE

As the foundation document of God's final revelation, the Qur'an has left a deep stamp on all spheres of Islam. What the Torah is for Jews and Christ is for Christians, the Qur'an is for Muslims: 'the way, the truth and the life'. In fact, for all Muslims the Qur'an is:
- the truth, the original source of the experience of God and piety and the obligatory criterion of right belief;
- the way, the true possibility of coping with the world and an eternally valid guideline for right action, ethics;
- the life, the abiding foundation of Islamic law and the soul of the Islamic liturgy. It is used for the instruction of Muslim children; it is the inspiration of Muslim art and the all-permeating spirit of Muslim culture. It is not so much concerned with dogmas as with practice. For,

## WHO IS REALLY A MUSLIM?

In cities like Marseilles, even the streets in front of the mosque fill with people for Friday prayer. Prayer carpets are laid out all over them. But all these people praying together are aware that one is not a true Muslim simply by making the confession of faith. The only true Muslim is the one who submits quite practically to God in life, in other words who attempts to live in accordance with God's will. And all this is done by following the example of the Prophet Muhammad. But who was this Muhammad? In the case of some other founders of religion the historical figure tends to get lost in legend and myth, but that is not the case with Muhammad.

## ARABIA: THE BIRTHPLACE OF ISLAM

Northern Arabia is fundamentally different from rich South Arabia (Yemen, the Hadramut), which because of its favourable climate, its impressive monopoly in incense and its trade with India was known as 'happy' Arabia (*Arabia felix*). It is poor in water, barren, sandy, stony, rocky, with no seas and rivers, only wadis. It is a land which requires of plants, animals and human beings extremes of hardness, perseverance and militancy.

This northern area of wildernesses, steppes and mountains also contains oases, which made it possible for the Bedouins to settle, to engage in agriculture and trade (breeding camels and later horses, which became increasingly important for the army). However, it was to change fundamentally because of the caravan trade, which increased tremendously with the 'Incense Road'. The caravan trade needed to be organized, protected and encouraged. And it was precisely this northern area, or more precisely north-west Arabia, that was the real homeland of the Arabs, and with its rising cities of Mecca, Ta'if, Medina and Najran was the birthplace of Islam. The future was to belong to it.

## A PROPHET ARISES

Muhammad was born in Mecca around 570. He came from the tribe of the Quraysh and the clan of the Hashim. Originally an orphan who was brought up by his grandfather and then by his uncle, the head of the clan, he became business manager for a rich merchant's widow and finally, at the age of 25, her husband. He engaged in long trade journeys through the desert to Palestine and Syria on her behalf. But more and more frequently he withdrew from business into the solitude of the mountains. Over the years prayer and meditation became more important to him than trade, with all its precious goods. At that time in pre-Islamic pagan Arabia, with its gods, sons and daughters of gods, there were quite a few god-seekers (*hanif*) who longed for a purer faith, faith in the one God.

And yet what a surprise it was when one day Muhammad, now 40 years old, appeared with the report that he had received revelations from God! He proclaimed these revelations only in the circle of his family and friends. And here finally he won over a small group of believers. Only in time did he become clear about all the implications of his prophetic calling. For he kept receiving new revelations, which he presented to his followers.

## A PROVOCATIVE MESSAGE

But when Muhammad proclaimed the revelations publicly after three years, he was almost universally rejected, indeed ridiculed, as one who 'warned' and 'admonished'. There were two understandable reasons for this:

Muhammad made a plea for an ethic of justice in the midst of the busy trading city of Mecca on the Incense Road at a time when the caravan trade from Yemen to Gaza and Damascus was at its height. He confronted his fellow citizens with the coming judgment, threatened severe punishments in the other world and called for conversion and social solidarity. This was a threat to the selfishness and materialism of the rich merchants and traders.

Secondly, Muhammad pleaded for submission to the one and only God, the just and merciful one. This was a threat to the cult of gods and the trade round the Ka'ba, the whole pilgrimage business, and thus Mecca's system of finance and business. Indeed the unity and prestige of his tribe, the Quraysh, was endangered. The social and religious problems were closely interwoven. Business life and social structure on the one hand and religion and moral views on the other formed an almost undistinguishable fabric of ideas and institutions.

Nevertheless, a Muslim community came into being. Its basis was not a particular social status but common faith, ritual prayer, piety with an eschatological focus and an ethic of justice. The consequence was a bitter conflict which lasted for ten years. Finally the Prophet's situation in Mecca became untenable. His wife died, and soon afterwards his uncle and guardian. Another uncle, who had married a wife from the clan of the Umayya which was hostile to Muhammad, turned against him. The quest for a place of refuge outside his tribe in the region of Mecca remained unsuccessful.

## MEDINA: THE FORMATION OF A COMMUNITY

There was only one way out, emigration, the Hijra. In the year 622 – which later became year 1 of the new Islamic chronology – the Prophet emigrated to Yathrib, which was later to be called Medina (al-Madina = 'city' of the Prophet). Medina was not a city of trade, pilgrimage and markets like Mecca, but rather an oasis of date palms and grain, a centre of agriculture, which was being practised effectively here above all by Jewish tribes. But in Medina several tribes and clans were entangled in disputes: they needed an arbitrator and peacemaker. At an earlier date, men from this city around 180 miles to the north had secretly met with Muhammad in Mecca at pilgrimage time and taken heed of his message.

Now the Muslims went away in small groups: this was an exodus from their own tribe in which they broke off relations with their own clan – for the sake of the faith. Truly it was a transition to another world. What counted was no longer tribal affinity, but the faith community; no longer the old gods but the one God. The community of Arabs became the community of Muslims. In Medina the Prophet founded the first Muslim community, which today is still called umma, as it was then.

From the beginning the umma was both a religious fellowship and a political community. So there was no separation between religion and state. From the start the Islamic state was a 'theocracy', the rule of God. But Muhammad was deeply disappointed: in particular the three Jewish tribes in Medina rejected his claim to be a prophet: for them he was not a prophet. Muhammad's image of the Jews became a negative one. He forced two of these tribes to emigrate and massacred the third. This, too, is a characteristic of the Arab prophet: he is both a statesman and a general at the same time.

For six years Muhammad waged war against his home tribe. But in 630 he re-entered Mecca peacefully as a victor, though he then continued to reside in Medina. The original model of all mosques is here. It is the house which Muhammad himself had built: there is a rectangular courtyard surrounded by clay walls, containing two halls with awnings to give shade, standing on palm trunks; there is a sign to orientate prayer towards Mecca and a simple pulpit; adjacent to the east wall were huts made of palm branches for the Prophet and his wives.

## MUSLIM PRACTICE: THE FIVE PILLARS OF ISLAM

From Medina, in 632 Muhammad made another pilgrimage to Mecca. This was to be his farewell pilgrimage. Terminally ill, his head in the lap of his favourite wife Aisha, the Prophet died at the age of 62 on 8 July 632 in Medina – today the second holiest city in Islam after Mecca. By now Muhammad had brought the whole of the Arabian peninsula under his control and made Arabia the heartland of Islam.

Prayer was now longer orientated towards Jewish Jerusalem but towards Mecca. At the centre of Mecca was the Ka'ba, which Muhammad had purged of local deities in 630. This was of the utmost significance for the integration of the Muslim populations, which were now steadily increasing. For with its prayer niche in the direction of Mecca, every mosque all over the world keeps reminding Muslims of their starting-point, their origin, the homeland of their religion. One only needs to think in a line as the crow flies to know where one absolutely must travel, at least once in one's lifetime. Every adult male Muslim has to make this pilgrimage once in his life, even if even now in fact only a small number of Muslims can afford it (so they can also send a representative instead).

Already in the earliest Muslim community, five pillars of Islam formed on the basis of the Qur'an; on them the whole house of Islam is built: as well as the confession of faith in the one God and his Prophet, whose tomb is venerated in Medina, and the obligation to pray every day,
– every year alms must be given or the social tax (*zakat*) paid;
– every year Ramadan, the month of fasting, must be observed, with a complete fast from dawn to sunset; and
– once in a lifetime pilgrimage, the hajj, must be made to Mecca. This is the fifth pillar of Islam.

## MECCA: THE DESTINATION OF THE GREAT PILGRIMAGE

The great pilgrimage of Muslims to Mecca is possible only in the pilgrimage month. At least once in a lifetime the Muslim is to turn away from the world and wholly towards God. However, this has nothing in common with the relatively pleasant pilgrimages that Christians make to Lourdes or to Rome.

A whole series of sometimes strenuous rituals have to be performed. First of all the pilgrims have to put themselves in a state of dedication: the women wear a seamless white garment, the men two white cloths; they do not shave or comb their hair. No one is to cut hair or nails, to use perfume or to have sexual intercourse, and if shoes are worn at all, they must be unsewn. Identical dress reinforces a sense of the equality of all men and women before God.

In the Muslim view, Abraham and his son Ishmael erected the Ka'ba (Arabic for 'cube') and cleansed the place of idolatry. This age-old central sanctuary of Mecca must be circled seven times, and the black stone, probably a basalt meteorite, has to be greeted, touched, even kissed. The Muslims regard the Ka'ba as a place of special divine presence. Everything that comes into contact with it receives part of God's power of blessing.

The 'lesser' pilgrimage – which is possible all through the year – consists merely of walking round the Ka'ba. But in the 'great' pilgrimage, people go into the plain of Arafat and climb Rahma, the mountain of grace, where they receive forgiveness of sins. Moreover, on subsequent days of the great pilgrimage there is another series of rites at holy places around Mecca. The main rite involves collecting pebbles, which are thrown at a stone pillar. This pillar is a symbol of the devil, who is said to live in ruins, tombs and in 'unclean places'; he is said to love music and dance and to be able to assume every possible form.

Unlike Jews and Christians, Muslims still practise age-old animal sacrifice to atone for transgressions. The animals to be sacrificed – a sheep, a goat or a camel, often for a whole group of pilgrims – are driven together. With the invocation of the name of God their throats are cut in the direction of the Ka'ba. The pilgrims are given a small portion of the meat to eat; the rest is for the poor. All in all, this is a joyful sacrificial feast, involving more than a million people and hundreds of thousands of sacrificial animals; it certainly cannot be performed without major rationalized organization. After the sacrifice the men shave, cut their hair and put on new clothes.

At the end of the second week the pilgrims go round the Ka'ba again. Then follows the great closing prayer, 'Allahu akbar', 'Allah alone is great'. There is no doubt that for any Muslim man or woman this pilgrimage is the experience of a lifetime of faith.


## WHO WILL SUCCEED THE PROPHET?

The foundations for the primal Islamic community paradigm were already laid under the Prophet, and were further developed by his successors, whom he himself did not nominate. We often read on Muslim tombstones that the death of the Prophet was 'the greatest misfortune'. What were the consequences?

– Direct jurisdiction by the Prophet, who was the recipient, interpreter and executor of divine revelations, was replaced by jurisdiction through the representative (*chalifa*) of the Prophet.

– Authority was no longer constantly renewed by ever new divine revelations. There was only the derived human authority of a non-prophetic leadership: there was no longer a 'spokesman' of God but at best a 'conversation partner' of God.

– The charismatic leader was replaced by the institution of the caliphate: charisma was replaced by office, prophecy by tradition, and thus charismatic rule was legalized and institutionalized.

The representative of the Prophet was not himself a prophet, nor primarily a merely religious authority. At the same time he was a political and legal authority, something like a supreme tribal chief who had to lead the whole Muslim community, mediate and be an arbiter in disputes. He also had to assume supreme command of the army. The tasks of a caliph were so novel that they had not been set down anywhere. Granted, the word 'caliph' occurs in the Qur'an several times, but at no point does it clearly denote a political and religious successor to the Prophet in leading the community. Is it surprising that at a very early stage there were disputes among Muslims about the characteristics and competence of the caliph and how he should be appointed?

However, the Muslims were now increasingly aware of one thing: though the Prophet was no longer among the living, the Qur'an would remain. As the eternal word of God it is alive and remains indestructible. In the political succession, the statesman Muhammad was replaced in the earliest Islamic community by the caliph. The caliphate would in fact in time become an institution. But in the religious succession, there was no supreme doctrinal authority. The Prophet Muhammad's place was taken by the Qur'an as God's Word, and along with it the example of God's emissary, the tradition about the Prophet, the Sunna. In the long run Qur'an and Sunna became the religious authority (and indirectly also the political authority).

## THE FIRST ARAB EXPANSION:
## THE POWER OF THE NEW RELIGION

Already under the first four 'righteous' caliphs (632–61) there was a first wave of conquest. After that, enormous areas became Muslim: once-Christian Syria with Damascus and Jerusalem; the Persian Sassanid empire with Mesopotamia and Azerbaijan; and finally Christian Egypt. No other religion has expanded so broadly and so lastingly in so short a time as Islam.

Beyond doubt non-religious factors also made a contribution: the policy of conquest and settlement planned by the élites in Mecca and Medina to control the militant rival Bedouin tribes; the voluntary nature of the associations; the superior military tactics of small and highly mobile units; and the prospect of lower taxes for those who had been conquered. But the decisive factor – and here most recent research confirms the traditional Islamic view – was the spiritual power of the new religion of the book, which gave the Muslims a powerful faith and a sense of mission, a motivation for religious war and moral justification for their conquests.

Primarily the caliphs were in fact concerned to achieve a territorial extension of the Islamic state and not to extend Islam spiritually. Christians, Jews and Zoroastrians were not to be converted but were to pay a poll tax and finance the Islamic state. They were regarded as protected minorities (dhimmi), albeit second-class citizens with markedly reduced legal status. They enjoyed internal autonomy and protection for their bodies, their lives and their property, but were excluded from state service and the army.


## KAIROUAN: THE OLDEST MOSQUE IN NORTH AFRICA

Who would think, going through the quiet and rather miserable old city of Kairouan in Tunis, that this was the 'camp city' of the Arab army in the second great wave of expansion; the great headquarters and the first Muslim city to be founded in North Africa, far from the coast and protected against attacks from the Byzantine fleet. It was the starting-point of all further military operations against Berbers and Byzantines throughout the Maghreb as far as the Atlantic. Even today, Kairouan is the fourth holiest city of Islam after Mecca, Medina and Jerusalem. Its wool and carpet businesses recall Kairouan's heyday in the ninth century.

And even today the mosque of Sidi-Oqba, who at that time was general and governor of the Roman province of Africa, i.e. North Africa, Arabic *ifri-qiya*, is the destination of millions of pilgrims. The inner court with several doors and, as is customary in mosques, a spring for ritual washing is dominated by the powerful minaret. This mosque is the oldest and most important Islamic building in North Africa, the model for all Moorish sacred architecture. All in all it has a forest of 414 Roman pillars which come from Carthage and other ruined cities.

### AN ETHICAL HIGH RELIGION

It would be wrong to dismiss Islam as a religion of fire and sword and not to see its religious substance. For there is no doubt that through the Prophet Muhammad, the Arabs were raised to the level of an ethical high religion based on faith in the one God and on a fundamental ethic of humanity with clear demands for greater humanity and justice. In origin Islam was less a religion of the law than a religion of ethics. And so there is also something like the Ten Commandments, the foundation of a shared ethic of humankind, in Islam.

There is no doubt that Muhammad was an authentic prophet, in many respects not dissimilar to the prophets of Israel. But Muslims attach great importance to the fact that Muhammad does not stand at the centre of Islam as Jesus Christ stands at the centre of Christianity. For the Muslims, God's Word did not become a man but a book. And the Qur'an, which in its original version lies with God himself, forms the centre of Islam.

Moreover Islam is a religion of the book *par excellence*. The Qur'an completes and replaces the Torah of the Jews and the Gospel of the Christians. For Muslims it is unsurpassable, perfect and absolutely reliable. Moreover it is solemnly recited and above all also learned by heart by the experts. But Muslim theologians, too, have discussed the question whether as the Word of God the Qur'an is not also the word of human beings, the word of the Prophet Muhammad.

## JERUSALEM: A SANCTUARY OF THE GOD OF ABRAHAM

In their very first thrust against the Christian Byzantine province of Syria, in 635 the Arabs conquered Jerusalem, the 'holy city' of Jews and Christians. That still has consequence for Jews and Christians today. Apart from the century of the Crusades, from then until our times Jerusalem remained Muslim: it is called 'al-Quds', the sanctuary. And it should not be forgotten that now the Jews, who after the complete destruction of Jerusalem by the Romans in 135 had been banned from the city (the prohibition was maintained by the Christian emperors), were allowed by the Muslims to enter their city once again. So it is not surprising that the Jews who were living in Palestine at that time felt that the Muslim conquest of Palestine was a liberation.

For Muslims the old temple courtyard is the 'noble, holy place' (*haram esh-sherif*). After Mecca and Medina it is the third holiest place in the world, which Muslims treasure as the apple of their eye. No services take place under the golden cupola of the Dome of the Rock. The strict order of prayer which is customary for Muslims certainly could not be carried out in this circular building.

Immediately under the cupola there is the enormous, uneven, bare rock of Mount Moriah. Here, according to the ancient tradition, Abraham was graciously preserved from sacrificing his son Isaac. Here the first human being is said to have been created, and here the Prophet Muhammad is said to have ascended into heaven – his footprints are still pointed out today. Finally, it is here that one day the judgment of the world will take place. For Muslims the Dome of the Rock (*kubbet es sachra*) is thus not a mosque but a tremendous place to think of the one God of Abraham. It is a place of silent prayer.

The Dome of the Rock, often wrongly called the Umar Mosque, although Caliph Umar did not himself capture Jerusalem, is a unique architectural masterpiece, built, it is said, on the site of the original Holy of Holies in the year 72 after the Hijra, 691/692 by our reckoning, under the Umayyad Abd al-Malik. It is regarded as the oldest, most beautiful and most perfect achievement of Islamic architecture; amazingly enough it has not been imitated anywhere in the Muslim world.

This most holy temple court of the Jews was desecrated by the Romans and neglected by the Byzantine Christians. Has it not been hallowed again by twelve centuries of Muslim worship? At any rate, with the Dome of the Rock we already have a sanctuary of the one God of Abraham. Could it not become a shared ecumenical sanctuary in that time that we hope for, when there is peace between the three Abrahamic religions?

## ISLAM SPLIT

It was not disputes over orthodox faith but disputes about the true succession to the Prophet that were the occasion for the first Muslim civil war, though such a war was strictly forbidden in the Qur'an. Indeed, these disputes led to a crisis in the original Islamic community paradigm. This resulted in the splitting of the umma into three 'parties' which still exist today. They are:
– the Sunni party, which to the present day embraces the vast majority of Muslims, who want to recognize the 'Sunna' and all four righteous caliphs;
– the Shi'ites, the 'party' (*shia*) of Ali, Muhammad's murdered cousin and son-in-law, which to the present day forms the minority (around 10 per cent) of Muslims (in Iran, Iraq and Lebanon). It recognizes only Ali as the legitimate successor to the Prophet;
– the Kharijite party, 'the seceders'. Regardless of allegiance to any tribe or family, these now wanted to accept the best Muslim as successor (even if he were an Abyssinian slave). For a long time the Kharijites, with their puritanical orientation, carried on a bitter war with the Sunni caliphs, and today they are represented only among the Berbers, in Oman and in Zanzibar.

After battles against the Shi'ite party in which they suffered great losses, the Meccan family of the Umayyads, which had originally been hostile to Muhammad, came out on top. With them the majority party of the Sunnis triumphed. The Umayyads moved the residence of the caliph to Damascus and made Syria the leading Muslim power. The first of the thirteen

Umayyad caliphs, Mu'awiya, united the Arab tribes, and in place of the
Arab tribal federation established a centralized and bureaucratic state with
an army, a chancery, and a postal and information service.

## THE ARABIAN EMPIRE OF THE UMAYYADS:
## THE SECOND EXPANSION

Thus a monarchical Arab imperial paradigm replaced the original Islamic
paradigm of the community. The succession of the 'representative of God'
(not just of the Prophet) was regulated by the dynastic principle: the status
of caliph became hereditary. The second great caliph of the Umayyad
dynasty, Abd al-Malik, who built the Dome of the Rock, introduced
Arabic instead of Greek as the official language. The whole of public life –
from currency through the existing common law to art – was Islamicized
as far as possible: this was a demonstration of the triumph of Islam over
Christian Byzantium.

The great mosque of the Umayyad caliph Walid, son of the builder of
the Dome of the Rock, in Damascus, is a towering example of this process.
This shows what the Islamicization of an architecture largely taken over
from Byzantium actually means: houses and landscapes are brought into
the foreground, and all the depictions of angels, human beings and animals
are replaced by floral and geometrical figures. The new Arabic ornamental
script and ceramics – along with the stucco work – are the most important
signs of Islamic art.

But no dynastic principle and no central authority could dissuade the
opposition party within the Arabic imperial paradigm, the party of Ali,
later to become the Shi'ites, from unshakeably maintaining allegiance to
Ali and above all to his younger son Husayn, the grandson of the Prophet.
A second civil war, in which Husayn was killed in Kerbela, intensified the
split in the umma and made Husayn the object of a martyr cult which is
unique in Islam. Thus in Islam the Shia became a separate confession, for
whom Ali is the one true caliph and Husayn its key witness. Indeed, the
stories of his suffering, the passion plays and in part bloody martyr cult
(with self-inflicted wounds and flagellation), still play an important role in
the Shi'ite sphere. Instead of the hereditary dynasty of the Umayyad
caliphs, the Shi'ites accept only the succession of the imams (spiritual
supreme heads), the last of whom is hidden and will one day return.

The Umayyads unleashed a second great wave of conquest, both
westwards and eastwards. Barely a century after the death of the Prophet,
their Arab empire (661–750) extended from India and the frontiers of
China to Morocco and Spain, from the Himalayas to the Pyrenees. In the
history of the religions no victorious progress took place so rapidly, over so

wide an area, and proved so permanent. This is a cause for Muslim pride even today.

There were fortified bases all along the frontiers of the Islamic empire. Like members of a religious order, the fighters for the faith lived in 'ribats'. There was a strange combination of military service and strict religious practice, of a kind which later also characterized the Christian crusaders and knights.

---

**RELIGION AND VIOLENCE**

At a very early stage, in strategically favourable locations all along the coast of North Africa the Arabs established defensive monasteries on the lines of Byzantine monastic fortifications. The ribat, the defensive monastery of Monastir, has taken its name from the Greek *monasterion*, monastery, and is one of the oldest and most imposing Muslim fortresses in North Africa. From here the Muslims waged their wars against nearby Christian Sicily. However, I do not want in any way to give the impression that there were wars of faith only in Islam. There were also wars of faith in Judaism in the name of God. And of course in Christianity there were the Crusades, and colonial conquests and missions to almost the whole of the Muslim world. This is even now a trauma for Muslims.

The problem of violence arises in all religions. There is violence in all religions. But in particular there is violence in the prophetic religions, which are orientated outwards, and are active, militant and missionary. In particular there is violence in Islam, since Muhammad himself was not only a prophet but also a successful general – and the Muslims are proud of that.

Even now, of course, the Qur'an is quoted, with its summons to the 'jihad'. But 'jihad' should not be translated 'holy war'. Literally, 'jihad' means 'effort': moral effort for God, against one's own imperfections. And in the view of many Muslims, only in extreme cases should this 'toiling on the way to God' be understood as a 'duty to fight against the unbelieving enemy'.

---

## A TURNING POINT: THE ABBASIDS

After a century of powerful expansion the empire of the Arabs was in a dangerous crisis. The contrast between the Arab Muslims and the disadvantaged non-Arab neo-Muslims was too great. The latter put

Arab rule in question in the very name of Islam. All this led to a revolution.

It was the Abbasids, the descendants of Abbas, the Prophet's uncle, who brought about 'the change' (*daula*) violently in 750: this was a renewal of the empire on an Islamic rather than an Arab basis. Instead of a purely Arab empire, the imperial rule of all Muslims was propagated and established. The change to the new capital, Baghdad, is symptomatic of the paradigm shift to the classic paradigm of Islam as a world religion. Baghdad was a city of many peoples in a state of many peoples.

Under the Abbasids (750–1258) Islam was no longer just an Arab religion but a universal religion embracing all peoples. Instead of the traditional Arab tribal loyalty there was now the universal Muslim order and brotherhood. All the differences between Arabs and non-Arabs were to disappear, but as 'representatives of God' and 'princes of the believers' the caliphs themselves were to be exalted even more highly above the people and indeed the aristocracy as sovereign rulers. Their absolutism and luxury were soon to surpass those of the Umayyads.

The palaces of the caliphs and the spiral minaret of the Grand Mosque of the temporary residence of the Abbasids in Samarra are only modest monuments to this era; there is also the mosque of the Turkish governor Ibn Tulun in Cairo, which was built in the Abbasid imperial style; this also has a spiral minaret.

## CLASSICAL ISLAM

The early Abbasid period – and at the same time in Moorish Spain the rule of the Umayyads of Cordoba who had fled there – is still regarded as the era in which Islam attained its classical form: now Arabia was economically and politically peripheral. Mesopotamia was central and the influence of Persia strong.

Now Islam was a world religion in the real sense. A specifically Islamic culture developed in the framework of this paradigm of Islam as a world religion. Based on classical Arabic, a Persian lifestyle and Hellenistic philosophy and science, it was far ahead of the early medieval culture of Christian Europe. Islamic law and then theological scholasticism developed centuries before Roman church law and scholastic theology, and both were rich in books.

## ISLAMIC LAW

Classical Islamic law (*fiqh*) was formed in the early Abbasid period. At that time the strict 'traditionalists' who appealed to some oral prophetic tradition, the higher 'Sunna of the Prophet', in principle became established in the face of the freer and older schools of law.

In time, four classical schools of law formed, which still exist today: the strict Malikite (and later also the Hanbalite), the more generous Hanafite, and finally the mediating Shafite. Shafi'i above all ensured that tradition was elevated to a universal principle, which in the longer term must result in immovability and rigidity. Only now was the religious law, the Shariah, that totality of canonical legal precepts, comprehensively shaped and structured. Even today, it is still the norm for Muslims who think traditionally.

## ISLAMIC THEOLOGY

Islamic theology (*kalam*) is secondary to the sacral law, but it likewise attained its classical form in the Abbasid period. A school theology or scholasticism came into being which took great trouble to give a rational explanation of the essence of Islam.

After the Muslim civil war between the two sons of Haroun al-Rashid and the victory of al-Mamun, the younger, a rational understanding of the transcendence of God, the freedom of the human will and above all the created nature of the Qur'an seems to have been established. Earlier it had been said that the Qur'an was neither Creator nor created. But now the pronounced thesis that the Qur'an was created (since nothing is like God) produced the sharply opposed thesis that the Qur'an is 'uncreated', 'eternal', 'perfect'. And not even the inquisitorial means introduced by Caliph Mamun helped here. At the end of the great controversy between rational theology and traditional scholarship over whether revelation (Qur'an and Sunna) or reason (philosophy) had priority in theology as in law, the principle of the Hadith scholars, who favoured tradition, prevailed.

What the great legal scholar Shafi'i had achieved in Islamic law in the ninth century, the great theologian Ashari achieved in Islamic theology in the tenth: he grounded and developed the position of those who preserved tradition with the rational arguments of those who were at that time 'moderns'. And he did this in a way which was not dissimilar to that adopted by Thomas Aquinas in the thirteenth century, who reinforced and differentiated the traditional theology of Augustine with the means of 'modern' Aristotelian philosophy.

Of course, the question of the relationship between scripture and tradition arose. Jews have Torah and Talmud, and many Christians are obligated to both scripture and tradition. For Muslims, Qur'an and Sunna now in fact stood side by side on an equal basis. The question was: did this not in fact subordinate the 'Sunna of the Prophet' to the Qur'an as the source of jurisprudence and theology? And would this not lead to a fossilization and absolutizing of the tradition by preventing any progress?

## AN ISLAMIC PARADIGM WITHOUT A CALIPH?

After two centuries the Abbasid empire collapsed: there was a crisis in the caliphate, the army revolted, the bureaucracy was corrupt and the economy declined. After 945 there was in fact no longer an empire, three centuries before the Mongol wave which swept everything away, when Baghdad was conquered in 1258 and with the last caliph the Abbasid dynasty perished for ever. Since then there has been no generally recognized central political authority and no symbol of unity in Islam.

Regionalization followed. Small states came into being with no central government but with bureaucratic élites; these were replaced by the domination of military leaders, great landlords and sultans. At the end of the eleventh century the Christian Crusaders were even able to settle in Palestine and Syria for a century and establish a kingdom of Jerusalem. However, this was won back in 1187 by Saladin, the sultan of Egypt and Syria, who enjoyed high esteem even in the Christian West, and who was later to become the wise representative of Islam in Lessing's play *Nathan the Wise*.

## TUNIS: THE TEACHING PLACES OF ISLAM

Islam would probably hardly have survived the new period without caliphs but for the Islamic religious teachers, the Ulama, who were particularly active at the Zituna of Tunis. This Olive Tree Mosque (*Djama ez Zituna*, also called the 'Great Mosque') is the most important sanctuary in Tunisia after the Sidi-Oqba mosque in Kairouan. As early as 732, under the Umayyads, a modest house of God was built here. In 864, under the Aghlabids (emirs by the grace of the Abbasids), a completely new mosque was built, which under the Hafsids between the thirteenth and fifteenth centuries became a college complex with numerous ancillary buildings. At this time the Zituna also developed into the most famous theological and legal teaching place in Islam alongside Al Azhar in Cairo and the Qarawiyin of Fes in Morocco.

In or around every mosque there is an opportunity for ritual washings, for cleansing from impurity caused by relieving oneself, sexual intercourse, menstruation and also sleep. This involves washing face, hands, armpits and feet: where there is no water, sand is enough. Only after this is one ready for prayer. That is what the religious scholars, the Ulama, teach.

## THE POWER OF THE ULAMA

These scholars, expert in the Qur'an and the Sunna, more specifically the Hadith – the sayings and actions of the Prophet – now had an autonomous authority in religious affairs. Of course, these lawyer-theologians did not replace the authority of the ruler in matters of state. But to the present day they do claim authority in all religious questions, because these can be rightly judged only in the light of the Qur'an and the Sunna. Now a separation of the élites and institutions of the state and religion increasingly replaced the earlier sacral regime under a 'representative of God' who determined both religion and politics.

The Ulama could now also substantially strengthen their authority even under foreign regimes in this completely new constellation without a caliph. They did so by training personnel in legal schools, by the formation of a religious community (with merchants, craftsmen, and so on), and by an international network of communication. Now more than ever their interpretation of Qur'an and Sunna influenced the whole of religious and secular life. The madrasas, which became the higher Islamic places of education, were a new form of organization: a mosque, a law school and a theological seminary in one. At the same time they were centres of charitable, educational and religious work, and in some circumstances also of political and religious propaganda and agitation. It was easy to mobilize the masses from them.

As ever, here Muslims studied the Qur'an and recited it rhythmically together. And anyone who after the downfall of the caliphate was in search of political power took note of the fact that in religion, ethics and law the Muslim masses were not so much influenced by the 'caliphs' and the sultan as by the Ulama and the mystics and their religious orders.

## THE MYSTICAL PATH OF THE SUFIS

More and more Muslim men and women were dissatisfied with the Ulama's all too sober study of the law and its legalism. They preferred to follow the mystical path. 'Mystics', called 'Sufis' in Arabic, were originally simply ascetics. They wore a penitential garment of coarse wool, Arabic *suf*, of the kind that was already the customary dress of Christian monks. They were often also called the 'poor': 'poor' in Arabic is *faqir*, in Persian *darwesh*, hence our terms fakir and dervish. They were solitaries, men and women; often they included drop-outs who scorned and provoked existing society, or active fighters for the faith in the Muslim frontier settlements.

However, mysticism in the real sense means more than asceticism; it also means a struggle for direct inner experience of the reality of God. Mysticism is not primally Islamic. Rather, it has existed in Islam only since the late ninth century, the time of the Abbasids, among individual 'friends of God' who at that time still remained a peripheral social phenomenon. These did not cultivate the mournfulness of ascetic renunciation but celebrated joy, love, union with God and remaining in God. What could help them more here, what could be more important, than studying the law and observing it scrupulously?

– First of all music: in this way brotherhood was cultivated and the feeling of the love of God was aroused and intensified.

– Then ritualized dance: by intense movement the new ecstasy was to be expressed to the point of going into a trance.

– And along with all this the most important thing was the thought of God, the *dhikr Allah*: Allah and his many names were invoked incessantly, and his greatness and eternity were praised as in a litany.

All in all, this was a way for the individual believer from the Islamic law (*sharia*) on the mystical path (*tariqa*) to the truth (*haqiqa*), to God; it was an inner understanding of religion, a strong, psychologically orientated, 'knowledge from within', a 'doctrine of the works of the heart'. However, for Muslims there was no question of complete union with God, even self-divinization: this last boundary between human beings and God may not be crossed, and respect for God's transcendence must not be lost. However, communion with God may be striven for in order to live a life that comes from God in the world. In this way the selfish efforts of men and women are to be transformed by the fire of the divine love.

The ascetic, who is regarded as poor, *faqir*, before God, performs ascetic exercises, but sometimes also shows skills with a knife, and can swallow poison; these seem to Western observers more like conjuring tricks than 'miracles'. The mystical background is the notion that the human being who is filled with the power of God can become insensitive to bodily pains, indeed has the capacity to perform miracles.

## SUFISM AS A MASS MOVEMENT

The Sufi movement developed into a mass movement with its own theology, its own religious practices and institutions, only between the tenth and the fourteenth centuries. Only then did the Sufi brotherhoods proper come into being. They were organized like a religious order under a sheikh as military leader, with regulations, superiors and a distinctive dress; there were sometimes also disputes among the orders. In many spheres these brotherhoods transcended the law schools. Sufi centres (hospices, lodges) on the model of the ribats were formed everywhere, and they engaged in social, charitable and missionary activities. They often became a whole network. At this time India, Indonesia, black Africa and Albania were Islamicized largely by Sufi preachers.

In the thirteenth century the Sufis, who normally practised a profession and had a family, took the place of the school lawyers as the most respected leaders of the people. And even those who were not members of the order often felt loosely associated with them. At all events they celebrated the great annual festival (*urs*) of the founder of the order, in order to receive his blessing. The clans met every year in Tunisia at their marabouts (from the Arabic *murabit* – 'inhabitant of a ribat', 'frontier fighter', 'hermit', 'ascetic'). The term could denote the saint buried there or his white monument or memorial, which usually was set somewhat apart. There people expected spiritual and material blessing (*baraka*) in an often magical way. The cult at the tomb of the saint became the main vehicle of the Sufi form of Islam. Many Ulama were now also at the same time Sufi. In fact the Ulama-Sufi paradigm without a caliph was now solidly established.

## A RELIGION OF THE HEART INSTEAD OF A RELIGION OF REASON?

Every religion must tolerate some things which it initially repudiated. Even Islam, wholly focused on the one God, still tolerates the veneration of saints, whose tombs and memorials can be found even in the Sahara. The sober piety of the teachers of the law, who reflected on the Sunna and the Qur'an, could hardly satisfy the religious need for experience. Religion was not to address only the head, the mind, but also the heart, the disposition.

Of course, such a religion of the heart can easily lose itself in irrationalism, superstition and the quest for miracles. And a religion which cannot also be understood, thought through and taught is not much use. However, religion should not just address an intellectual élite, but also meet the religious needs of the people. Sufism did this through poetry, song, music, dance and festivals.

But from the Middle Ages on, criticism of the Sufi veneration of saints, music and even magic, often taken over from pagan cults, became increasingly loud. Muslim reformers called for a return to pure Islam. And the political authorities were often afraid of the influence of the Sufi orders. For some Sufi 'saints' and leaders played a role in politics which was highly undesirable. That also explains why in some places the Sufi orders were repressed, and why Atatürk, the father of modern Turkey, actually banned the dervish orders, Sufi orders, which were reactionary in both religion and politics.

## THE CONFRONTATION BETWEEN ISLAM
## AND MODERNITY

So far Islam has already undergone a whole series of paradigm shifts and survived them. But what will it make of the new modern constellation? The European 'age of discoveries' also made an impact on the Muslim world. The three Islamic empires which arose after the sixteenth century could not simply close themselves to the invasion of the European powers.
- In India the Mogul empire found itself confronted with the gradual conquest of India by the British (more Muslims live on the Indian subcontinent than in the Arab states). Similarly, Indonesia was occupied by the Dutch.
- In Persia the Shi'ite Safawid empire underwent a first (unsuccessful) modernization in the nineteenth century under the Qajars and came under the dominant influence of Russia and England.
- Turkey formed the centre of the Sunni Ottoman empire, *the* Islamic power set over against the Christian nations. This mighty empire also embraced Egypt, Arabia and the Balkans, and manifested itself in Istanbul in mosques of unprecedented number, size and splendour. However, we cannot overlook the geopolitical change: the discovery of America and the circumnavigation of Africa made the Mediterranean, the great trading power of Egypt and the Eastern trade through Persia and the Ottoman Empire, of secondary importance. Cheap silver from South America shattered the currency.

## A CRISIS OF IDENTITY FOR ISLAM

Thus after the seventeenth century, even the powerful Ottoman empire went on the defensive. European modernity advanced on all sides, with trade, science, technology, industry and also democracy. Thus the European powers, unhindered in any way, became stronger and stronger, and the Ottomans increasingly weak: in economic, political and military terms. This process of European modernization and secularization seemed unstoppable.

For all too long the self-confident Islamic rulers trusted in the power over the earth given them by God. They neglected to take the technical and cultural changes in Europe seriously. Even in the Ottoman empire, cultural and social life threatened to rigidify under the influence of a traditionalist Ulama and reactionary Sufis.

Certainly the integrating power of Islam and the cohesion of its faith over the centuries were great. For a long time its expansion was unhampered: there was a unique and imposing history of victors and victories, which are attested by the gigantic mosques in Istanbul.

However, the political decline of the Ottoman empire was already evident in the nineteenth century and with it the identity crisis in Islam: a feeling of impotence and alienation was spreading, a loss of Muslim self-confidence and dignity. Granted, Hagia Sophia, transformed by the Muslims, was still a sign of the victory of Islam over Christianity, but already in the nineteenth century Europeans were mocking the 'sick man by the Bosphorus'.


## MODERNIZATION AND SECULARIZATION: ATATÜRK

Beyond question the Turkish sultans – like the Albanian Muhammad Ali in Egypt after Napoleon's departure, with European capital and advisers – made considerable attempts at modernization in the nineteenth century. But even then the reforms of the army, the administration, the economy and the constitution did not progress far. And at the beginning of the twentieth century the colonial powers of France, England, Holland and Italy had the whole of North Africa, the Middle East, Persia, India and Indonesia under their control.

For the last sultans, Dolmabahce, the splendid 'Versailles' of Istanbul, newly built on the Bosphorus, now became the sign of their dwindling power and the revolutionary unrest among the people. For the First World War brought about the downfall of the Ottoman empire. After the capitulation in 1918 the sultanate was abolished. Five years later Mustafa Kemal proclaimed the Turkish Republic. After that, soon to bear the name Atatürk, the 'Father of the Turks', he resided in the Dolmabahce Palace as president of the republic. He banished the sultan, and moved the capital from the Bosphorus to Ankara in the centre of Anatolia. Far-reaching changes were immediately initiated: a separation between the state and religion, a Europeanizing of the constitution and the law, of education, script and dress.

The First World War brought about a great political upheaval for Islam generally. The Arab Middle East was not united but divided: there were areas under European mandates, and kingdoms in Transjordan and in Iraq. In Arabia there was a kingdom under the Wahhabi Saudi family, which struggled back from Sufism to an Islam of original purity and thus formed the conservative Muslim counterpart to Turkey. When Kemal Atatürk died in 1938, Turkey seemed to be solidly established as a secular republic. In particular, great strides seemed to have been made over the equal status of women under the law.

## ISTANBUL: BETWEEN CHADOR AND WESTERN DRESS

Educated Muslim women who know their Qur'an rightly point out that the Qur'an accords women a better position than the sacral law, the Sharia, which arose later. In fact in the Qur'an the status of women is in many respects far better than it was in pre-Muslim Arabia. Male and female are equal before God; both partners in a marriage are to show understanding and love; the woman has a right to property; there are restrictions on polygamy and divorce; and the exposure or killing of new-born girls is prohibited.

However, the fact cannot be concealed that the Qur'an too (not unlike the Bible) already requires the submission of the wife to her husband's will and allows the husband (here it differs from the Bible) even to strike his wife if she is stubbornly disobedient. In the laws relating to marriage, family and inheritance, and before the courts, the woman is always clearly at a disadvantage. However, only after the Abbasid period did the veil become customary, as did the banishment of women from public life.

In the twentieth century, reforms were carried through in Turkey (as in Tunisia and Egypt): the vote has given women in Turkey a legal footing in political life. Recently women have also been allowed to join the Friday prayers in the mosque and to attend burials. They often form the majority in universities, banks, the editorial boards of journals and advertising agencies. The one thing they fall short in is having an equal status in law. The wife still needs the consent of the 'head of the family' to engage in a profession. But their education and their capacity to earn their own living are giving women increasing independence. And the mass media, education and economic developments are increasingly levelling down the differences between the women in Istanbul with a Western orientation and the women in the towns and villages of Anatolia, whose daughters, with a university education, quite naturally follow Western forms in their outward appearance.

## FOR OR AGAINST THE VEIL

It is surprising that today young women in particular are again covering their heads, but this need not necessarily be a sign of regression. Besides, when convinced secularists in France or in Turkey want to purge public life of all religious symbols, these women are making a dogmatic point.

Some Muslim women fought and still fight against the head covering, which seems to them to threaten their equal rights in society. They do not want religion once again to be a system of rules which intervenes and permeates life down to the last detail. They do not want Islam to dominate everything, from the economy and politics, through culture, to personal lifestyle. They approve of a spiritual and moral orientation, but not of petty regimentation.

But other educated younger women deliberately wear a headdress in order to express their Muslim identity in the face of Western ideals of femininity. Be this as it may, Christian churches which at the beginning of the third millennium forbid their priests to marry, do not allow women to be ordained, and do not even let girls serve at the altar, are hardly in a position to criticize the alleged misogyny in Islam.

## THE REVIVAL OF ISLAM:
## DOUBT IN THE MODERN PARADIGM

There is one thing at any rate which Atatürk, who believed in Europe, never expected: the revival of Islam which has taken place since the Second World War. The decisive factors are well known:
– The political liberation of Muslim lands from colonial rule in the 1950s and 1960s;
– The military and economic successes in the 1970s after the war between Arabs and Israel, the oil embargo and the victory of Ayatollah Khomeini over the Shah and the United States in 1979.

But in the end disillusionment over the West – its crises, its partisan support of Israel, its immorality and godlessness – was no less momentous than this increased self-confidence and sense of power.

So the Muslim revival (which was already called for in the nineteenth century by the Muslim reformer Jamaleddin al-Afghani in the face of European colonialism) must not be seen just as a militant political reaction to Western colonialism and imperialism. Nor should it be seen just as a disturbing and ambivalent indication of the failure of the Western policy of development through the transfer of technology. It should not even be seen just as a reactionary and religious ebbing of the revolutionary secular wave which has surged in vain.

Here we have fundamental doubts about the modern paradigm, which are also widespread today in Europe and America. So today Muslim men and women with a 'Muslim' orientation see the Muslim state as the great religious and political alternative to the secular state of Atatürk. In the face of the widespread irreligious and immoral materialism in both West and East they are looking for a new spiritual basis for trade, culture and society, through belief in the one God (*tawhid*), in submission (*islam*) to his will and his commandments. But others, thinking in 'lay' terms, are calling more than ever for a radical separation of religion from politics. In the face of the Muslim and secularist position the basic question which arises for the future is:

## IS A REFORMED POSTMODERN ISLAM POSSIBLE?

The problems of Islam are focused in Turkey as in a burning glass. The land is in the midst of a process of economic, political and social change, and is struggling towards a democratic transformation. In Turkey, where there are 71,000 mosques, this certainly also raises deep moral and religious questions, and is ultimately a reflection of the foundations of the nation in Islam, which remains fundamental in the cultural world of these peoples. The 'death of God' announced by modern European prophets of atheism has come about far less in Islam than in the 'Christian' West.

And it cannot be disputed that the ethical imperatives of the Qur'an which call for more justice, fairness, restraint, moderation, compassion and forgiveness have had and can have an effect. Here those who are renewing Islam by no means totally reject European modernity. But in modernity they want to hold on to Islamic identity. They want, at least in principle, to live out an Islam which rejects Westernization and total secularization but accepts development and modernization.

So for Islam, as for Catholic Christianity before the Second Vatican Council, the problem of religion and the future arises: will Islam remain only a conservative and preservative force or will it become a progressive and liberating social force? How far can there be a renewal of Islam which in principle seeks to be orientated towards the future, with an awareness of problems and a readiness for change? And how far will a readiness for change go in the face of the world of the twenty-first century which is now beginning? Despite a partially spectacular technological modernization, will the state be dominated by religious institutions which are still governed by medieval theology, medieval law and a medieval social constitution?

## WHO WILL PREVAIL?

Indeed, who will finally prevail politically, in jurisprudence and jurisdiction, umma and state, science and society?

– Will it be the orthodox traditionalists? Unconcerned about all the developments in science, law and society generally, they want to carry through a literal application of the detailed religious prescriptions of the Sharia to the present-day economic and social order and in fact to fix this to the medieval paradigm.

– Or will it be the religious and political innovators? Aware of the paradigm shifts which have taken place in the meantime – in the face of all the insistence on tradition (*taqlid*) – they want to open the door of independent interpretation (*ijtihad*) which has been closed since around 900. They want to attempt a translation of the message of the Qur'an for the present day, in order to make possible an economy, science and society which is capable of competition in the interests of human well-being.

Turks sometimes say that in the twenty-first century the Turks would give Islam, which has been tainted with terror by extremist Arabs and Iranians, a friendly face. That is to be hoped for, but it presupposes an unambiguous Muslim foundation for universal human rights and a resolution of the Kurdish question. Human rights now demand an equal status under law for both women and non-Muslims. In this respect the 'Cairo Declaration of Human Rights in Islam' which was passed by the 40 member states of the 'Orgaization of the Islamic Conference' falls short of the 1948 United Nations Declaration of Human Rights (as it also does in respect of bodily integrity).

### WE NEED BRIDGE-BUILDERS

When one stands in front of the mighty suspension bridge over the Bosphorus, which earlier no one would have believed possible, a bridge between Europe and Asia, West and East, new times and old, we ask ourselves: What will be the future of this city, this state full of oppositions? What will be the future of Islam here and in other countries? Who will be the heir of this 1300-year-old religion and culture?

– Will it be the modernists and secularists who think that they can dispense with Islam, and with religion in general?

– Or will it be the traditionalists and fundamentalists, who think that by precisely observing the religious writings they can again give these societies a new spiritual and moral foundation?

I would like to hope that neither one nor the other will completely prevail, but that once again more importance will be attached to those who want to preserve the substance of Islam but at the same time are attempting to translate the message of the Qur'an for the present time. I would hope to see neither a godless secularism nor a fundamentalism alien to the world, but rather a religion which can again give people of today a horizon of meaning, and ethical standards, and a spiritual home.

At any rate I hope that it will be a religion which does not divide and split, but binds and reconciles. For what our time needs above all are bridge-builders, in matters great and small. It needs bridge-builders who in all difficulties, conflicts and confrontations, nevertheless see the things that we share: above all, the ethical values and attitudes that we share. I would like to see bridge-builders who confess these shared values and standards and also attempt to live by them.

## NO SURVIVAL FOR THE WORLD WITHOUT A GLOBAL ETHIC

There are also such politically innovative bridge-builders in present-day Islam. They stand for a postmodern reformed Islam, which takes the Qur'an only as a guideline. There are humane values, standards and attitudes in the Qur'an, though they have not established themselves as the right of the individual before the state (along the lines of the constitutions of Western states), any more than they have in the Bible. On the basis of the Qur'an, Muslims from within Islam can attain human rights and at the same time work for a global ethic, for the well-being of global peace and global justice. 'If you wish for others what you wish for yourself, you become a Muslim,' the prophet Muhammad once remarked and thus gave expression to the Golden Rule.

Who of us could not complain endlessly about all the suffering and misery of this world? But who of us could dispute that time and again, men and women – in great things as in small – can change this torn world, have changed it and want to change it for the better? In the seven chapters of this book I want to give them above all courage, not with a lofty utopia but rather with a realistic vision. To repeat and sum up what governs the principles of my work and of countless men and women wherever they live:

No peace among the nations without peace among the religions.
No peace among the religions without dialogue between the religions.
No dialogue between the religions without global ethical standards.
No survival of our globe without a global ethic.

# *Epilogue*

It was Lord Menuhin, that brilliant musician and humanist, who unintentionally gave me the idea of this book, long before he became my friend. In 1979 he was an enthusiastic guide through the realm of music as author and presenter of an eight-part Canadian Broadcasting Company television series entitled 'The Music of Man'. What could be better, I thought at the time, than a similar guided tour through the realm of the religions?

At the same time, though, I was aware that the realm of the religions was considerably more difficult to research and even more difficult to describe. Yehudi Menuhin only had to pick up his violin or his conductor's baton to open even ignorant and perhaps unmusical ears and hearts to the fascinating world of music. But how could one open people's ears and hearts to the world of religion, which in quite a different way was just as mysterious?

Besides, I still had a tremendous amount to learn before daring to embark on such an adventure, if it was practicable at all. I had been in a favourable position to get to know Europe immediately after the Second World War. I went to Muslim North Africa as early as 1955 and made my first trip round the world only a few years later. Over four decades a tremendous number of conversations and meetings, talks and lectures, symposia and congresses, as well as several semesters in America, followed; these provided me with the experience that is needed, particularly in religious matters, if one is to have more than abstract book learning.

Above all I had to get to know my own religion, Christianity, thoroughly so that I could enter more deeply into critical discussion with other religions. Those who carry on dialogue with others without knowing their own standpoint bring more confusion than anything else. It was only over the course of decades of study and dialogue lectures with experts in other religions that I acquired the theological foundations and basic insights without which the Global Ethic Project, this book and the German television series which was made in connection with it would have been impossible:
– Unqualified openness and readiness for dialogue with other religions and deep roots in one's own religion are not mutually exclusive.

– Salvation is possible for people outside the Catholic Church, and indeed outside Christianity: the question of truth and the question of salvation are not identical.

– God does not exist above or outside this world but in this world; there is transcendence in the immanence.

– Jesus Christ must be understood in terms of his earthly career and not a speculative doctrine of the Trinity: Christianity 'from below'.

– But Jesus of Nazareth can be compared with the other great figures of the world religions. In this way he takes on an unmistakable profile: it becomes clear what he has in common with these other figures and what distinguishes him from them.

– Non-Christians, indeed agnostics and atheists, can also have a morality; this should be acknowledged in particular if one is convinced of the abiding importance of religion.

– A fundamental trust in reality (the opposite of nihilism and cynicism) can be the basis for a fundamental morality which is open to anyone.

– The world of religions is not utterly chaotic. Rather, it is possible to distinguish three rivers of religion, of Near Eastern, Indian and Chinese origin.

– Every religion has undergone fundamental reorientations, revolutionary upheaval and epoch-making paradigm shifts in its river systems. But paradigms which have been displaced can go on existing . . .

So there needs to be a time for everything in life, and once again I had the experience that when the time comes, the necessary opportunity will also present itself. In 1984 the BBC enquired whether I would be prepared to act as author and presenter of a big television series on contemporary Christian belief. Such an offer seemed to me too good to refuse, so I worked out a basic plan, which in fact was accepted at the planning level. However, at the same time I had considerable doubts whether I could complete such a tremendous project in addition to my teaching duties in Tübingen. Here once again, in retrospect, I think I can detect a 'hidden' hand guiding my life: the BBC turned down the project at the highest level because it looked like being too expensive.

However, some years later, when I was telling this story in confidence, the then television director of Süddeutscher Rundfunk, Dr Hans Heiner Boelte, spontaneously remarked, 'We'll do it.' And so a television series and a book were born.

I am often asked, 'How long did this or that book take you?' In the case of this book I can justifiably say: my whole life, or at least the five decades of my life as a theologian. It must already have become clear that I could not approach this project as a 'religious expert', after the manner of a television journalist. I did not want to have topical or interesting film sequences shot and then comment on them. I had to choose another approach, which may have seemed complicated to those routinely engaged in making television programmes.

The method which I followed took a great deal of time and intensive research. I was grateful to be able to discuss every step with my advisers, Dr Karl-Josef Kuschel and Stephan Schlensog. All the manuscripts in the various stages of development were read, criticized and corrected by colleagues in the Global Ethic Foundation. Many different phases, from a first extended draft document which made use of my previous researches into the different religions, through the shooting script and making of the television film, to the final text of this book, were involved. I am most grateful to all those who have made such a complex project possible. There are too many of them to mention here. With so much ground to cover I cannot expect to have avoided misunderstandings, but I hope that readers will feel that this book has helped to shed more light on some of the most important questions or our time.

# Index

Printed in the United Kingdom
by Lightning Source UK Ltd.
136085UK00001B/85/A